Potatoes

Potatoes

This is a Parragon Publishing Book
This edition published in 2003

Parragon Publishing
Queen Street House
4 Queen Street
Bath BA1 1HE, UK

ISBN: 0-75258-324-7

Printed in China

NOTE

Cup measurements in this book are for American cups.
Tablespoons are assumed tobe 15ml. Unless otherwise stated,
milk is assumed to be full fat, eggs are medium
and pepper is freshly ground black pepper.

Recipes using uncooked eggs should be
avoided by infants, the elderly, pregnant women and anyone
suffering from an illness.

Contents

Introduction 8 Regional Cooking 10–13
Using Potatoes 14 How to Use This Book 16

Soups, Appetizers & Salads

Light Meals & Side Dishes

Light Meals & Side Dishes

(continued)

Vegetarian & Vegan Suppers

Vegetable Savories

Fish Dishes

Poultry & Meat

Bread & Desserts

Introduction

Easy to grow and cook, inexpensive, marvelously tasty, extremely nutritious, and highly versatile, the potato has unsurprisingly become one of the world's most popular vegetables and an important staple food, which is cultivated almost everywhere.

There is a vast range of different varieties—around 3,000 in all—although only about 100 of these are regularly grown. Each variety has its own distinctive shape, texture, even color, and reflects its country of origin, from the firm yellow flesh of the Jersey Royal new potato to the rich, warm orange of the Caribbean yam.

Possibly dating as far back as 3000 bce, the potato originated in South America, where it was known as the "papa." It was eaten by the Incas, fresh when it was in season and dried in winter. It was unknown to the rest of the world, however, until the 16th century, when Peru fell to the Spanish conquistador Francisco Pizarro. Peru was well known to be rich in minerals, and it was the mineral traders who began to introduce the potato elsewhere.

In Europe, the potato arrived via Spain, and its name gradually evolved from "papa" to "battata." It became famous not only for its nutritional value, but also for its healing properties. The Italians believed that the cooked flesh would heal a wound if rubbed into the infected area, and Pope Pious IV was sufficiently convinced of this to plant his own crop. From here, the potato moved northward through Switzerland, France, Germany, and Belgium, reaching the New World with the explorer Francis Drake, who shared his cargo of potatoes with the starving English colonists. Sir Walter Raleigh later brought the potato to Britain. He also took it to Ireland, where the soil was perfect for growing it, and it became a dietary mainstay for the Irish peasantry, who survived for generations on little else.

Nutritionally, potatoes are an excellent source of starch for energy and fiber. They have a higher protein value than most plant foods, are very rich in vitamin C, and also contain vitamin B-complex, as well as minerals, especially potassium. However, many of the nutrients are found in or just below the skin, so it is essential to cook them in ways that will retain their health-promoting properties.

Although potatoes were once considered to be forbidden to slimmers, they are in fact a positive aid to weight control when cooked and served with the minimum of fat. Sufferers from stomach ulcers and arthritis will also benefit from drinking raw potato juice, although their taste buds may object to the flavor!

This book is a collection of some of the most delicious potato recipes, which have been gathered from around the world. Whatever the occasion, these inspiring dishes will showing you how this adaptable vegetable can be used in a multitude of ways to enhance your everyday eating.

Regional Cooking

Although the potato is known and grown throughout the world, the ways in which it is cooked and served vary enormously from country to country, and often depend on whether it is the main staple of a nation's diet.

The highest consumers are Russia, Poland, and Germany, followed by Holland, Cyprus, and Ireland. Elsewhere, the potato may be less popular than pasta, rice, or bread in the daily diet.

As Spain was the first European country to discover the potato, it is appropriate that it is used in one of the most popular and well-known classic Spanish dishes, tortilla. This is a substantial, crispy-coated

vegetable omelet based on eggs and thinly sliced waxy potatoes, to which may be added bell peppers, tomatoes, corn—the choice is unlimited. Variations of this omelet can be found all around the Mediterranean—a Greek version, for example, is to fill the potato omelet with a melting mixture of feta cheese and spinach.

In Italy, mealy potatoes are used in another classic dish—gnocchi. Here, the cooked potatoes are mixed with flour, egg yolks, and olive oil to make little dumplings, which are cooked in boiling water and served with a sauce. Herbs or cheese may be added to the recipe, and a delicious variation is to add spinach. A similar base can also be used to make potato noodles.

From Ireland comes Colcannon —a marvelous mixture of mashed potatoes and shredded cabbage, topped with a pool of melted butter—which is usually served with a piece of bacon.

Regional Cooking

Worldwide, the potato is often used as a basis for a hearty salad. On the Mediterranean coast of France, for example, potatoes are combined with tuna and eggs as the base for the famous Salade Niçoise. In India, they may be mixed with broccoli and mango, and topped with a spicy yogurt dressing, while in Mexico sliced potatoes are topped with tomatoes, chilies, and ham and served with guacamole.

In Italy, potatoes are layered with sausage, radicchio, sun-dried tomatoes, and basil and drizzled with a tomato-flavored olive oil dressing, and in Russia the classic combination of cucumber and dill is often made more substantial by the addition of potatoes and beets.

The potato makes an excellent ingredient in soups, and in European cuisine, potatoes are used in a number of classic soup recipes—Vichyssoise, Pistou, and Bouillabaisse. Different cultures have their own variations of chowder, a filling soup based on potatoes and milk. In New England, for example, fresh clams are added, while in Scotland the soup is flavored with smoked haddock to make the intriguingly named Cullen Skink.

Even as an accompaniment, potatoes are served in a variety of ways. In India, they are mixed with other vegetables, readily absorbing the curry flavors. In France, layers of waxy potatoes are topped with heavy cream and sometimes cheese to make Potatoes Dauphinois. In Britain they are served roasted to a crisp with the traditional Sunday lunch, and in Belgium French fries are served with mayonnaise, for dipping.

Using Potatoes

The potato is without doubt one of the most versatile food items. However, not all types of potato are suitable for all purposes, and the following list gives the uses for some of the most popular varieties:

Craig Royal Red

This waxy main crop potato is best for deep-frying and boiling, or using in salads or tortillas.

Desirée

One of the best and most versatile varieties, this pink-skinned mealy potato is good for baking, deep-frying, boiling, and mashing.

King Edward

A large, high-quality, creamy white potato, this popular variety is ideal for all purposes.

Maris Piper

This medium-firm variety has creamy white flesh, and is good for boiling and deep-frying.

New Potatoes

These are harvested in early summer, and are best boiled and eaten warm with chopped mint and melted butter, or cold in salads. Jersey Royals have a superb flavor, and their appearance often heralds warmer weather.

Pentland Crown

This creamy white, mealy potato is ideal for mashing and baking.

Yam

An orange-fleshed sweet potato, which is best mashed in cakes and soufflés, or roasted.

Buying and Storing

When choosing potatoes, make sure they are firm and well-shaped with a smooth, tight skin. New potatoes should be eaten as fresh as possible, but old potatoes can be stored in a cool, dark, dry place—exposure to light makes them turn green, resulting in an unpleasant flavor and a higher level of glycoalkaloids, which are naturally occurring toxins.

Preparation and Cooking

To preserve the nutritional value of potatoes, they should ideally be baked in their skins, or scrubbed rather than peeled. If peeled potatoes are required, they should be cooked in their skins and then peeled afterward.

Mashing or Creaming

Boil the potatoes, then drain well. Add a knob of butter, season, then mash, preferably with an electric hand-whisk, or by hand, first with a potato masher and then stirring briskly with a fork. As a variation, add cream or crème fraîche as well as butter; use garlic-infused olive oil instead of butter; or add some fresh pesto sauce.

Roasting

Simmer the potatoes in boiling water for 10 minutes. Drain them, then shake them in the pan to roughen their surfaces. Tip them carefully into a roasting pan of very hot fat, and cook on the top shelf of the oven at 425°F/220°C for about 45 minutes until golden and crispy.

Boiling

For new and old potatoes, put them in a pan, pour in enough boiling water to cover them, then add a lid to the pan, and boil gently until tender.

Steaming

To steam new and old potatoes, put them in a steamer over a pan of boiling water, and cook them gently until they are tender.

Baking

Scrub, then dry the potatoes. Prick the skins, then rub them with olive oil and salt. Bake at 425°F/220°C for between 1—1½ hours.

How to Use This Book

Each recipe contains a wealth of useful information, including a breakdown of nutritional quantities, preparation and cooking times, and level of difficulty. All of this information is explained in detail below.

● This amount of time represents the actual cooking time.

The nutritional information provided for each recipe is per serving or per portion. Optional ingredients, variations, or serving suggestions have not been included in the calculations. ●

The number of chef's ● hats represents the difficulty of each recipe, ranging from easy (1 chef's hat) to difficult (5 chef's hats).

This amount of ● time represents the preparation of ingredients, including cooling, chilling, and soaking times.

The ingredients for ● each recipe are listed in the order that they are used.

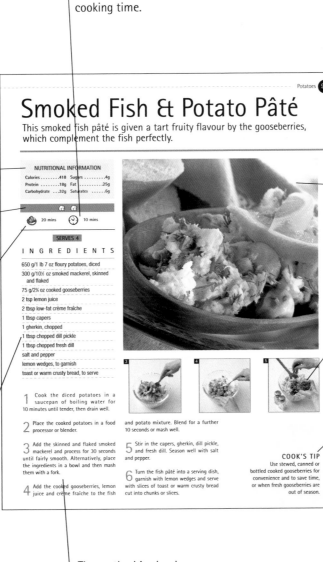

Potatoes 97

Smoked Fish & Potato Pâté
This smoked fish pâté is given a tart fruity flavour by the gooseberries, which complement the fish perfectly.

NUTRITIONAL INFORMATION

Calories . . . . .418 Sugars 4g
Protein . . . . .18g Fat 25g
Carbohydrate . . .32g Saturates 6g

20 mins   10 mins

SERVES 4

INGREDIENTS

650 g/1 lb 7 oz floury potatoes, diced

300 g/10½ oz smoked mackerel, skinned and flaked

75 g/2¾ oz cooked gooseberries

2 tsp lemon juice

2 tbsp low-fat crème fraîche

1 tbsp capers

1 gherkin, chopped

1 tbsp chopped dill pickle

1 tbsp chopped fresh dill

salt and pepper

lemon wedges, to garnish

toast or warm crusty bread, to serve

1 Cook the diced potatoes in a saucepan of boiling water for 10 minutes until tender, then drain well.

2 Place the cooked potatoes in a food processor or blender.

3 Add the skinned and flaked smoked mackerel and process for 30 seconds until fairly smooth. Alternatively, place the ingredients in a bowl and then mash them with a fork.

4 Add the cooked gooseberries, lemon juice and crème fraîche to the fish

and potato mixture. Blend for a further 10 seconds or mash well.

5 Stir in the capers, gherkin, dill pickle, and fresh dill. Season well with salt and pepper.

6 Turn the fish pâté into a serving dish, garnish with lemon wedges and serve with slices of toast or warm crusty bread cut into chunks or slices.

COOK'S TIP
Use stewed, canned or bottled cooked gooseberries for convenience and to save time, or when fresh gooseberries are out of season.

● A full-color photograph of the finished dish.

● The method is illustrated with step-by-step photographs, making the recipe easy to follow.

● Variations and cook's tips provide useful information regarding ingredients or cooking techniques.

● The method is clearly explained with step-by-step instructions that are easy to follow.

Soups, Appetizers &Salads

Potatoes form the basis of many delicious and easy-to-prepare home-made soups, because they are the perfect thickening agent while adding a subtle flavor. With the addition of just a few ingredients, you can have a

selection of soups at your fingertips.

Also featured in this chapter are appetizers and salads based on potatoes. In addition to the creamy potato salads that are so popular, there

are many other recipes to tempt your palate, including

dishes suitable for light lunches as well

as hearty entrées. Many are also ideal

for barbecues and picnics.

Creamy Corn Soup

This filling combination of tender corn kernels and a creamy stock is extra delicious with lean diced ham sprinkled on top.

NUTRITIONAL INFORMATION

Calories	.307	Sugars	.15g
Protein	.19g	Fat	.14g
Carbohydrate	.28g	Saturates	.5g

15 mins   25 mins

SERVES 4

INGREDIENTS

1 large onion, chopped

1¾ cups diced potatoes

1 quart skim milk

1 bay leaf

½ tsp ground nutmeg

1 lb/450 g corn kernels, canned or frozen, drained or thawed

1 tbsp cornstarch

3 tbsp cold water

4 tbsp plain lowfat unsweetened yogurt

salt and pepper

TO GARNISH

⅔ cup lean ham, diced

2 tbsp fresh chives, snipped

1 Place the onion and potatoes in a large pan and pour over the milk.

2 Add the bay leaf, nutmeg, and half the corn to the pan. Bring to a boil, then cover and simmer gently for 15 minutes until the potato is softened. Stir the soup occasionally and keep the heat low so that the milk does not burn on the bottom of the pan.

3 Discard the bay leaf and let the liquid cool for 10 minutes. Transfer to a

blender and process for a few seconds. Alternatively, rub through a strainer.

4 Pour the smooth liquid into a pan. Blend the cornstarch with the cold water to make a paste and stir it into the soup.

5 Bring the soup back to a boil, stirring until it thickens, and add the remaining corn. Heat through for

2–3 minutes until piping hot.

6 Remove the soup from the heat and season well with salt and pepper to taste. Stir in the yogurt until well blended.

7 Ladle the creamy corn soup into warm bowls and serve sprinkled with the diced ham and snipped chives.

Sweet Potato & Onion Soup

This simple recipe uses the sweet potato with its distinctive flavor and color, combined with a hint of orange and cilantro.

NUTRITIONAL INFORMATION

Calories	320	Sugars	........26g
Protein	.........7g	Fat	...........7g
Carbohydrate	...62g	Saturates	......1g

🥔 15 mins   🕐 30 mins

SERVES 4

INGREDIENTS

2 tbsp vegetable oil

generous 5 cups diced sweet potatoes

1 carrot, diced

2 onions, sliced

2 garlic cloves, crushed

2½ cups vegetable bouillon

1¼ cups unsweetened orange juice

1 cup plain lowfat unsweetened yogurt

2 tbsp chopped fresh cilantro

salt and pepper

TO GARNISH

cilantro sprigs

orange zest

1 Heat the vegetable oil in a large pan and add the diced sweet potatoes and carrot, sliced onions, and garlic. Sauté the vegetables gently for 5 minutes, stirring constantly.

2 Pour in the vegetable bouillon and orange juice and bring them to a boil.

3 Reduce the heat to a simmer, then cover the pan and cook the vegetables for 20 minutes or until the sweet potato and carrot cubes are tender.

4 Transfer the mixture to a food processor or blender in batches and process or blend for 1 minute until puréed. Return the purée to the rinsed-out pan.

5 Stir in the unsweetened yogurt and chopped cilantro and season to taste.

6 Serve the soup in warm bowls and garnish with cilantro sprigs and orange zest.

VARIATION

This soup can be chilled before serving, if preferred. If chilling it, stir the yogurt into the dish just before serving. Serve in chilled bowls.

Potato & Garbanzo Soup

From pantry ingredients, this spicy and substantial soup makes a delicious meal-in-a-bowl, ideal for a mid-week supper.

NUTRITIONAL INFORMATION

Calories	40	Sugars	.......1.6g
Protein	........1.8g	Fat	...........1g
Carbohydrate	...6.5g	Saturates	.....0.1g

🥄 5 mins   🕐 50 mins

SERVES 4

INGREDIENTS

1 tbsp olive oil

1 large onion, finely chopped

2–3 garlic cloves, finely chopped or crushed

1 carrot, quartered and thinly sliced

2 cups diced potatoes

¼ tsp ground turmeric

¼ tsp garam masala

¼ tsp mild curry powder

14 oz/400 g canned chopped tomatoes in juice

3¾ cups water

¼ tsp chili paste, or to taste

14 oz/400 g canned garbanzo beans, rinsed and drained

3 oz/85 g fresh or frozen peas

salt and pepper

chopped fresh cilantro, to garnish

1 Heat the olive oil in a large saucepan over a medium heat. Add the onion and garlic and cook for 3–4 minutes, stirring occasionally, until the onion is beginning to soften.

2 Add the carrot, potatoes, turmeric, garam masala, and curry powder and continue cooking for 1–2 minutes.

3 Add the tomatoes, water, and chili paste with a large pinch of salt.

Reduce the heat, then cover and simmer for 30 minutes, stirring occasionally.

4 Add the garbanzo beans and peas to the pan and continue cooking for about 15 minutes, or until all the vegetables are tender.

5 Taste the soup and adjust the seasoning, if necessary, adding a little more chili if wished. Ladle into warm soup bowls and sprinkle with cilantro.

Apple & Arugula Soup

Arugula is a fashionable salad leaf which has a slightly bitter flavor. It also gives a delicate green coloring to this soup.

NUTRITIONAL INFORMATION

Calories	.59	Sugars	.2.7g
Protein	.20g	Fat	.20g
Carbohydrate	.8.5g	Saturates	.1.2g

🥔 5 mins ⏱ 35 mins

SERVES 4

INGREDIENTS

4 tbsp butter

generous 5 cups diced waxy potatoes

1 red onion, quartered

1 tbsp lemon juice

4½ cups chicken bouillon

1 lb/450 g eating apples, peeled and diced

pinch of ground allspice

1¾ oz/50 g arugula leaves

salt and pepper

TO GARNISH

slices of red apple

chopped scallions

1 Melt the butter in a large pan and add the diced potatoes and sliced red onion. Sauté gently for 5 minutes, stirring constantly.

2 Add the lemon juice, chicken bouillon, diced apples, and ground allspice.

3 Bring to a boil, then reduce the heat to a simmer, cover the pan, and cook for 15 minutes.

4 Add the arugula to the soup and cook for another 10 minutes until the potatoes are cooked through.

5 Transfer half of the soup to a food processor or blender and process for 1 minute. Return to the pan and stir the purée into the remaining soup.

6 Season to taste with salt and pepper. Ladle into hot soup bowls and garnish with the apple slices and chopped scallions. Serve at once with warm crusty bread.

COOK'S TIP

If arugula is unavailable, use baby spinach instead for a similar flavor.

Indian Potato & Pea Soup

A slightly hot and spicy Indian flavor is given to this soup with the use of garam masala, chili, cumin, and cilantro.

NUTRITIONAL INFORMATION

Calories . . . . .160 Sugars 8g
Protein . . . . .6g Fat 7g
Carbohydrate . . .21g Saturates 1g

5 mins   35 mins

SERVES 4

I N G R E D I E N T S

2 tbsp vegetable oil

1¼ cups diced mealy potatoes

1 large onion, chopped

2 garlic cloves, crushed

1 tsp garam masala

1 tsp ground cilantro

1 tsp ground cumin

3¾ cups vegetable bouillon

1 red chili, chopped

3½ oz/100 g frozen peas

4 tbsp plain unsweetened yogurt

salt and pepper

chopped cilantro, to garnish

warm bread, to serve

VARIATION

For slightly less heat, seed the chili before adding it to the soup. Always wash your hands after handling chilies because they contain volatile oils that can irritate the skin and make your eyes burn if you touch your face.

1 Heat the vegetable oil in a large pan and add the diced potatoes, onion, and garlic. Sauté gently for about 5 minutes, stirring constantly.

2 Add the ground spices and cook for 1 minute, stirring all the time.

3 Stir in the vegetable bouillon and chopped red chili and bring the mixture to a boil. Reduce the heat, then cover the pan and simmer for 20 minutes, until the potatoes begin to break down.

4 Add the peas and cook for a further 5 minutes. Stir in the yogurt and season to taste.

5 Pour into warmed soup bowls. Garnish with chopped fresh cilantro and serve hot with warm bread.

Broccoli & Potato Soup

This creamy soup has a delightful pale green coloring and rich flavor from the blend of tender broccoli and blue cheese.

NUTRITIONAL INFORMATION

Calories 452   Sugars 4g
Protein . . . . .14g   Fat 35g
Carbohydrate . . .20g   Saturates 19g

5–10 mins   35 mins

SERVES 4

INGREDIENTS

2 tbsp olive oil

2⅔ cups diced potatoes

1 onion, diced

8 oz/225 g broccoli florets

4½ oz/125 g blue cheese, crumbled

4½ cups vegetable bouillon

⅔ cup heavy cream

pinch of paprika

salt and pepper

1 Heat the oil in a large pan and add the diced potatoes and onion. Sauté gently for 5 minutes, stirring constantly.

2 Reserve a few broccoli florets for the garnish and add the remaining broccoli to the pan. Add the cheese and bouillon.

COOK'S TIP

This soup freezes very successfully. Follow the method described here up to step 4, and freeze the soup after it has been puréed. Add the cream and paprika just before serving. Garnish and serve.

3 Bring to a boil, then reduce the heat, cover the pan, and simmer for 25 minutes, until the potatoes are tender.

4 Transfer the soup to a food processor or blender in 2 batches and process until the mixture is a smooth purée.

5 Return the purée to a clean pan and stir in the cream and a pinch of paprika. Season to taste with salt and pepper.

6 Blanch the reserved broccoli florets in a little boiling water for approximately 2 minutes, then drain with a slotted spoon.

7 Pour the soup into warmed bowls and garnish with the broccoli florets and a sprinkling of paprika. Serve immediately.

Potato & Mushroom Soup

The many varieties of dried mushrooms available are relatively expensive, but the concentrated flavor that they add to a dish justifies the cost.

NUTRITIONAL INFORMATION

Calories	81	Sugars	.......0.7g
Protein	........3.8g	Fat	..........4g
Carbohydrate	...7.6g	Saturates	.....1.8g

🕑 5 mins   🕐 30 mins

SERVES 4

I N G R E D I E N T S

2 tbsp vegetable oil

1 lb 5 oz/600 g mealy potatoes, sliced

1 onion, sliced

2 garlic cloves, crushed

4½ cups beef bouillon

1 oz/25 g dried mushrooms

2 celery stalks, sliced

2 tbsp brandy

salt and pepper

T O P P I N G

3 tbsp butter

2 thick slices white bread, crusts removed

3 tbsp Parmesan cheese, freshly grated

T O G A R N I S H

rehydrated dried mushrooms

parsley sprigs

COOK'S TIP

Probably the most popular dried mushroom is the cep, but any variety will add a lovely flavor to this soup. If you do not wish to use dried mushrooms, add 4½ oz/ 125 g sliced fresh mushrooms of your choice to the soup.

1 Heat the vegetable oil in a large skillet and add the potato and onion slices and the garlic. Sauté gently for 5 minutes, stirring constantly.

2 Add the beef bouillon, dried mushrooms, and sliced celery. Bring to a boil, then reduce the heat to a simmer, cover the pan and cook the soup for 20 minutes until the potatoes are tender.

3 Meanwhile, melt the butter for the topping in the skillet. Sprinkle the bread slices with the grated cheese and cook the slices in the butter for 1 minute on each side until crisp. Cut each slice into triangles.

4 Stir the brandy into the soup. Season with salt and pepper. Pour into warmed bowls and top with the triangles. Serve garnished with mushrooms and parsley.

Field Pea & Cheese Soup

Field green peas are sweeter than other varieties of field pea and reduce down to a purée when cooked, which acts as a thickener in soups.

NUTRITIONAL INFORMATION

Calories 260   Sugars 5g
Protein . . . . .11g   Fat 10g
Carbohydrate . . .32g   Saturates 3g

5–10 mins   45 mins

SERVES 4

INGREDIENTS

2 tbsp vegetable oil

2⅔ cups diced mealy potatoes, unpeeled

2 onions, diced

2¾ oz/75 g field green peas

4½ cups vegetable bouillon

2¼ oz/60 g grated Gruyère cheese

salt and pepper

CROUTONS

3 tbsp butter

1 garlic clove, crushed

1 tbsp chopped parsley

1 thick slice white bread, cubed

1 Heat the vegetable oil in a large pan. Add the potatoes and onions and sauté over a low heat, stirring constantly, for about 5 minutes.

2 Add the field green peas to the pan and stir to mix together well.

3 Pour the vegetable bouillon into the pan and bring to a boil. Reduce the heat to low and simmer for 35 minutes, until the potatoes are tender and the field peas cooked.

4 Meanwhile, make the croûtons. Melt the butter in a skillet. Add the garlic, parsley, and bread cubes and cook, turning frequently, for about 2 minutes, until the bread cubes are golden brown on all sides.

5 Stir the grated cheese into the soup and season to taste with salt and pepper. Heat gently until the cheese is starting to melt.

6 Pour the soup into warmed individual bowls and sprinkle the croûtons on top. Serve at once.

VARIATION

For a richly colored soup, red lentils could be used instead of field green peas. Add a large pinch of brown sugar to the recipe for extra sweetness if red lentils are used.

Vegetable & Corn Chowder

This is a really filling soup, which should be served before a light main course. It is easy to prepare and filled with flavor.

NUTRITIONAL INFORMATION

Calories . . . . . . .378 Sugars 20g
Protein . . . . .16g Fat 13g
Carbohydrate . . .52g Saturates 6g

15 mins   30 mins

SERVES 4

INGREDIENTS

1 tbsp vegetable oil

1 red onion, diced

1 red bell pepper, seeded and diced

3 garlic cloves, crushed

1¾ cups diced potatoes

2 tbsp all-purpose flour

2½ cups milk

1¼ cups vegetable bouillon

1¾ oz/50 g broccoli florets

3 cups canned corn, drained

¾ cup Cheddar cheese, grated

salt and pepper

1 tbsp chopped cilantro, to garnish

COOK'S TIP

Vegetarian cheeses are made with rennets of non-animal origin, using microbial or fungal enzymes.

1 Heat the oil in a large pan. Add the onion, bell pepper, garlic, and potato and sauté over a low heat, stirring frequently, for 2–3 minutes.

2 Stir in the flour and cook, stirring for 30 seconds. Gradually stir in the milk and stock.

3 Add the broccoli and corn. Bring the mixture to a boil, stirring constantly,

then reduce the heat and simmer for about 20 minutes, or until all the vegetables are tender.

4 Add ½ cup of the cheese and stir until it melts.

5 Season and spoon the chowder into a warm soup tureen. Garnish with the remaining cheese and the chopped cilantro and serve.

Fava Bean & Mint Soup

Fresh fava beans are best for this delicious soup, but if they are unavailable, use frozen beans instead.

NUTRITIONAL INFORMATION

Calories	224	Sugars 4g
Protein	........12g	Fat 6g
Carbohydrate	...31g	Saturates 1g

15 mins   40 mins

SERVES 4

INGREDIENTS

2 tbsp olive oil

1 red onion, chopped

2 garlic cloves, crushed

2⅔ cups diced potatoes

3 cups fava beans, thawed if frozen

3¾ cups vegetable bouillon

2 tbsp freshly chopped mint

mint sprigs and unsweetened yogurt, to garnish

1 Heat the olive oil in a large pan. Add the onion and garlic and sauté for 2–3 minutes, until softened.

2 Add the potatoes and cook, stirring constantly, for 5 minutes.

3 Stir in the beans and the bouillon. Cover and simmer for 30 minutes, or until the beans and potatoes are tender.

4 Remove a few vegetables with a slotted spoon and set aside. Place the remainder of the soup in a food processor or blender and process until smooth.

5 Return the soup to a clean pan and add the reserved vegetables and chopped mint. Stir thoroughly and heat through gently.

6 Transfer the soup to a warm tureen or individual serving bowls. Garnish with swirls of yogurt and sprigs of fresh mint and serve immediately.

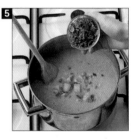

VARIATION

Use fresh cilantro and ½ teaspoon ground cumin as flavorings in the soup, if you prefer.

Sweet Potato & Squash Soup

When there's a chill in the air, this vivid soup is just the thing to serve—it's very warm and comforting.

NUTRITIONAL INFORMATION

Calories	57	Sugars	.......1.5g
Protein	........2.3g	Fat	..........2.5g
Carbohydrate	...6.6g	Saturates	.....0.8g

15 mins   1 hr 15 mins

SERVES 6

INGREDIENTS

12 oz/350 g sweet potatoes

1 acorn squash

4 shallots

olive oil

5–6 garlic cloves, unpeeled

3¾ cups chicken bouillon

½ cup light cream

salt and pepper

snipped chives, to garnish

1 Cut the sweet potato, squash and shallots in half lengthwise. Brush the cut sides with oil.

2 Put the vegetables, cut sides down, in a shallow roasting pan. Add the garlic cloves. Roast in a preheated oven, 375°F/190°C for about 40 minutes until tender and light brown.

3 When cool, scoop the flesh from the potato and squash halves, and put in a pan with the shallots. Remove the garlic peel and add the soft insides to the other vegetables.

4 Add the stock and a pinch of salt. Bring just to a boil, then reduce the heat and simmer, partially covered, for about 30 minutes, stirring occasionally, until the vegetables are very tender.

5 Let the soup cool slightly, then transfer to a blender or food processor and purée until smooth, working in batches, if necessary. (If using a food processor, strain off the cooking liquid and reserve. Purée the soup solids with enough cooking liquid to moisten them, then combine with the remaining liquid.)

6 Return the soup to the pan and stir in the cream. Season to taste, then simmer for 5–10 minutes until completely heated through. Ladle into warm bowls and serve hot.

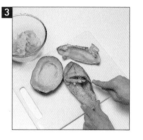

Celery Root & Leek Soup

It is hard to imagine that celery root, a coarse, knobbly vegetable, can taste so sweet. It makes a marvelously flavorful soup.

NUTRITIONAL INFORMATION

Calories 20   Sugars 1.3g
Protein ....0.8g   Fat 0.7g
Carbohydrate ...2.7g   Saturates 0.4g

10 mins   35 mins

SERVES 4

INGREDIENTS

1 tbsp butter

1 onion, chopped

2 large leeks, halved lengthwise and sliced

1 large celery root, peeled and cubed

8 oz/225 g potatoes, cubed

1 carrot, quartered and thinly sliced

5 cups water

⅛ tsp dried marjoram

1 bay leaf

freshly grated nutmeg

salt and pepper

celery leaves, to garnish

1 Melt the butter in a large saucepan over a medium-low heat. Add the onion and leeks and cook for about 4 minutes, stirring frequently, until just softened; do not allow to color.

2 Add the celery root, potato, carrot, water, marjoram, and bay leaf, with a large pinch of salt. Bring to a boil, then reduce the heat, cover, and simmer for about 25 minutes until the vegetables are tender. Remove the bay leaf.

3 Let the soup cool slightly. Transfer to a blender or food processor and purée until smooth. (If using a food processor, strain off the cooking liquid and reserve. Purée the soup solids with enough cooking liquid to moisten them, then combine with the remaining liquid.)

4 Return the puréed soup to the pan and stir to blend. Season with salt, pepper, and nutmeg. Simmer over a medium-low heat until reheated.

5 Ladle the soup into warm bowls. Garnish with celery leaves and serve.

Roasted Garlic & Potato Soup

The combination of potato, garlic, and onion works marvelously in soup. In this recipe the garlic is roasted to give it added dimension and depth.

NUTRITIONAL INFORMATION

Calories	240	Sugars	.........7g
Protein	.........8g	Fat	..........10g
Carbohydrate	...33g	Saturates	.......5g

🍽 10 mins   🕐 1 hour

SERVES 4

INGREDIENTS

1 large bulb garlic with large cloves, peeled (about 3½ oz/100 g)

2 tsp olive oil

2 large leeks, thinly sliced

1 large onion, finely chopped

2¾ cups diced potatoes

5 cups chicken or vegetable bouillon

1 bay leaf

⅔ cup light cream

freshly grated nutmeg

fresh lemon juice, optional

salt and pepper

snipped fresh chives, to garnish

1 Put the garlic cloves in a baking dish. Lightly brush with oil and bake in a preheated oven at 350°F/180°C for about 20 minutes until golden.

2 Heat the oil in a large pan over a medium heat. Add the leeks and onion, then cover and cook for about 3 minutes, stirring frequently, until they begin to soften.

3 Add the potatoes, roasted garlic, bouillon, and bay leaf. Season with salt (unless the stock is salty) and pepper. Bring to a boil, then reduce the heat, cover, and cook gently for about 30 minutes until the vegetables are tender. Remove the bay leaf.

4 Let the soup cool slightly, then transfer to a blender or food processor and purée until smooth, working in batches if necessary. (If using a food processor, strain off the cooking liquid and reserve. Purée the soup solids with enough cooking liquid to moisten them, then combine with the remaining liquid.)

5 Return the soup to the pan and stir in the cream and a generous grating of nutmeg. Taste and adjust the seasoning, if necessary, adding a few drops of lemon juice, if wished. Reheat over a low heat. Ladle into warm soup bowls, then garnish with chives or parsley and serve.

Sweet Potato & Apple Soup

This soup makes a marvelous late-fall or winter appetizer. It has a delicious texture and cheerful golden color.

NUTRITIONAL INFORMATION

Calories 57	Sugars 3.8g	
Protein 0.7g	Fat 2.9g	
Carbohydrate ...7.4g	Saturates 1.8g	

10 mins   45 mins

SERVES 6

INGREDIENTS

1 tbsp butter

3 leeks, thinly sliced

1 large carrot, thinly sliced

1 lb 5 oz/600 g sweet potatoes, peeled and cubed

2 large tart eating apples, peeled and cubed

5 cups water

freshly grated nutmeg

1 cup apple juice

1 cup whipping or light cream

salt and pepper

snipped fresh chives or cilantro, to garnish

1 Melt the butter in a large pan over a medium-low heat. Add the leeks, then cover and cook for 6–8 minutes, or until softened, stirring frequently.

2 Add the carrot, sweet potatoes, apples, and water. Season lightly with salt, pepper, and nutmeg. Bring to the boil, then reduce the heat and simmer, covered, for about 20 minutes, stirring occasionally, until the vegetables are very tender.

3 Allow the soup to cool slightly, then transfer to a blender or food processor and purée until smooth, working in batches if necessary. (If using a food processor, strain off the cooking liquid and reserve. Purée the soup solids with enough cooking liquid to moisten them, then combine with the remaining liquid.)

4 Return the puréed soup to the pan and stir in the apple juice. Place over a low heat and simmer for about 10 minutes until heated through.

5 Stir in the cream and continue simmering for about 5 minutes, stirring frequently, until heated through. Taste and adjust the seasoning, adding more salt, pepper, and nutmeg, if necessary. Ladle the soup into warm bowls, then garnish with chives or cilantro and serve.

Vichyssoise

This is a classic creamy soup made from potatoes and leeks. To achieve the delicate pale color, be sure to use only the white parts of the leeks.

NUTRITIONAL INFORMATION

Calories 208	Sugars 5g	
Protein 5g	Fat 12g	
Carbohydrate ...20g	Saturates 6g	

🍲 10 mins   🕐 40 mins

SERVES 6

INGREDIENTS

3 large leeks

3 tbsp butter or margarine

1 onion, thinly sliced

1 lb 2 oz/500 g potatoes, chopped

3½ cups vegetable bouillon

2 tsp lemon juice

pinch of ground nutmeg

¼ tsp ground coriander

1 bay leaf

1 egg yolk

⅔ cup light cream

salt and white pepper

freshly snipped chives, to garnish

1 Trim the leeks and remove most of the green part. Slice the white part of the leeks very finely.

2 Melt the butter or margarine in a pan. Add the leeks and onion and bouillon, stirring occasionally, for about 5 minutes without browning.

3 Add the potatoes, vegetable bouillon, lemon juice, nutmeg, coriander, and bay leaf to the pan. Season to taste with salt and pepper and bring to a boil. Cover and simmer for about 30 minutes, until all the vegetables are very soft.

4 Cool the soup a little. Remove and discard the bay leaf and then press through a strainer or process in a food processor or blender until smooth. Pour into a clean pan.

5 Blend the egg yolk into the cream. Add a little of the soup to this mixture and then whisk it all back into the soup. Reheat gently, without boiling. Adjust the seasoning to taste. Cool and then chill thoroughly in the refrigerator.

6 Serve the soup sprinkled with freshly snipped chives.

Watercress Vichyssoise

The addition of watercress to a traditional vichyssoise gives it a refreshing flavor and lovely cool color.

NUTRITIONAL INFORMATION

Calories 42   Sugars 0.8g
Protein ....2.1g   Fat 2.2g
Carbohydrate ...3.6g   Saturates 1g

15 mins   35 mins

SERVES 6

INGREDIENTS

1 tbsp olive oil

3 large leeks, thinly sliced

2 cups finely diced potatoes

2½ cups chicken or vegetable bouillon

2 cups water

1 bay leaf

6 oz/175g prepared watercress

¾ cup light cream

salt and pepper

watercress leaves, to garnish

1 Heat the oil in a heavy-based pan over a medium heat. Add the leeks and cook for about 3 minutes, stirring frequently, until they begin to soften.

2 Add the potato, bouillon, water, and bay leaf. Add salt if the stock is unsalted. Bring to a boil, then reduce the heat, cover, and cook gently for about 25 minutes until the vegetables are tender. Remove the bay leaf.

3 Add the watercress and continue to cook for another 2–3 minutes, stirring frequently, until the watercress is completely wilted.

4 Allow the soup to cool slightly, then transfer to a blender or food processor and purée until smooth, working in batches if necessary. (If using a food processor, strain off the cooking liquid and reserve. Purée the soup solids with enough cooking liquid to moisten them, then combine with the remaining liquid.)

5 Put the soup in a large bowl and stir in half the cream. Season with salt, if needed, and plenty of pepper. Let cool.

6 Refrigerate until cold. Taste and adjust the seasoning, if necessary. Ladle into chilled bowls, then drizzle the remaining cream on top and garnish with watercress leaves. Serve at once.

Mixed Fish Soup

Any mixture of fish is suitable for this recipe, from simple smoked and white fish to salmon or mussels, depending on the occasion.

NUTRITIONAL INFORMATION

Calories ....458 Sugar 5g
Protein ....28g Fats 25g
Carbohydrates ...22g Saturates 12g

10 mins   35 mins

SERVES 4

INGREDIENTS

2 tbsp vegetable oil

1 lb/450 g small new potatoes, halved

1 bunch scallions, sliced

1 yellow bell pepper, sliced

2 garlic cloves, crushed

1 cup dry white wine

2½ cups fish bouillon

8 oz/225 g white fish fillet, skinned and cubed

8 oz/225 g smoked cod fillet, skinned and cubed

2 tomatoes, peeled, seeded, and chopped

3½ oz/100 g shelled cooked shrimp

⅔ cup heavy cream

2 tbsp shredded fresh basil

1 Heat the vegetable oil in a large pan and add the halved potatoes with the sliced scallions, bell pepper, and garlic. Sauté gently for 3 minutes, stirring constantly.

2 Add the white wine and fish bouillon to the pan and bring to a boil. Reduce the heat and simmer for 10–15 minutes.

3 Add the cubed fish fillets and the tomatoes to the soup and continue to cook for 10 minutes or until the fish is cooked through.

4 Stir in the shrimp, cream, and shredded basil and cook for 2–3 minutes. Pour the soup into warmed bowls and serve immediately.

COOK'S TIP

For a soup which is slightly less rich, omit the wine and stir plain yogurt into the soup instead of the heavy cream.

Smoked Haddock Soup

This chunky aromatic soup is perfect for a cold weather lunch or supper served with crusty bread and a salad.

NUTRITIONAL INFORMATION

Calories	80	Sugar	........2.9g
Protein	........4.3g	Fats	...........3g
Carbohydrates	..9.6g	Saturates	.....1.4g

5–10 mins

40 mins

SERVES 4

INGREDIENTS

1 tbsp oil

⅓ cup bacon, cut into thin matchsticks

1 large onion, finely chopped

2 tbsp all-purpose flour

4 cups milk

1 lb 9 oz/700 g potatoes, cubed

6 oz/175 g skinless smoked haddock

salt and pepper

finely chopped fresh parsley, to garnish

1 Heat the oil in a large pan over a medium heat. Add the bacon and cook for 2 minutes. Stir in the onion and continue cooking for 5–7 minutes, stirring frequently, until the onion is soft and the bacon golden. Tip the pan and spoon off as much fat as possible.

2 Stir in the flour and continue cooking for 2 minutes. Add half of the milk and stir well, scraping the bottom of the pan to mix in the flour.

3 Add the potatoes and remaining milk and season with pepper. Bring just to a boil, stirring frequently, then reduce the heat and simmer, partially covered, for 10 minutes.

4 Add the fish and continue cooking, stirring occasionally, for about 15 minutes, or until the potatoes are tender and the fish breaks up easily.

5 Taste the soup and adjust the seasoning (salt may not be needed). Ladle into a warm tureen or bowls and sprinkle generously with chopped parsley.

COOK'S TIP

Cutting the potatoes into small cubes not only looks attractive, but lets them cook more quickly and evenly.

Breton Fish Soup with Cider

Fishermen's soups vary, depending on the season and the catch.
Monkfish has a texture like lobster, but cod is equally appealing.

NUTRITIONAL INFORMATION

Calories	103	Sugars	1.5g
Protein	5.2g	Fat	6.3g
Carbohydrate	6.6g	Saturates	3.8g

5–10 mins   40 mins

SERVES 4

I N G R E D I E N T S

2 tsp butter

1 large leek, thinly sliced

2 shallots, finely chopped

½ cup hard cider

1¼ cups fish bouillon

9 oz/250 g potatoes, diced

1 bay leaf

4 tbsp all-purpose flour

¾ cup milk

¾ cup heavy cream

2¼ oz/60 g fresh sorrel leaves

12 oz/350 g skinless monkfish or cod fillet,
    cut into 1 inch/2.5 cm pieces

salt and pepper

COOK'S TIP

Be careful not to overcook the
fish—tender fish, such as cod,
break up into smaller flakes and
firm fish, like monkfish, can
become tough.

1 Melt the butter in a large pan over a medium-low
heat. Add the leek and shallots and cook for about
5 minutes, stirring frequently, until they start to soften.
Add the cider and bring to a boil.

2 Stir in the bouillon, potatoes, and bay leaf with a large
pinch of salt (unless the bouillon is salty) and bring
back to a boil. Reduce the heat, then cover and cook gently
for 10 minutes.

3 Put the flour in a small bowl and very slowly whisk in
a few tablespoons of the milk to make a thick paste.
Stir in a little more to make a smooth liquid.

4 Adjust the heat so the soup bubbles gently. Stir in the
flour mixture and cook, stirring frequently, for 5 minutes.
Add the remaining milk and half the cream. Continue cooking
for about 10 minutes until the potatoes are tender.

5 Chop the sorrel finely and combine with the remaining
cream. (If using a food processor, add the sorrel and
chop, then add the cream and process briefly.)

6 Stir the sorrel cream into the soup and add the fish.
Continue cooking, stirring occasionally, for about
3 minutes, until the monkfish stiffens or the cod just
begins to flake. Taste the soup and adjust the seasoning, if
needed. Ladle into warm bowls and serve.

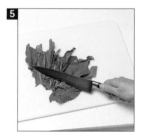

Fennel & Tomato Soup

This light and refreshing soup is also good served cold. An ideal starter for a summer meal, served with crunchy Melba toast.

NUTRITIONAL INFORMATION

Calories	 110	Sugars	. . . . .8g
Protein	. . . . .10g	Fat	. . . . .2g
Carbohydrate	. . .13g	Saturates	. . . . . . .0g

30 mins   40 mins

SERVES 4

INGREDIENTS

2 tsp olive oil

1 large onion, halved and sliced

2 large fennel bulbs, halved and sliced

1 small potato, diced

3¾ cups water

1⅔ cups tomato juice

1 bay leaf

4½ oz/125 g cooked shelled small shrimp

2 tomatoes, skinned, seeded, and chopped

½ tsp snipped fresh dill

salt and pepper

dill sprigs or fennel fronds, to garnish

1 Heat the olive oil in a large pan over a medium heat. Add the onion and fennel and cook for 3–4 minutes, stirring occasionally, until the onion is just softened.

2 Add the potato, water, tomato juice, and bay leaf with a large pinch of salt. Reduce the heat, then cover and simmer for about 25 minutes, stirring once or twice, until the vegetables are soft.

3 Let cool slightly, then transfer to a blender or food processor. Purée until

smooth, working in batches if necessary. (If using a food processor, strain off the cooking liquid and reserve. Purée the solids with enough cooking liquid to moisten them, then mix with the remaining liquid.)

4 Return the soup to the pan and add the shrimp. Simmer gently for about 10 minutes, to reheat the soup and let it absorb the shrimp flavor.

5 Stir in the tomatoes and dill. Taste and adjust the seasoning, adding salt, if needed, and pepper. Thin the soup with a little more tomato juice, if wished. Ladle into warm bowls, then garnish with dill or fennel fronds and serve.

Cullen Skink

This is a traditional, creamy Scottish soup. Some fresh cod has been added to balance the strong flavor of the smoked haddock.

NUTRITIONAL INFORMATION

Calories 108   Sugars 2.3g
Protein . . . . .7.4g   Fat 6.4g
Carbohydrate . . .5.6g   Saturates 3.9g

🐚 🐚 🐚

🍲 20 mins   🕐 40 mins

SERVES 4

I N G R E D I E N T S

8 oz/225 g undyed smoked haddock fillet

2 tbsp butter

1 onion, finely chopped

2½ cups milk

2 cups diced potatoes

12 oz/350 g cod, boned, skinned and cubed

⅔ cup heavy cream

2 tbsp chopped fresh parsley

lemon juice, to taste

salt and pepper

T O   G A R N I S H

lemon slices

parsley sprigs

1 Put the haddock fillet in a large skillet and cover with boiling water. Leave for 10 minutes. Drain, reserving 1¼ cups of the soaking water. Flake the fish, taking care to remove all the bones.

2 Heat the butter in a large pan and add the onion. Cook gently for 10 minutes until softened. Add the milk and bring to a gentle simmer before adding the potato. Cook for 10 minutes.

3 Add the reserved haddock flakes and cod. Simmer for 10 minutes more until the cod is tender.

4 Remove about one third of the fish and potatoes, then put in a food processor and blend until smooth. Alternatively, push through a strainer into a bowl. Return to the soup with the cream, parsley, and seasoning. Taste and add a little lemon juice, if desired. Add a little of the reserved soaking water if the soup seems too thick. Reheat gently then serve immediately, garnished with the lemon and parsley.

COOK'S TIP

Look for Finnan haddock, if you can find it. Do not use yellow dyed haddock fillet, which is often actually whiting and not haddock at all.

New England Clam Chowder

A chowder is made from milk and potatoes, to which other flavors are added. This classic version comes from New England.

NUTRITIONAL INFORMATION

Calories	136	Sugars	.........2g
Protein	........7.7g	Fat	..........9.5g
Carbohydrate	...5.4g	Saturates	.....5.4g

15 mins   30 mins

SERVES 4

INGREDIENTS

2 lb/900 g live clams, reserving 8, in their shells, to garnish

4 rashers rindless lean bacon, chopped

2 tbsp butter

1 onion, chopped

1 tbsp chopped fresh thyme

1¾ cups diced potato

1¼ cups milk

1 bay leaf

1⅔ cups heavy cream

1 tbsp chopped fresh parsley

salt and pepper

1 Scrub the clams and put into a large pan with a splash of water. Cook over a high heat for 3–4 minutes until all the clams have opened. Discard any that remain closed. Strain the clams, reserving the cooking liquid. Set aside until cool enough to handle.

2 Remove the clams from their shells. Chop coarsely if large, and set aside.

3 In a clean pan, fry the bacon until browned and crisp. Drain on paper towels. Add the butter to the same pan and when it has melted, add the onion. Cook for 4–5 minutes until softened but not colored. Add the thyme and cook briefly before adding the diced potato, reserved clam cooking liquid, milk, and bay leaf. Bring to a boil and simmer for 10 minutes until the potato is tender but not falling apart. Remove the bayleaf.

4 Transfer to a food processor and blend until smooth or push through a strainer into a bowl.

5 Add the reserved clams, bacon, and the cream. Simmer for another 2–3 minutes until heated through. Season to taste. Stir in the chopped parsley and serve.

COOK'S TIP

For a smart presentation, reserve 8 clams in their shells. Sit 2 on top of each bowl of soup to serve.

Creamy Scallop Soup

This delicately flavored soup should not be overcooked. A sprinkling of parsley before serving makes a pretty contrast to the creamy color.

NUTRITIONAL INFORMATION

Calories 98	Sugars 1.4g	
Protein 6.5g	Fat 5.6g	
Carbohydrate . . .5.9g	Saturates 3.2g	

🕒 10 mins   🕐 35 mins

SERVES 4

I N G R E D I E N T S

4 tbsp butter

1 onion, finely chopped

2⅔ cups diced potatoes

2½ cups hot fish bouillon

12 oz/350 g prepared scallops, including corals if available

1¼ cups milk

2 egg yolks

6 tbsp heavy cream

salt and pepper

1 tbsp chopped fresh parsley, to garnish

1 Melt the butter in a large pan over a gentle heat. Add the onions and cook very gently for 10 minutes until softened but not colored. Add the potatoes and seasoning, then cover and cook for a further 10 minutes over a very low heat.

2 Pour on the hot fish bouillon, bring to a boil and simmer for another 10–15 minutes until the potatoes are tender.

3 Meanwhile, prepare the scallops. If the corals are available, chop coarsely and set aside. Coarsely chop the white meat and put in a second pan with the milk. Bring to a gentle simmer and cook for 6–8 minutes until the scallops are just tender.

4 When the potatoes are cooked, transfer them and their cooking liquid

to a food processor or blender and blend to a purée. Alternatively, press through a strainer. Return the mixture to a clean pan with the scallops and their milk and the pieces of coral, if using.

5 Whisk together the egg yolks and cream and add to the soup, off the heat. Return the soup to a very gentle heat. Stirring constantly, reheat the soup until it thickens slightly. Do not boil or the soup will curdle. Adjust seasoning and serve immediately, sprinkled with fresh parsley.

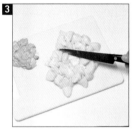

COOK'S TIP

The soup can be made in advance up to the point where the cream and eggs are added. This should be done only just before serving.

Pistou

This hearty soup of beans and vegetables is from Nice and gets its name from the fresh basil sauce stirred in at the last minute.

NUTRITIONAL INFORMATION

Calories 55   Sugars 1.2g
Protein . . . . .3.8g   Fat 2.6g
Carbohydrate . . .4.2g   Saturates 0.6g

🍲 10 mins   🕐 25 mins

SERVES 6

INGREDIENTS

2 young carrots

1 lb/450 g potatoes

7 oz/200 g fresh peas in the shells

7 oz/200 g thin beans

5½ oz/150 g young zucchini

2 tbsp olive oil

1 garlic clove, crushed

1 large onion, finely chopped

10 cups vegetable bouillon or water

1 bouquet garni of 2 sprigs fresh parsley and 1 bay leaf tied in a 3 inch/7.5 cm piece of celery

3 oz/85 g dried small soup pasta

1 large tomato, skinned, seeded, and chopped or diced

pared Parmesan cheese, to serve

PISTOU SAUCE

1½ cups fresh basil leaves

1 garlic clove

5 tbsp fruity extra-virgin olive oil

salt and pepper

1 To make the pistou sauce, put the basil leaves, garlic, and olive oil in a food processor and process until well blended. Season with salt and pepper to taste. Transfer to a bowl, then cover and chill until required.

2 Peel the carrots and cut them in half lengthwise, then slice. Peel the potatoes and cut into quarter lengths, then slice. Set aside.

3 Shell the peas. Top and tail the beans and cut them into 1 inch/2.5 cm pieces. Cut the zucchini in half lengthwise, then slice.

4 Heat the oil in a large pan or flameproof casserole. Add the garlic and cook for 2 minutes, stirring. Add the onion and continue cooking for 2 minutes until soft. Add the carrots and potatoes and stir for about 30 seconds.

5 Pour in the bouillon and bring to a boil. Lower the heat, then partially cover and simmer for 8 minutes, until the vegetables are starting to become tender.

6 Stir in the peas, beans, zucchini, bouquet garni, pasta, and tomato. Season and cook for 4 minutes, or until the vegetables and pasta are tender. Stir in the pistou or sauce and serve with Parmesan.

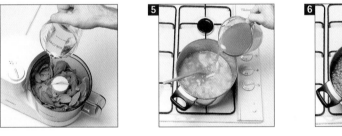

Spinach & Ginger Soup

This mildly spiced, rich green soup is delicately scented with ginger and lemon grass. It makes a good light appetizer or summer lunch dish.

NUTRITIONAL INFORMATION

Calories ....38 Sugars 0.8g
Protein ....3.2g Fat 1.8g
Carbohydrate ...2.4g Saturates 0.2g

5–10 mins   25 mins

SERVES 4

INGREDIENTS

2 tbsp sunflower oil

1 onion, chopped

2 garlic cloves, finely chopped

2 tsp fresh ginger root, finely chopped

4 cups fresh young spinach leaves

1 small lemon grass stem, finely chopped

4 cups chicken or vegetable bouillon

8 oz/225 g potato, peeled and chopped

1 tbsp rice wine or dry sherry

1 tsp sesame oil

salt and pepper

fresh spinach, finely shredded, to garnish

1 Heat the oil in a large pan. Add the onion, garlic, and ginger, and cook gently for 3–4 minutes until softened but not browned.

2 Reserve 2–3 small spinach leaves. Add the remaining leaves and lemon grass to the pan, stirring until the spinach is wilted. Add the bouillon and potato to the pan and bring to a boil. Lower the heat, cover, and simmer for about 10 minutes.

3 Tip the soup into a blender or food processor and process until completely smooth.

4 Return the soup to the pan and add the rice wine, then adjust the seasoning to taste with salt and pepper. Heat until just about to boil.

5 Finely shred the 2–3 reserved spinach leaves and scatter some over the top. Drizzle with a few drops of sesame oil and serve hot, garnished with more finely shredded fresh spinach leaves.

COOK'S TIP

To make a creamy-textured spinach and coconut soup, stir in about 4 tablespoons creamed coconut, or alternatively replace about 1¼ cups of the bouillon with coconut milk. Serve the soup with shavings of fresh coconut scattered over the surface.

Bouillabaisse

This soup makes a festive seafood extravaganza worthy of any special occasion or celebration.

NUTRITIONAL INFORMATION

Calories . . . . .55 Sugars 1.1g
Protein . . . . .7.2g Fat 1.8g
Carbohydrate . . .2.6g Saturates 0.3g

10 mins | 1 hr 5 mins

SERVES 6

INGREDIENTS

1 lb/450 g jumbo shrimp

1 lb 10 oz/750 g firm white fish fillets, such as sea bass, snapper, and monkfish

4 tbsp olive oil

grated zest of 1 orange

1 large garlic clove, finely chopped

½ tsp chili paste or harissa

1 large leek, sliced

1 onion, halved and sliced

1 red bell pepper, cored, seeded, and sliced

3–4 tomatoes, cored and cut into 8 pieces

4 garlic cloves, sliced

1 bay leaf

pinch of saffron threads

½ tsp fennel seeds

2½ cups water

5 cups fish bouillon

1 fennel bulb, finely chopped

1 large onion, finely chopped

8 oz/225 g potatoes, halved and thinly sliced

9 oz/250 g scallops

salt and pepper

toasted French bread slices, to serve

store-bought aïoli, to serve

1 Shell the shrimp and reserve the shells. Cut the fish into pieces 2 inches/5 cm square. Trim any ragged edges and reserve. Put the fish in a bowl with 2 tablespoons of the olive oil, the orange zest, crushed garlic, and chili paste. Turn to coat, cover, and chill the shrimp and fish separately.

2 Heat 1 tablespoon of the olive oil in a large pan over a medium heat. Add the leek, onion, and red bell pepper. Cover and cook for 5 minutes, stirring frequently, until the onion softens. Stir in the tomatoes, sliced garlic, bay leaf, saffron, fennel seeds, shrimp shells, water, and fish bouillon. Bring to a boil, reduce the heat and simmer, covered, for 30 minutes. Strain well.

3 Heat the remaining oil in a large pan. Add the fennel and onion and cook for 4–5 minutes until the onion softens, stirring frequently. Add the bouillon and potatoes and bring to a boil. Reduce the heat slightly, cover, and cook for 12–15 minutes, or until the potatoes are just tender.

4 Reduce the heat to a simmer and add the fish, starting with any thicker pieces and putting in the thinner ones after 2–3 minutes. Add the shrimp and scallops and continue simmering until all the seafood is cooked and opaque throughout.

5 Taste the soup and adjust the seasoning. Ladle into warm bowls. Spread the aïoli on the toasted bread slices and arrange on top of the soup.

Mussel & Potato Soup

This soup can be made in stages, so it is ideas for entertaining because some of it can be prepared in advance.

NUTRITIONAL INFORMATION

Calories . . . . .95 Sugars 1.8g
Protein . . . . .3.7g Fat 6.2g
Carbohydrate . . .6.4g Saturates 3.7g

15 mins   45 mins

SERVES 4

I N G R E D I E N T S

2 lb 4 oz/1 kg mussels

10½ oz/300 g potatoes

3 tbsp all-purpose flour

2½ cups milk

1¼ cups whipping cream

1–2 garlic cloves, finely chopped

6 cups curly parsley leaves (1 large bunch)

salt and pepper

1 Discard any broken mussels and those with open shells that do not close when tapped. Rinse under cold running water, pull off any "beards" and scrape off barnacles with a knife. Put the mussels in a large heavy-based pan. Cover tightly and cook over a high heat for about 4 minutes, or until the mussels open.

2 When cool enough to handle, remove the mussels from the shells, adding any additional juices to the cooking liquid. Strain the cooking liquid into a bowl through a cheesecloth-lined strainer and set aside.

3 Boil the potatoes, in their skins, in salted water for about 15 minutes until tender. When cool enough to handle, peel and cut into small dice.

4 Put the flour in a mixing bowl and very slowly whisk in a few tablespoons of the milk to make a thick paste. Stir in a little more to make a smooth liquid.

5 Put the remaining milk, cream, and garlic in a pan and bring to a boil. Whisk in the flour mixture. Reduce the heat to medium-low and simmer for about 15 minutes until the garlic is tender and the liquid has thickened slightly. Drop in the parsley leaves and cook for about 2–3 minutes until bright green and wilted.

6 Let the soup base cool slightly, then transfer to a blender or food processor and purée until smooth, working in batches if necessary. (If using a food processor, strain off the cooking liquid and reserve. Purée the soup solids with enough cooking liquid to moisten, then combine with the remaining liquid.)

7 Return the purée to the pan and stir in the mussel cooking liquid and the potatoes. Season to taste with salt, if needed, and pepper. Simmer the soup gently for 5–7 minutes until reheated. Add the mussels and continue cooking for about 2 minutes until the soup is steaming and the mussels are hot. Ladle the soup into warm bowls and serve.

Tom's Chicken Soup

This recipe is originally from the north of Ireland, in the beautiful area of Moira, Northern Ireland.

NUTRITIONAL INFORMATION

Calories	153	Sugars	.........6g
Protein	.........6g	Fat	...........6g
Carbohydrate	...18g	Saturates	.......1g

5 mins   1 hr 20 mins

SERVES 4

INGREDIENTS

3 smoked bacon slices, chopped

1 lb 2 oz/500 g skinless boneless chicken, chopped

2 tbsp butter

1½ lb/675 g potatoes, chopped

3 onions, chopped

2½ cups giblet or chicken bouillon

2½ cups milk

⅔ cup heavy cream

salt and pepper

2 tbsp chopped fresh parsley

soda bread, to serve

COOK'S TIP

Soda bread is not made with yeast as bread usually is. Instead it is made with baking soda as the raising agent. It can be made with all-purpose flour or whole-wheat flour.

1 Gently cook the bacon and chicken in a large pan for 10 minutes.

2 Add the butter, potatoes, and onions and cook for 15 minutes, stirring all the time.

3 Add the bouillon and milk, then bring the soup to a boil. Lower the heat and simmer for 45 minutes. Season with salt and pepper to taste.

4 Blend in the cream and simmer for 5 minutes. Stir in the chopped fresh parsley, then transfer the soup to a warm tureen or individual bowls and serve with Irish soda bread.

Chicken & Vegetable Soup

This creamy soup is filled with chunky vegetables and aromatic herbs.
Using baby vegetables give the soup an attractive look.

NUTRITIONAL INFORMATION

Calories	77	Sugar	. . . . .1.5g
Protein	. . . . .5.5g	Fats	. . . . .3.3g
Carbohydrates	. .6.9g	Saturates	. . . . .1.9g

5 mins   1 hour

SERVES 4

I N G R E D I E N T S

4 cups chicken bouillon

6 oz/175 g skinless boned chicken breast

fresh parsley and tarragon sprigs

2 garlic cloves, crushed

4½ oz/125 g baby carrots, halved or
quartered

8 oz/225 g small new potatoes, quartered

4 tbsp all-purpose flour

½ cup milk

4–5 scallions, sliced diagonally

3 oz/85 g asparagus tips, halved and cut
into 1½ inch/4 cm pieces

½ cup whipping or heavy cream

1 tbsp finely chopped fresh parsley

1 tbsp finely chopped fresh tarragon

salt and pepper

1 Put the bouillon in a pan with the
chicken, parsley and tarragon sprigs,
and garlic. Bring just to a boil, then reduce
the heat, cover, and simmer for 20
minutes, or until the chicken is cooked
through and firm to the touch.

2 Remove the chicken and strain the
stock. When the chicken is cool enough
to handle, cut into bite-sized pieces.

3 Return the stock to the pan and bring to a boil.
Adjust the heat so the liquid boils very gently. Add
the carrots, cover, and cook for 5 minutes. Add the
potatoes, cover again, and cook for about 12 minutes, or
until the vegetables are beginning to become tender.

4 Meanwhile, put the flour in a small mixing bowl and
very slowly whisk in the milk to make a thick paste.
Pour in a little of the hot stock mixture and stir to make a
smooth liquid.

5 Stir the flour mixture into the soup and bring just to
a boil, stirring. Boil gently for 4–5 minutes until it
thickens, stirring frequently.

6 Add the scallions, asparagus, and chicken. Reduce the
heat a little and simmer for about 15 minutes, until
all the vegetables are tender. Stir in the cream and herbs.
Season and serve.

Leek, Potato & Bacon Soup

Leek and potato soup is a classic recipe. Here the soup is enhanced with smoked bacon pieces and enriched with heavy cream for a little luxury.

NUTRITIONAL INFORMATION

Calories 93	Sugars 1g	
Protein 3.3g	Fat 7.8g	
Carbohydrate ...2.7g	Saturates 4.4g	

5 mins   30 mins

SERVES 4

I N G R E D I E N T S

2 tbsp butter

1 cup diced potatoes

4 leeks, shredded

2 garlic cloves, crushed

3½ oz/100 g smoked bacon, diced

3¾ cups vegetable bouillon

1 cup heavy cream

2 tbsp chopped fresh parsley

salt and pepper

TO GARNISH

vegetable oil, for deep-frying

1 leek, shredded

1 Melt the butter in a large pan and add the diced potatoes, shredded leeks, garlic, and diced bacon. Sauté gently for 5 minutes, stirring constantly.

2 Add the vegetable bouillon and bring to a boil. Reduce the heat, then cover the pan and simmer for 20 minutes until the potatoes are cooked. Stir in the heavy cream.

3 Meanwhile, make the garnish. Half-fill a pan with oil and heat to 350–375°F/180–190°C or until a cube of bread browns in 30 seconds. Add the shredded leek and deep-fry for 1 minute until browned and crisp, taking care as it contains water. Drain the shredded leek thoroughly on paper towels and reserve.

4 Reserve a few pieces of potato, leek, and bacon and set aside. Put the rest of the soup in a food processor or blender in batches and process each batch for 30 seconds. Return the puréed soup to a clean pan and heat through.

5 Stir in the reserved vegetables, bacon, and parsley and season to taste. Pour into warmed bowls and garnish with the fried leeks.

VARIATION

For a lighter soup, omit the cream and stir yogurt or crème fraîche into the soup at the end of the cooking time.

Potato & Chorizo Soup

Chorizo is a spicy sausage originating from Spain, where it is used to add its unique strong flavor to enhance many traditional dishes.

NUTRITIONAL INFORMATION

Calories 55   Sugars 1.2g
Protein ....3.0g   Fat 1.6g
Carbohydrate ...7.8g   Saturates 0.3g

5 mins   35 mins

SERVES 4

INGREDIENTS

2 tbsp olive oil

2 lb/900 g potatoes, cubed

2 red onions, quartered

1 garlic clove, crushed

4½ cups pork or vegetable stock

5½ oz/150 g Savoy cabbage, shredded

1¾ oz/50 g chorizo sausage, sliced

salt and pepper

paprika, to garnish

2 Add the pork or vegetable bouillon and bring to a boil. Reduce the heat and cover the pan. Simmer the vegetables for about 20 minutes until the potatoes are tender.

3 Process the soup in a food processor or blender in 2 batches for 1 minute each. Return the puréed soup to a clean pan.

4 Add the shredded Savoy cabbage and sliced chorizo sausage to the pan and cook for another 7 minutes. Season with salt and pepper to taste.

5 Ladle the soup into warmed soup bowls. Garnish with a sprinkling of paprika and serve.

1 Heat the olive oil in a large pan and add the cubed potatoes, quartered red onions, and garlic. Sauté gently for 5 minutes, stirring constantly.

COOK'S TIP

Chorizo sausage requires no pre-cooking. In this recipe, it is added toward the end of the cooking time so that it does not overpower the other flavors in the soup.

Lentil, Potato & Ham Soup

A comforting cold-weather soup, this is good served with bread as a main course, but can also be an appetizer, served in smaller portions.

NUTRITIONAL INFORMATION

Calories 61	Sugars 1.4g
Protein 5.4g	Fat 0.8g
Carbohydrate . . .8.6g	Saturates 0.3g

5 mins   45 mins

SERVES 4

I N G R E D I E N T S

10½ oz/300 g Puy lentils

2 tsp butter

1 large onion, finely chopped

2 carrots, finely chopped

1 garlic clove, finely chopped

2 cups water

1 bay leaf

¼ tsp dried sage or rosemary

4 cups chicken bouillon

1⅓ cup diced potatoes (see Cook's Tip)

1 tbsp tomato paste

⅔ cup smoked ham, finely diced

salt and pepper

chopped fresh parsley, to garnish

1 Rinse and drain the lentils and pick over to check for any small stones.

2 Melt the butter in a large pan or flameproof casserole over a medium heat. Add the onion, carrots, and garlic, then cover and cook for 4–5 minutes until the onion is slightly softened, stirring frequently.

3 Add the lentils to the vegetables with the water, bay leaf, and sage or rosemary. Bring to a boil, then reduce the heat, cover, and simmer for 10 minutes.

4 Add the bouillon, potatoes, tomato paste and ham. Bring back to a simmer. Cover and continue simmering for 25–30 minutes, or until the vegetables are tender.

5 Season to taste with salt and pepper and remove the bay leaf. Ladle into warm bowls, then garnish with parsley and serve.

COOK'S TIP

Cut the potatoes into small dice, about ¼ inch/5 mm, so they will be in proportion to the lentils.

Chinese Potato & Pork Broth

In this recipe the pork is seasoned with traditional Chinese flavorings—soy sauce, rice wine vinegar, and a dash of sesame oil.

NUTRITIONAL INFORMATION

Calories	166	Sugars	.........2g
Protein	........10g	Fat	...........5g
Carbohydrate	...26g	Saturates	.......1g

5 mins   20 mins

SERVES 4

INGREDIENTS

4½ cups chicken bouillon

3½ cups diced potatoes

2 tbsp rice wine vinegar

2 tbsp cornstarch

4 tbsp water

4½ oz/125 g pork fillet, sliced

1 tbsp light soy sauce

1 tsp sesame oil

1 carrot, cut into thin strips

1 tsp fresh ginger root, chopped

3 scallions, thinly sliced

1 red bell pepper, sliced

8 oz/225 g canned bamboo shoots, drained

VARIATION

For extra heat, add 1 chopped red chili or 1 teaspoon of chili powder to the soup in step 5.

1 Add the chicken bouillon, diced potatoes, and 1 tablespoon of the rice wine vinegar to a pan and bring to a boil. Reduce the heat until the stock is just simmering.

2 Mix the cornstarch with the water, then stir into the hot stock.

3 Bring the stock back to a boil, stirring until thickened, then reduce the heat until it is just simmering again.

4 Place the pork slices in a dish and season with the remaining rice wine vinegar, the soy sauce, and sesame oil.

5 Add the pork slices, carrot strips, and ginger to the bouillon and cook for 10 minutes. Stir in the scallions, red bell pepper, and bamboo shoots. Cook for another 5 minutes. Pour the soup into warmed bowls and serve immediately.

Chunky Potato & Beef Soup

This is a real winter warmer—pieces of tender beef and chunky mixed vegetables are cooked in a liquor flavored with sherry.

NUTRITIONAL INFORMATION

Calories 187	Sugars 3g	
Protein 14g	Fat 9g	
Carbohydrate ...12g	Saturates 2g	

5 mins | 35 mins

SERVES 4

INGREDIENTS

2 tbsp vegetable oil

8 oz/225 g lean braising or frying steak, cut into strips

8 oz/225 g new potatoes, halved

1 carrot, diced

2 celery stalks, sliced

2 leeks, sliced

3¾ cups beef bouillon

8 baby corn cobs, sliced

1 bouquet garni

2 tbsp dry sherry

salt and pepper

chopped fresh parsley, to garnish

1 Heat the vegetable oil in a large pan.

2 Add the strips of meat to the pan and cook for 3 minutes, turning constantly.

3 Add the halved potatoes, diced carrot, sliced celery, and leeks. Cook for a further 5 minutes, stirring.

4 Pour the beef bouillon into the pan and bring to a boil. Reduce the heat until the liquid is simmering, then add the sliced baby corn cobs and the bouquet garni.

5 Cook the soup for a further 20 minutes or until cooked through.

6 Remove the bouquet garni from the pan. Stir the dry sherry into the soup and season to taste with salt and pepper.

7 Pour the soup into warmed bowls and garnish with the chopped fresh parsley. Serve at once with crusty bread.

COOK'S TIP

Make double the quantity of soup and freeze the remainder in a rigid container for later use. When ready to use, leave in the refrigerator to defrost thoroughly, then heat until piping hot.

Indian Bean Soup

A thick and hearty soup, nourishing and substantial enough to serve as an entrée with whole-wheat bread.

NUTRITIONAL INFORMATION

Calories 237   Sugars 9g
Protein ....9g   Fat 9g
Carbohydrate ...33g   Saturates 1g

20 mins   50 mins

SERVES 6

INGREDIENTS

4 tbsp vegetable ghee or vegetable oil

2 onions, peeled and chopped

8 oz/225 g potatoes, cut into chunks

8 oz/225 g parsnips, cut into chunks

8 oz/225 g turnips or rutabagas, cut into chunks

2 celery stalks, sliced

2 zucchini, sliced

1 green bell pepper, seeded and cut into ½ inch/1 cm pieces

2 garlic cloves, crushed

2 tsp ground coriander

1 tbsp paprika

1 tbsp mild curry paste

5 cups vegetable bouillon

salt

14 oz /400 g canned black-eye beans, drained and rinsed

chopped cilantro, to garnish (optional)

1 Heat the ghee or oil in a pan, add all the prepared vegetables, except the zucchini and green bell pepper, and cook over a moderate heat, stirring frequently, for 5 minutes. Add the garlic, ground coriander, paprika, and curry paste and cook, stirring constantly, for 1 minute.

2 Stir in the bouillon and season with salt to taste. Bring to a boil, cover, and simmer over a low heat, stirring occasionally, for 25 minutes.

3 Stir in the black-eye beans, sliced zucchini, and green bell pepper, then replace the lid and continue cooking for a further 15 minutes, or until all the vegetables are tender.

4 Process 1¼ cups of the soup mixture (about 2 ladlefuls) in a food processor or blender. Return the puréed mixture to the soup in the pan and reheat until piping hot. Sprinkle with chopped cilantro if using, and serve hot.

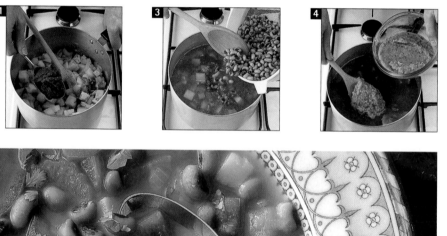

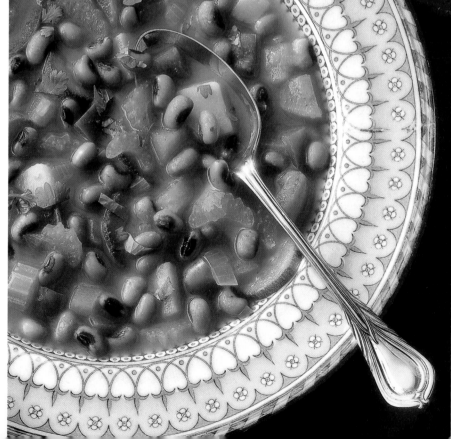

Potato Skins & Two Fillings

Potato skins are always a favorite. Prepare the skins in advance and warm them through before serving with the salad fillings.

NUTRITIONAL INFORMATION

Calories 279	Sugar 2g	
Protein 5g	Fats 011g	
Carbohydrates ...44g	Saturates 7g	

30 mins   1 hr 10 mins

SERVES 4

INGREDIENTS

4 large baking potatoes

2 tbsp vegetable oil

4 tsp salt

⅔ cup sour cream and 2 tbsp chopped fresh chives, to serve

snipped chives, to garnish

BEAN SPROUT SALAD

½ cup bean sprouts

1 celery stalk, sliced

1 orange, peeled and segmented

1 red eating apple, chopped

½ red bell pepper, chopped

1 tbsp chopped parsley

1 tbsp light soy sauce

1 tbsp clear honey

1 small garlic clove, crushed

BEAN FILLING

1½ cups canned, mixed beans, drained

1 onion, halved and sliced

1 tomato, chopped

2 scallions, chopped

2 tsp lemon juice

salt and pepper

1 Scrub the potatoes and put on a baking sheet. Prick the potatoes all over with a fork and rub the oil and salt into the skins.

2 Cook in a preheated oven at 400°F/200°C for 1 hour or until soft and cooked through.

3 Cut the potatoes in half lengthwise and scoop out the flesh, leaving a ½ inch/1 cm thick shell. Put the shells, skin side uppermost, in the oven for 10 minutes until crisp.

4 Mix the ingredients for the bean sprout salad in a bowl, then toss them in the soy sauce, honey, and garlic to coat.

5 Mix together the ingredients for the bean filling in a separate bowl.

6 Mix the sour cream and chives in another bowl.

7 Serve the potato skins hot, with the two salad fillings, garnished with snipped chives, and the sour cream and chive sauce.

Carrot & Potato Medley

This is a colorful dish of shredded vegetables in a fresh garlic and honey dressing. It is delicious served with crusty bread to mop up the dressing.

NUTRITIONAL INFORMATION

Calories 81   Sugars 4.1g
Protein . . . . .1g   Fat 5.6g
Carbohydrate . . . .7g   Saturates 0.8g

5 mins   5 mins

SERVES 4

INGREDIENTS

2 tbsp olive oil

8 oz/225 g potatoes, cut into thin strips

1 fennel bulb, cut into thin strips

2 carrots, grated

1 red onion, cut into thin strips

chopped chives and fennel fronds,
   to garnish

DRESSING

3 tbsp olive oil

1 tbsp garlic wine vinegar

1 garlic clove, crushed

1 tsp Dijon mustard

2 tsp clear honey

salt and pepper

1 Heat the olive oil in a skillet. Add the potato and fennel slices and cook for 2–3 minutes, until beginning to brown. Remove from the skillet with a slotted spoon and drain on paper towels.

2 Arrange the carrot, red onion, potato, and fennel in separate piles on a serving platter.

3 Mix the dressing ingredients together and pour over the vegetables. Toss well and sprinkle with chopped chives and fennel fronds. Serve immediately or leave in the refrigerator until required.

VARIATION

Use broiled, mixed bell peppers or shredded leeks in this dish for variety, or add beansprouts and a segmented orange, if desired.

Mixed Bean & Apple Salad

Use any mixture of beans you have to hand in this recipe, but the wider the variety, the more colorful the salad.

NUTRITIONAL INFORMATION

Calories 183	Sugars 8g
Protein 6g	Fat 7g
Carbohydrate ...26g	Saturates 1g

20 mins   20 mins

SERVES 4

INGREDIENTS

8 oz/225 g new potatoes, scrubbed and quartered

8 oz/225 g mixed canned beans, such as red kidney beans, lima beans, and borlotti beans, drained and rinsed

1 red eating apple, diced and tossed in 1 tbsp lemon juice

1 yellow bell pepper, seeded and diced

1 shallot, sliced

½ fennel bulb, sliced

oak-leaf lettuce leaves

DRESSING

1 tbsp red wine vinegar

2 tbsp olive oil

½ tbsp mustard

1 garlic clove, crushed

2 tsp chopped fresh thyme

VARIATION

Use Dijon or whole-grain mustard in place of ordinary mustard for a different flavor.

1 Cook the quartered potatoes in a pan of boiling water for 15 minutes, until tender. Drain and transfer to a mixing bowl.

2 Add the mixed beans to the potatoes, together with the apple, bell pepper, shallots, and fennel. Mix well, taking care not to break up the cooked potatoes.

3 To make the dressing, whisk all the dressing ingredients together until thoroughly combined, then pour over the potato salad.

4 Line a serving plate or salad bowl with the oak-leaf lettuce leaves and spoon the potato mixture into the center. Serve immediately.

Beet Salad & Dill Dressing

The beets add a rich color to this dish. The dill dressing with the potato salad is a classic combination.

NUTRITIONAL INFORMATION

Calories	174	Sugars	.........8g
Protein	.........4g	Fat	...........6g
Carbohydrate	...27g	Saturates	......1g

🍲 25 mins ⏱ 15 mins

SERVES 4

INGREDIENTS

2⅔ cups diced waxy potatoes

4 small cooked beets, sliced

½ small cucumber, thinly sliced

2 large dill pickles, sliced

1 red onion, halved and sliced

dill sprigs, to garnish

DRESSING

1 garlic clove, crushed

2 tbsp olive oil

2 tbsp red wine vinegar

2 tbsp chopped fresh dill

salt and pepper

COOK'S TIP

If making the salad in advance, do not mix the beets and potatoes until just before serving, as the beet will bleed its color.

1 Cook the potatoes in a pan of boiling water for 15 minutes or until tender. Drain and leave to cool.

2 When cool, mix the potato and beets together in a bowl and set aside.

3 Line a salad platter with the slices of cucumber, dill pickles, and red onion.

4 Spoon the potato and beet mixture into the center of the platter.

5 In a small bowl, whisk all the dressing ingredients together, then pour over the salad.

6 Serve the potato and beet salad immediately (see Cook's Tip, left), garnished with dill sprigs.

Radish & Cucumber Salad

The radishes and the herb and mustard dressing give this colorful salad a mild mustard flavor which complements the potatoes perfectly.

NUTRITIONAL INFORMATION

Calories 140	Sugars 3g	
Protein 3g	Fat 6g	
Carbohydrate ...20g	Saturates 1g	

50 mins   20 mins

SERVES 4

INGREDIENTS

1 lb 2 oz/500 g new potatoes, scrubbed and halved

½ cucumber, thinly sliced

2 tsp salt

1 bunch radishes, thinly sliced

DRESSING

1 tbsp Dijon mustard

2 tbsp olive oil

1 tbsp white wine vinegar

2 tbsp mixed chopped herbs

1 Cook the potatoes in a pan of boiling water for 10–15 minutes, or until tender. Drain and set aside to cool.

2 Meanwhile, spread out the cucumber slices on a plate and sprinkle with the salt. Leave to stand for 30 minutes, then rinse under cold running water and pat dry with paper towels.

3 Arrange the cucumber and radish slices on a serving plate in a decorative pattern and pile the cooked potatoes in the center of the slices.

4 In a small bowl, mix all the dressing ingredients together, whisking until thoroughly combined. Pour the dressing over the salad, tossing well to coat all of the ingredients. Chill in the refrigerator before serving.

COOK'S TIP

The cucumber adds not only color but also a real freshness to the salad. It is salted and left to stand to remove the excess water, which would make the salad soggy. Wash the cucumber well to remove all of the salt before adding to the salad.

Sweet Potato Salad

This hot, fruity salad combines sweet potato and fried bananas with colorful mixed bell peppers, tossed in a honey-based dressing.

NUTRITIONAL INFORMATION

Calories	424	Sugars	.......29g
Protein	.........5g	Fat	..........17g
Carbohydrate	...68g	Saturates	.......8g

15 mins   20 mins

SERVES 4

INGREDIENTS

2¾ cups diced sweet potatoes

4 tbsp butter

1 tbsp lemon juice

1 garlic clove, crushed

1 red bell pepper, seeded and diced

1 green bell pepper, seeded and diced

2 bananas, thickly sliced

2 thick slices white bread, crusts removed, diced

salt and pepper

DRESSING

2 tbsp clear honey

2 tbsp chopped chives

2 tbsp lemon juice

2 tbsp olive oil

1 Cook the sweet potatoes in a pan of boiling water for 10–15 minutes, until tender. Drain thoroughly and reserve.

2 Meanwhile, melt the butter in a skillet. Add the lemon juice, garlic, and bell peppers and cook, stirring constantly for 3 minutes.

3 Add the banana slices to the pan and cook for 1 minute. Remove the bananas from the pan with a slotted spoon and stir into the potatoes.

4 Add the bread cubes to the skillet and cook, stirring frequently, for 2 minutes, until they are golden brown on all sides.

5 Mix the dressing ingredients together in a small pan and heat until the honey is runny.

6 Spoon the potato mixture into a serving dish and season to taste with salt and pepper. Pour the dressing over the potatoes and sprinkle the croûtons over the top. Serve immediately.

COOK'S TIP

Use firm, slightly underripe bananas in this recipe as they won't turn soft and mushy when they are cooked.

Sweet Potato & Nut Salad

Pecan nuts with their slightly bitter flavor are mixed with sweet potatoes to make a sweet and sour salad with an interesting texture.

NUTRITIONAL INFORMATION

Calories	330	Sugars	.........5g
Protein	.........4g	Fat	..........20g
Carbohydrate	...36g	Saturates	.......2g

25 mins   10–15 mins

SERVES 4

INGREDIENTS

2¾ cups diced sweet potatoes

2 celery stalks, sliced

4½ oz/125 g celery root, grated

2 scallions, sliced

½ cup pecan nuts, chopped

2 heads endive, separated

1 tsp lemon juice

thyme sprigs, to garnish

DRESSING

4 tbsp vegetable oil

1 tbsp garlic wine vinegar

1 tsp soft light brown sugar

2 tsp chopped thyme

1 Cook the sweet potatoes in a large pan of boiling water for 10–15 minutes, until tender. Drain thoroughly and set aside to cool.

2 When cooled, stir in the sliced celery, celery root, scallions, and pecan nuts.

3 Line a salad plate with the endive leaves and sprinkle with lemon juice.

4 Spoon the sweet potato mixture into the center of the leaves.

5 In a small bowl, whisk the dressing ingredients together.

6 Pour the dressing over the salad and serve at once, garnished with fresh thyme sprigs.

COOK'S TIP

Sweet potatoes do not store as well as ordinary potatoes. It is best to store them in a cool, dark place (not the refrigerator) and use within 1 week of purchase.

Indian Potato Salad

There are many hot Indian-flavored potato dishes which are served with curry, but this fruity salad is delicious chilled.

NUTRITIONAL INFORMATION

Calories ....175 Sugars 8g
Protein ....6g Fat 1g
Carbohydrate ...38g Saturates 0.3g

25 mins   20 mins

SERVES 4

INGREDIENTS

generous 5 cups diced mealy potatoes

2¾ oz/75 g small broccoli florets

1 small mango, diced

4 scallions, sliced

salt and pepper

small cooked spiced poppadoms, to serve

DRESSING

½ tsp ground cumin

½ tsp ground coriander

1 tbsp mango chutney

⅔ cup lowfat unsweetened yogurt

1 tsp chopped fresh ginger root

2 tbsp chopped fresh cilantro

1 Cook the potatoes in a pan of boiling water for 10 minutes or until tender. Drain and place in a mixing bowl.

2 Meanwhile, blanch the broccoli florets in a separate pan of boiling water for 2 minutes. Drain the broccoli well and add to the potatoes in the bowl.

3 When the potatoes and broccoli have cooled, add the diced mango and sliced scallions. Season to taste with salt and pepper and mix well to combine.

4 In a small bowl, stir all of the dressing ingredients together.

5 Spoon the dressing over the potato mixture and mix together carefully, taking care not to break up the potatoes and broccoli.

6 Serve the salad immediately, accompanied by the small cooked spiced poppadoms.

COOK'S TIP

Mix the dressing ingredients together in advance and leave to chill in the refrigerator for a few hours in order for a stronger flavor to develop.

Mexican Potato Salad

The flavors of Mexico are echoed in this dish, in which potato slices are topped with tomatoes and chilies and served with guacamole.

NUTRITIONAL INFORMATION

Calories	260	Sugars	.........6g
Protein	.........6g	Fat	...........9g
Carbohydrate	...41g	Saturates	.......2g

20 mins   20 mins

SERVES 4

INGREDIENTS

2 lb 12 oz/1.25 kg waxy potatoes, sliced

1 ripe avocado

1 tsp olive oil

1 tsp lemon juice

1 garlic clove, crushed

1 onion, chopped

2 large tomatoes, sliced

1 green chili, chopped

1 yellow bell pepper, seeded and sliced

2 tbsp chopped fresh cilantro

salt and pepper

lemon wedges, to garnish

1 Cook the potato slices in a pan of boiling water for 10–15 minutes, or until tender. Drain and let cool.

2 Meanwhile, cut the avocado in half and remove the pit. Mash the avocado flesh with a fork (you could also scoop the avocado flesh from the 2 halves using a spoon and then mash it).

3 Add the olive oil, lemon juice, garlic, and chopped onion to the avocado flesh and stir to mix. Cover the bowl with plastic wrap, to minimize discoloration, and set aside.

4 Mix the tomatoes, chili, and yellow bell pepper together and transfer to a salad bowl with the potato slices.

5 Arrange the avocado mixture on top of the salad and sprinkle with the chopped fresh cilantro. Season to taste with salt and pepper and serve garnished with lemon wedges.

VARIATION

You can omit the green chili from this salad if you do not like hot dishes.

Nests of Chinese Salad

Crisp fried potato nests are perfect as an edible salad bowl and delicious when filled with a colorful Chinese-style salad of vegetables and fruit.

NUTRITIONAL INFORMATION

Calories ....272 Sugars 11g
Protein ....4g Fat 4g
Carbohydrate ...59g Saturates 0.4g

15 mins   15 mins

SERVES 4

INGREDIENTS

POTATO NESTS

2¼ cups grated mealy potatoes

1 cup cornstarch

vegetable oil, for deep-frying

fresh chives, to garnish

SALAD

4½ oz/125 g pineapple, cubed

1 green bell pepper, cut into strips

1 carrot, cut into thin strips

1¾ oz/50 g snow peas, thickly sliced

4 baby corn cobs, halved lengthwise

¼ cup beansprouts

2 scallions, sliced

DRESSING

1 tbsp clear honey

1 tsp light soy sauce

1 garlic clove, crushed

1 tsp lemon juice

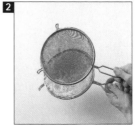

1 To make the nests, rinse the potatoes several times in cold water. Drain well on paper towels so they are completely dry. This is to prevent the potatoes spitting when they are cooked in the fat. Place the potatoes in a mixing bowl. Add the cornstarch, mixing well to coat the potatoes.

2 Half fill a wok with vegetable oil and heat until smoking. Line a 6 inch/ 15 cm diameter wire strainer with a quarter of the potato mixture and press another strainer of the same size on top.

3 Lower the strainers into the oil and cook for 2 minutes until the potato nest is golden brown and crisp. Remove from the wok, allowing the excess oil to drain off.

4 Repeat 3 more times to use up all of the mixture and make a total of 4 nests. Let cool.

5 Mix the salad ingredients together then spoon into the potato baskets.

6 Mix the dressing ingredients together. Pour the dressing over the salad. Garnish with chives and then serve immediately.

Arugula & Apple Salad

This green and white salad is made with creamy, salty-flavored goat cheese—its distinctive flavor is perfect with salad leaves.

NUTRITIONAL INFORMATION

Calories	104	Sugars	3.1g
Protein	3.1g	Fat	5.3g
Carbohydrate	11.8g	Saturates	1.5g

15 mins, plus 15 mins cooling time · 15 mins

SERVES 4

INGREDIENTS

1 lb 5 oz/600 g potatoes, unpeeled and sliced

2 green eating apples, diced

1 tsp lemon juice

1 oz/25 g walnut pieces

4½ oz/125 g goat cheese, cubed

5½ oz/150 g arugula leaves

salt and pepper

DRESSING

2 tbsp olive oil

1 tbsp red wine vinegar

1 tsp clear honey

1 tsp fennel seeds

COOK'S TIP

Serve this salad immediately to prevent the apple from discoloring. Alternatively, prepare all of the other ingredients in advance and add the apple at the last minute.

1 Cook the potatoes in a pan of boiling water for 15 minutes until tender. Drain and let cool. Transfer the cooled potatoes to a serving bowl.

2 Toss the diced apples in the lemon juice, then drain and stir them into the cold potatoes.

3 Add the walnut pieces, cheese cubes, and arugula leaves, then toss the salad to mix. Season to taste.

4 In a small bowl, whisk the dressing ingredients together and then pour the dressing over the salad. Serve the salad immediately.

Mixed Vegetable Salad

This salad is a medley of crunchy vegetables, mixed with sliced cooked potatoes and ham, then coated in a fresh-tasting lemon mayonnaise.

NUTRITIONAL INFORMATION

Calories 105	Sugars 2.5g	
Protein 3.9g	Fat 7.2g	
Carbohydrate . . .6.6g	Saturates 1.2g	

5 mins, plus 15 mins cooling time   15 mins

SERVES 4

I N G R E D I E N T S

1 lb/450 g waxy new potatoes, scrubbed

1 carrot, cut into thin sticks

8 oz/225 g cauliflower florets

8 oz/225 g baby corn cobs, halved lengthwise

6 oz/175 g green beans

1 cup ham, diced

1¾ oz/50 g mushrooms, sliced

salt and pepper

DRESSING

2 tbsp chopped fresh parsley

⅔ cup mayonnaise

⅔ cup unsweetened yogurt

4 tsp lemon juice

zest of 1 lemon

2 tsp fennel seeds

1 Cook the potatoes in a pan of boiling water for 15 minutes or until tender. Drain and let cool. When the potatoes are cold, slice them thinly.

2 Meanwhile, cook the carrot sticks, cauliflower florets, baby corn cobs, and green beans in a pan of boiling water for 5 minutes. Drain well and let cool.

3 Reserving 1 teaspoon of the chopped parsley for the garnish, mix the remaining dressing ingredients together in a bowl.

4 Arrange the vegetables on a salad platter and top with the diced ham and sliced mushrooms.

5 Spoon the dressing over the the salad and garnish with the reserved parsley. Serve at once.

COOK'S TIP

For a really quick salad, use a frozen packet of mixed vegetables, thawed, instead of fresh vegetables.

Broiled New Potato Salad

Broiled new potatoes are tossed in oil for a char-grilled flavor and color. Served warm with a garlic mayonnaise, they make a delicious salad.

NUTRITIONAL INFORMATION

Calories 162   Sugars 1.1g
Protein . . . . .3.2g   Fat 11.4g
Carbohydrate . .12.3g   Saturates 2.2g

5 mins   25 mins

SERVES 4

INGREDIENTS

1½ lb/675 g new potatoes, scrubbed

3 tbsp olive oil

2 tbsp chopped fresh thyme

1 tsp paprika

4 slices smoked bacon

salt and pepper

parsley sprig, to garnish

DRESSING

4 tbsp mayonnaise

1 tbsp garlic wine vinegar

2 garlic cloves, crushed

1 tbsp chopped fresh parsley

1 Cook the new potatoes in a pan of boiling water for 10 minutes. Drain thoroughly.

2 Mix the olive oil, chopped thyme, and paprika together and pour the mixture over the warm potatoes.

3 Place the bacon slices under a preheated medium broiler and cook for 5 minutes, turning once until crisp. When cooked, coarsely chop the bacon and keep warm.

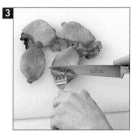

4 Transfer the potatoes to the broiler pan and cook for 10 minutes, turning once.

5 Mix the dressing ingredients in a small serving bowl. Transfer the potatoes and bacon to a large serving bowl. Season with salt and pepper and mix together.

6 Spoon over the dressing. Garnish with a parsley sprig and serve immediately for a warm salad. Alternatively, let cool and serve chilled.

VARIATION

Add spicy sausage to the salad in place of bacon—you do not need to cook it under the broiler before adding it to the salad.

Potato & Tuna Salad

This colorful dish is a variation of the classic Salade Niçoise.
Packed with tuna and vegetables, it is both filling and delicious.

NUTRITIONAL INFORMATION

Calories ....225 Sugars 5g
Protein ....21g Fat 5g
Carbohydrate ...27g Saturates 2g

40 mins   20 mins

SERVES 4

INGREDIENTS

1 lb/450 g new potatoes, scrubbed and
  quartered

1 green bell pepper, sliced

1¾ oz/50 g canned corn, drained

1 red onion, sliced

10½ oz/300 g canned tuna in brine, drained
  and flaked

2 tbsp chopped pitted black olives

salt and pepper

lime wedges, to garnish

DRESSING

2 tbsp lowfat mayonnaise

2 tbsp sour cream

1 tbsp lime juice

2 garlic cloves, crushed

finely grated zest of 1 lime

1 Cook the potatoes in a pan of boiling water for
approximately 15 minutes until tender. Drain and let
cool in a mixing bowl.

2 Gently stir in the sliced green bell pepper, corn, and
sliced red onion.

3 Spoon the potato mixture into a large serving bowl
and arrange the flaked tuna and chopped black olives
over the top.

4 Season the salad generously with salt and pepper.

5 To make the dressing, mix together the mayonnaise,
sour cream, lime juice, garlic, and lime zest in a bowl.

6 Spoon the dressing over the tuna and olives. Garnish
with lime wedges and serve.

COOK'S TIP

Green beans and hard-cooked egg
slices can be added to the salad for
a more traditional Salade Niçoise.

Tuna Niçoise Salad

This is a classic version of the French Salade Niçoise. It is a substantial salad, suitable for a lunch or light summer supper.

NUTRITIONAL INFORMATION

Calories . . . . .109 Sugars 1.1g
Protein . . . . .7.2g Fat 7.0g
Carbohydrate . . .4.8g Saturates 1.2g

10 mins   20 mins

SERVES 4

INGREDIENTS

4 eggs

1 lb/450 g new potatoes

1 cup dwarf green beans, trimmed and halved

2 x 6 oz/175 g tuna steaks

6 tbsp olive oil, plus extra for brushing

1 garlic clove, crushed

1½ tsp Dijon mustard

2 tsp lemon juice

2 tbsp chopped fresh basil

2 Boston lettuces

1½ cups cherry tomatoes, halved

2 cups cucumber, peeled, cut in half and sliced

½ cup pitted black olives

1¾ oz/50 g canned anchovies in oil, drained

salt and pepper

1 Bring a small pan of water to a boil. Add the eggs and then cook for 7–9 minutes from when the water returns to a boil—7 minutes for a slightly soft center, 9 minutes for a firm center. Drain and refresh under cold running water. Set aside.

2 Cook the potatoes in boiling salted water for 10–12 minutes until tender. Add the beans 3 minutes before the end of the cooking time. Drain both vegetables well and refresh under cold water. Drain well.

3 Wash and dry the tuna steaks. Brush with a little olive oil and season. Cook on a preheated ridged grill pan for 2–3 minutes each side, until just tender but still slightly pink in the center. Set aside to rest.

4 Whisk together the garlic, mustard, lemon juice, basil, and seasoning. Whisk in the olive oil.

5 To assemble the salad, break apart the lettuces and tear into large pieces. Divide between individual serving plates. Next add the potatoes and beans, tomatoes, cucumber, and olives. Toss lightly together. Shell the eggs and cut into quarters lengthwise. Arrange these on top of the salad. Scatter over the anchovies.

6 Flake the tuna steaks and arrange on the salads. Pour over the dressing and serve.

Lobster Salad & Lime Dressing

The lobster makes this a special occasion salad, both in cost and flavor. The richness of the lobster meat is offset by the tangy lime dressing.

NUTRITIONAL INFORMATION

Calories 181	Sugars 0.8g
Protein 6.8g	Fat 13.9g
Carbohydrate . . .7.6g	Saturates 2.2g

5 mins

10–15 mins

SERVES 4

INGREDIENTS

1 lb/450 g waxy potatoes, scrubbed and sliced

8 oz/225 g cooked lobster meat

⅔ cup mayonnaise

2 tbsp lime juice

finely grated zest of 1 lime

1 tbsp chopped fresh parsley

2 tbsp olive oil

2 tomatoes, seeded and diced

2 hard-cooked eggs, quartered

1 tbsp quartered pitted green olives

salt and pepper

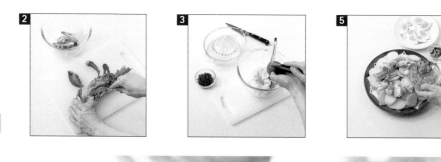

1 Cook the potatoes in a pan of boiling water for 10–15 minutes or until cooked through. Drain and reserve.

2 Remove the lobster meat from the shell and then separate it into large pieces.

3 In a bowl, mix together the mayonnaise, 1 tbsp of the lime juice, half the grated lime zest, and half the chopped parsley, then set aside.

4 In a separate bowl, whisk the remaining lime juice with the olive oil and pour the dressing over the potatoes. Arrange the potatoes on a serving plate.

5 Top with the lobster meat, tomatoes, eggs, and olives. Season with salt and pepper and sprinkle with the reserved parsley.

6 Spoon the mayonnaise on to the center of the salad. Top with the reserved zest and serve.

COOK'S TIP

As shellfish is used in this salad, serve it immediately, or keep covered and chilled for up to 1 hour before serving.

Indonesian Chicken Salad

The spicy peanut dressing served with this salad may be prepared in advance and left to chill a day before required.

NUTRITIONAL INFORMATION

Calories	802	Sugars	........15g
Protein	........35g	Fat	..........55g
Carbohydrate	...45g	Saturates	......10g

5 mins   15 mins

SERVES 4

INGREDIENTS

2 lb 12 oz/1.25 kg waxy potatoes

10½ oz/300 g fresh pineapple, diced

2 carrots, grated

1¾ cups beansprouts

1 bunch scallions, sliced

1 large zucchini, cut into thin sticks

3 celery stalks, cut into thin sticks

6 oz/176 g unsalted peanuts

2 cooked chicken breast fillets, about
    4½ oz/125 g each, sliced

DRESSING

6 tbsp crunchy peanut butter

6 tbsp olive oil

2 tbsp light soy sauce

1 red chili, chopped

2 tsp sesame oil

4 tsp lime juice

1 Using a sharp knife, cut the potatoes into small dice. Bring a pan of water to the boil.

2 Cook the diced potatoes in a pan of boiling water for 10 minutes or until tender. Drain them and let cool until required.

3 Transfer the cooled potatoes to a salad bowl.

4 Add the pineapple, carrots, bean sprouts, scallions, zucchini, celery, peanuts, and sliced chicken to the potatoes. Toss well to mix all the salad ingredients together.

5 To make the dressing, put the peanut butter in a small mixing bowl and gradually whisk in the olive oil and light soy sauce.

6 Stir in the chopped red chili, sesame oil, and lime juice. Mix until well combined.

7 Pour the spicy dressing over the salad and toss lightly to coat all of the ingredients. Serve the potato and chicken salad immediately.

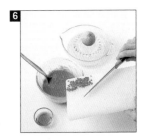

COOK'S TIP

Unsweetened canned pineapple may be used in place of the fresh pineapple for convenience. If only sweetened canned pineapple is available, drain it and rinse under cold running water before using.

Spicy Chicken Salad

Tender chicken breast meat is perfect for salads. It cooks quickly in small pieces and these are perfect for tossing with other salad ingredients.

NUTRITIONAL INFORMATION

Calories	.105	Sugars	.2.8g
Protein	.6.7g	Fat	.4.9g
Carbohydrate	.9.2g	Saturates	.1.8g

5 mins, plus 15 mins cooling time   15 mins

SERVES 4

INGREDIENTS

2 skinned chicken breast fillets, about 4½ oz/125 g each

2 tbsp butter

1 red chili, chopped

1 tbsp clear honey

½ tsp ground cumin

2 tbsp chopped fresh cilantro

3½ cups diced potatoes

1¾ oz/50 g green beans, halved

1 red bell pepper, cut into thin strips

2 tomatoes, seeded and diced

DRESSING

2 tbsp olive oil

pinch of chili powder

1 tbsp garlic wine vinegar

pinch of superfine sugar

1 tbsp chopped fresh cilantro

1 Cut the chicken into thin strips. Melt the butter in a pan over a medium heat and add the chicken, chili, honey, and cumin. Cook for 10 minutes, turning until cooked through.

2 Transfer the mixture to a bowl and let cool, then stir in the cilantro.

3 Meanwhile, cook the diced potatoes in a pan of boiling water for 10 minutes until they are tender. Drain and let cool.

4 Blanch the green beans in boiling water for 3 minutes. Drain and leave to cool. Mix the green beans and potatoes together in a salad bowl.

5 Add the bell pepper strips and the diced tomatoes to the potatoes and green beans. Stir in the spicy chicken mixture.

6 In a small bowl, whisk the dressing ingredients together and pour the dressing over the salad, tossing well. Serve the salad at once.

VARIATION

If you prefer, use lean turkey meat instead of the chicken for a slightly stronger flavor. Use the white meat for the best appearance and flavor.

Italian Sausage Salad

Sliced Italian sausage blends well with the other Mediterranean flavors of sun-dried tomato and basil in this salad.

NUTRITIONAL INFORMATION

Calories 450	Sugars 6g	
Protein 13g	Fat 28g	
Carbohydrate ...38g	Saturates 1g	

25 mins

25 mins

SERVES 4

INGREDIENTS

1 lb/450 g waxy potatoes

1 radicchio or lollo rosso lettuce

1 green bell pepper, sliced

6 oz/175 g Italian sausage, sliced

1 red onion, halved and sliced

4½ oz/125 g sun-dried tomatoes, sliced

2 tbsp shredded fresh basil

DRESSING

1 tbsp balsamic vinegar

1 tsp tomato paste

2 tbsp olive oil

salt and pepper

COOK'S TIP

Any sliced Italian sausage or salami can be used in this salad. Italy is home of the salami and there are numerous varieties to choose from—those from the south tend to be more highly spiced than those from the north of the country.

1 Cook the potatoes in a pan of boiling water for 20 minutes or until cooked through. Drain and let cool.

2 Line a large serving platter with the radicchio or lollo rosso lettuce leaves.

3 Slice the cooled potatoes and arrange them in layers on the lettuce-lined serving platter together with the sliced green bell pepper, sliced Italian sausage, red onion, sun-dried tomatoes, and shredded fresh basil.

4 In a small bowl, whisk the balsamic vinegar, tomato paste, and olive oil together and season to taste with salt and pepper. Pour the dressing over the potato salad and serve immediately.

Light Meals & Side Dishes

Potatoes are very versatile and can be used as a base to create an array of tempting light meals and satisfying snacks. They are also nutritious, and their carbohydrate gives a welcome energy boost. As potatoes have a fairly neutral flavor, they can be teamed with a variety of other ingredients and flavors.

This chapter contains a range of delicious yet light meals—try Feta & Spinach Omelet, or Sour Cream & Salmon Crêpes. Potatoes can be cooked in a variety of ways, such as mashing, roasting, deep-frying, and baking, making them an adaptable and valuable component of any meal.

Potatoes with a Spicy Filling

These twice-baked potatoes have an unusual filling made from the Middle Eastern flavors of garbanzo beans, cumin, and cilantro.

NUTRITIONAL INFORMATION

Calories 335   Sugars 7g
Protein . . . . .15g   Fat 7g
Carbohydrate . . .57g   Saturates 1g

20 mins   1 hr 30 mins

SERVES 4

INGREDIENTS

4 large baking potatoes

1 tbsp vegetable oil, optional

15½ oz/425 g canned garbanzos, drained

1 tsp ground coriander

1 tsp ground cumin

4 tbsp cilantro, chopped

⅔ cup plain lowfat unsweetened yogurt

salt and pepper

SALAD

2 tomatoes

½ cucumber

½ red onion

4 tbsp chopped fresh cilantro

1 Preheat the oven to 400°F/200°C. Scrub the potatoes and pat them dry with paper towels. Prick the potatoes all over with a fork. Brush with oil (if using) and season with salt and pepper.

2 Place the potatoes on a baking sheet and bake for 1–1¼ hours or until cooked through. Cool for 10 minutes.

3 Mash the garbanzo beans in a large mixing bowl. Stir in the ground coriander, cumin, and half the cilantro. Cover with plastic wrap and set aside.

4 Halve the cooked potatoes and scoop the flesh into a bowl, keeping the shells intact. Mash the flesh until smooth and gently mix into the garbanzo mixture with the unsweetened yogurt. Season well with salt and pepper to taste.

5 Place the potato shells on a baking sheet and fill with the potato and garbanzo mixture. Return the potatoes to the oven and bake for 10–15 minutes until heated through.

6 Meanwhile, make the salad. Using a sharp knife, chop the tomatoes. Slice the cucumber and cut the red onion into thin slices. Toss all the ingredients together with the cilantro in a serving dish.

7 Serve the potatoes sprinkled with the remaining chopped cilantro and the prepared salad.

COOK'S TIP

For an even lower fat version of this recipe, bake the potatoes without oiling them first.

Vegetable Samosas

These Indian snacks are perfect for a quick or light meal. Served with a salad, they can be made in advance and frozen for ease.

NUTRITIONAL INFORMATION

Calories 291	Sugars 2g
Protein 4g	Fat 23g
Carbohydrate . . .18g	Saturates 3g

20 mins

30 mins

MAKES 12

I N G R E D I E N T S

FILLING

2 tbsp vegetable oil

1 onion, chopped

½ tsp ground coriander

½ tsp ground cumin

pinch of turmeric

½ tsp ground ginger

½ tsp garam masala

1 garlic clove, crushed

1½ cups diced potatoes

1 cup frozen peas, thawed

5½ oz/150 g spinach, chopped

PASTRY

12 oz/350 g phyllo pastry

vegetable oil, for deep-frying

1 To make the filling, heat the oil in a skillet. Add the onion and sauté, stirring frequently, for 1–2 minutes, until softened. Stir in all of the spices and garlic and cook for 1 minute.

2 Add the potatoes and cook over a low heat, stirring frequently, for 5 minutes, until they begin to soften.

3 Stir in the peas and spinach and cook for another 3–4 minutes.

4 Lay the phyllo pastry sheets out on a clean counter and fold 12 sheets in half lengthwise.

5 Place 2 tablespoons of the vegetable filling at one end of each folded pastry sheet. Fold over one corner to make a triangle. Continue folding in this way to make a triangular package and seal the edges with water.

6 Repeat with the remaining pastry and the remaining filling.

7 Heat the oil for deep-frying to 350°F/180°C or until a cube of bread browns in 30 seconds. Fry the samosas, in batches, for 1–2 minutes until golden. Drain on absorbent paper towels and keep warm while cooking the remainder. Serve immediately.

Gnocchi with Tomato Sauce

These gnocchi or small dumplings are made with potato and flavored with spinach and nutmeg, then served in a tomato and basil sauce.

NUTRITIONAL INFORMATION

Calories 337   Sugars 4g
Protein ....9g   Fat 10g
Carbohydrate ...52g   Saturates 4g

25 mins   1 hour

SERVES 4

INGREDIENTS

1 lb/450 g baking potatoes

2¾ oz/75 g spinach

1 tsp water

3 tbsp butter or margarine

1 small egg, beaten

¾ cup all-purpose flour

fresh basil sprigs, to garnish

TOMATO SAUCE

1 tbsp olive oil

1 shallot, chopped

1 tbsp tomato paste

8 oz/225 g canned chopped tomatoes

2 tbsp chopped basil

6 tbsp red wine

1 tsp superfine sugar

salt and pepper

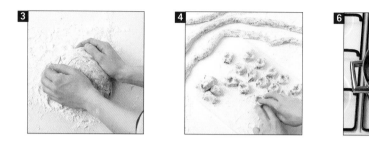

1 Cook the potatoes in their skins in a pan of boiling salted water for 20 minutes. Drain well and press through a strainer into a bowl.

2 Cook the spinach in the water for 5 minutes or until wilted. Drain and pat dry with paper towels. Chop and stir into the potatoes.

3 Add the butter or margarine, egg, and half of the flour to the spinach mixture, mixing well. Turn out on to a floured surface, gradually kneading in the remaining flour to form a soft dough.

4 With floured hands, roll the dough into thin ropes and cut off ¾ inch/ 2 cm pieces. Press the center of each dumpling with your finger, drawing it toward you to curl the sides of the gnocchi. Cover the gnocchi and leave to chill.

5 Heat the oil for the sauce in a pan and sauté the chopped shallots for 5 minutes. Add the tomato paste, tomatoes, basil, red wine, and sugar and season well. Bring to the boil and then simmer for 20 minutes.

6 Bring a pan of salted water to a boil and cook the gnocchi for 2–3 minutes or until they rise to the top of the pan. Drain well and transfer to serving dishes. Spoon the tomato sauce over the gnocchi. Garnish and serve.

Vegetable Burgers & Fries

These spicy vegetable burgers are delicious, especially when served in a warm bun or roll with light oven fries.

NUTRITIONAL INFORMATION

Calories 461	Sugars 4g	
Protein 18g	Fat 17g	
Carbohydrate . . .64g	Saturates 2g	

🥔 45 mins   🕐 1 hour

SERVES 4

I N G R E D I E N T S

VEGETABLE BURGERS

3½ oz/100 g spinach

1 tbsp olive oil

1 leek, chopped

2 garlic cloves, crushed

1½ cups chopped mushrooms

10½ oz/300 g firm bean curd, chopped

1 tsp chili powder

1 tsp curry powder

1 tbsp chopped cilantro

1½ cups fresh whole-wheat bread crumbs

1 tbsp olive oil

burger roll and salad, to serve

FRIES

2 large potatoes

2 tbsp flour

1 tsp chili powder

2 tbsp olive oil

1 To make the burgers, cook the spinach in a little boiling water for 2 minutes. Drain thoroughly and pat dry with paper towels.

2 Heat the oil in a skillet and sauté the leek and garlic for 2–3 minutes. Add the remaining mushrooms, bean curd, spices, and cilantro, and cook for 5–7 minutes, until the vegetables have softened. Toss in the spinach and cook for 1 minute.

3 Transfer the mixture to a food processor and process for 30 seconds, until almost smooth. Transfer to a bowl and stir in the bread crumbs, mixing well. Let stand until cool enough to handle. Using floured hands, form the mixture into four equal-size burgers. Let chill for 30 minutes.

4 To make the fries, cut the potatoes into thin wedges and cook in a pan of boiling water for 10 minutes. Drain and toss in the flour and chili powder. Lay the chips on a cookie sheet and sprinkle with the oil. Cook in a preheated oven, 400°F/200°C, for 30 minutes, or until golden.

5 Meanwhile, heat 1 tablespoon oil in a skillet and cook the burgers for 8–10 minutes, turning once. Serve with salad in a bap with the fries.

Puff Potato Pie

This pie with its rich filling is a great alternative to serving potatoes as a side dish with any meal. Alternatively, serve with salad for a light lunch.

NUTRITIONAL INFORMATION

Calories ....198 Sugars 1.4g
Protein ....3.7g Fat 12.4g
Carbohydrate ..19.8g Saturates 2.9g

5–10 mins   50 mins, plus
             20–30 mins
             cooling time

SERVES 6

INGREDIENTS

1 lb 9 oz/700 g potatoes, peeled and thinly sliced

2 scallions, finely chopped

1 red onion, finely chopped

⅔ cup heavy cream

1 lb 2 oz/500 g fresh ready-made pie dough

2 eggs, beaten

salt and pepper

1 Lightly grease a baking sheet. Bring a pan of water to a boil, and add the sliced potatoes. Bring back to a boil and then simmer for a few minutes. Drain the potato slices and let cool. Dry off any excess moisture with paper towels.

2 In a bowl, mix together the scallions, red onion, and the cooled potato slices. Stir in 2 tablespoons of the cream and plenty of seasoning.

3 Divide the pie dough in half and roll out one piece to a 9 inch/23 cm round. Roll the remaining pie dough to a 10 inch/25 cm round.

4 Place the smaller circle on to the baking sheet and top with the potato mixture, leaving a 1 inch/2.5 cm border. Brush this border with a little of the beaten egg.

5 Top with the larger circle of pie dough, then seal well and crimp the edges of the pie dough. Cut a steam vent in the middle of the pie dough and, using the back of a knife, mark with a pattern. Brush with the beaten egg and bake in a preheated oven, 400°F/200°C, for 30 minutes.

6 Mix the remaining beaten egg with the rest of the cream and pour into the pie through the steam vent. Return to the oven for 15 minutes, then let cool for 30 minutes. Serve warm or cold.

COOK'S TIP

The filling may be prepared up to 4 hours in advance.

Potato & Bean Pâté

This pâté is easy to prepare and may be stored in the refrigerator for up to two days. Serve with small toasts, Melba toast, or crudités.

NUTRITIONAL INFORMATION

Calories	84	Sugars	.......3.0g
Protein	........5.1g	Fat	..........0.5g
Carbohydrate	..15.7g	Saturates	.....0.1g

🖐 🖐 🖐

🥔 3 mins 🕐 10 mins

SERVES 4

I N G R E D I E N T S

⅔ cup diced mealy potatoes, diced

8 oz/225 g mixed canned beans, such as borlotti beans, lima beans, and kidney beans, drained

1 garlic clove, crushed

2 tsp lime juice

1 tbsp chopped fresh cilantro

2 tbsp unsweetened yogurt

salt and pepper

chopped fresh cilantro, to garnish

1 Cook the potatoes in a pan of boiling water for 10 minutes until tender. Drain well and mash.

2 Transfer the potato to a food processor or blender and add the beans, garlic, lime juice, and the fresh cilantro. Season the mixture and process for 1 minute to make a smooth purée. Alternatively, mix the beans with the potato, garlic, lime juice, and cilantro and mash.

3 Turn the pâté into a bowl and add the yogurt. Mix well.

4 Spoon the pâté into a serving dish and garnish with the chopped cilantro. Serve at once or let chill.

COOK'S TIP

To make Melba toast, toast ready-sliced bread lightly on both sides under a preheated high broiler. Remove the crusts. Holding the bread flat, slide a sharp knife through the slice to split it horizontally. Cut into triangles and toast the untoasted side until the edges curl.

Mixed Mushroom Cakes

These cakes will be loved by vegetarians and meat-eaters alike, packed with creamy potato and as wide a variety of mushrooms as possible.

NUTRITIONAL INFORMATION

Calories 298   Sugars 0.8g
Protein . . . . .5g   Fat 22g
Carbohydrate . . .22g   Saturates 5g

20 mins | 25 mins

SERVES 4

INGREDIENTS

2¾ cups diced mealy potatoes

2 tbsp butter

6 oz/175 g mixed mushrooms, chopped

2 garlic cloves, crushed

1 small egg, beaten

1 tbsp chopped fresh chives, plus extra
   to garnish

flour, for dusting

vegetable oil, for deep-frying

salt and pepper

1 Cook the potatoes in a pan of lightly salted boiling water for 10 minutes, or until cooked through.

2 Drain the potatoes well. Mash with a potato masher or fork and set aside.

3 Meanwhile, melt the butter in a skillet. Add the mushrooms and garlic and cook, stirring constantly, for 5 minutes. Drain well.

4 Stir the mushrooms and garlic into the potato, together with the beaten egg and chives.

5 Divide the mixture equally into 4 portions and shape them into round cakes. Toss them in the flour until the outsides of the cakes are completely coated.

6 Pour the oil into the skillet until it is half-full, then heat it until i is hot. Add the potato cakes and cook over a medium heat for 10 minutes until they are golden brown, turning them over halfway through. Serve the cakes at once, with a simple crisp salad.

COOK'S TIP

Prepare the cakes in advance: cover and leave to chill in the refrigerator for up to 24 hours, if you wish.

Cheese & Onion Rostis

These grated potato cakes are also known as straw cakes, as they resemble a straw mat! Serve them with a tomato sauce or salad.

NUTRITIONAL INFORMATION

Calories 307   Sugars 4g
Protein . . . . .8g   Fat 13g
Carbohydrate . . .42g   Saturates 6g

10 mins   40 mins

SERVES 4

INGREDIENTS

2 lb/900 g potatoes

1 onion, grated

½ cup grated Gruyère cheese

2 tbsp chopped parsley

1 tbsp olive oil

2 tbsp butter

salt and pepper

TO GARNISH

1 shredded scallion

1 small tomato, quartered

1 Parboil the potatoes in a pan of lightly salted boiling water for 10 minutes and let cool. Peel the potatoes and grate with a coarse grater. Place the grated potatoes in a large mixing bowl.

COOK'S TIP

The potato cakes should be flattened as much as possible during cooking, otherwise the outside will be cooked before the center.

2 Stir in the onion, cheese, and parsley. Season well with salt and pepper. Divide the potato mixture into 4 portions of equal size and form them into cakes.

3 Heat half of the olive oil and butter in a skillet. Cook two of the potato cakes over a high heat for 1 minute, then reduce the heat and cook for 5 minutes, until they are golden underneath. Turn them over and cook for another 5 minutes.

4 Repeat with the other half of the oil and the remaining butter to cook the remaining 2 cakes. Transfer to warm individual serving plates. Garnish and serve immediately.

Potato & Cauliflower Fritters

These fritters make a filling snack. They are a great way to use up leftover cooked vegetables.

NUTRITIONAL INFORMATION

Calories 665	Sugars 5g	
Protein 18g	Fat 25g	
Carbohydrate . . .98g	Saturates 4g	

🕙 10 mins   🕐 15–20 mins

SERVES 4

INGREDIENTS

1½ cups diced mealy potatoes

8 oz/225 g cauliflower florets

scant ½ cup freshly grated Parmesan cheese

1 egg

1 egg white for coating

vegetable oil, for deep-frying

paprika, for dusting (optional)

salt and pepper

crispy bacon slices, chopped, to serve

1 Cook the potatoes in a pan of boiling water for 10 minutes until cooked through. Drain well and mash.

2 Meanwhile, cook the cauliflower florets in a separate pan of boiling water for 10 minutes.

3 Drain the cauliflower florets and mix into the mashed potato. Stir in the grated Parmesan cheese and season well with salt and pepper.

4 Separate the whole egg and beat the yolk into the potato and cauliflower, mixing well.

5 Lightly whisk both the egg whites in a clean bowl, then carefully fold into the potato and cauliflower mixture.

6 Divide the potato mixture into 8 equal portions and shape them into rounds.

7 Pour the oil in a skillet until half-full, then heat it until hot. Cook the fritters for 3–5 minutes, turning once halfway through cooking.

8 Dust the cooked fritters with a little paprika, if preferred, and serve at once accompanied by the crispy chopped bacon.

VARIATION

Any other vegetable, such as broccoli, can be used in this recipe instead of the cauliflower florets, if you prefer.

Fritters with Garlic Sauce

Chunks of cooked potato are coated first in Parmesan cheese, then in a light batter before being fried until golden for a delicious hot snack.

NUTRITIONAL INFORMATION

Calories 599   Sugars 9g
Protein . . . . .22g   Fat 39g
Carbohydrate . . .42g   Saturates 13g

20 mins   20–25 mins

SERVES 4

INGREDIENTS

1 lb 2 oz/500 g waxy potatoes, cubed

1¼ cups freshly grated Parmesan cheese

vegetable oil, for deep-frying

SAUCE

2 tbsp butter

1 onion, halved and sliced

2 garlic cloves, crushed

¼ cup all-purpose flour

1¼ cups milk

1 tbsp chopped fresh parsley

BATTER

½ cup all-purpose flour

1 small egg

⅔ cup milk

1 To make the sauce, melt the butter in a pan and cook the sliced onion and garlic over a low heat, stirring frequently, for 2–3 minutes. Add the flour and cook, stirring constantly, for 1 minute.

2 Remove from the heat and stir in the milk and parsley. Return to the heat and bring to a boil. Keep warm.

3 Meanwhile, cook the cubed potatoes in a pan of boiling water for 5–10 minutes, until just firm. Do not overcook or they will fall apart.

4 Drain the potatoes and toss them in the Parmesan cheese. If the potatoes are still slightly wet, the cheese sticks to them and coats them well.

5 To make the batter, place the flour in a mixing bowl and gradually beat in the egg and milk until smooth. Dip the potato cubes into the batter to coat them.

6 In a large pan, heat the oil to 350°F/180°C or until a cube of bread browns in 30 seconds. Add the fritters and cook for 3–4 minutes, or until golden.

7 Remove the fritters with a slotted spoon and drain well. Transfer them to a warm serving bowl and serve immediately with the garlic sauce.

Hash Browns & Tomato Sauce

Hash Browns are popular fried potato squares, often served as brunch. This version includes extra vegetables.

NUTRITIONAL INFORMATION

Calories 339   Sugars 9g
Protein . . . . .10g   Fat 21g
Carbohydrate . . .29g   Saturates 7g

20 mins   45 mins

SERVES 4

INGREDIENTS

1 lb 2 oz/500 g waxy potatoes

1 carrot, diced

1 celery stalk, diced

2¼ oz/60 g white mushrooms, diced

1 onion, diced

2 garlic cloves, crushed

¼ cup frozen peas, thawed

⅔ cup grated freshly grated Parmesan
   cheese

4 tbsp vegetable oil

2 tbsp butter

salt and pepper

SAUCE

1¼ cups strained tomatoes

2 tbsp chopped fresh cilantro

1 tbsp vegetarian Worcestershire sauce

½ tsp chili powder

2 tsp brown sugar

2 tsp mustard

⅓ cup vegetable bouillon

1 Cook the potatoes in a saucepan of lightly salted boiling water for 10 minutes. Drain and let cool. Meanwhile, cook the carrot in lightly salted boiling water for 5 minutes.

2 Set the potato aside to cool. When cool enough to handle, grate it with a coarse grater.

3 Drain the carrot and add it to the grated potato, together with the celery, mushrooms, onion, garlic, peas, and cheese. Season to taste with salt and pepper.

4 Put all of the sauce ingredients in a small pan and bring to a boil. Reduce the heat to low and simmer for 15 minutes.

5 Divide the potato mixture into 8 portions of equal size and shape into flattened rectangles with your hands.

6 Heat the oil and butter in a skillet and cook the hash browns in batches over a low heat for 4–5 minutes on each side, until crisp and golden brown.

7 Transfer the hash browns to a serving plate and serve immediately with the tomato sauce.

Feta & Spinach Omelet

This quick chunky omelet has pieces of potato cooked into
the egg mixture and is then filled with feta cheese and spinach.

NUTRITIONAL INFORMATION

Calories	564	Sugars	.........6g
Protein	........30g	Fat	..........39g
Carbohydrate	...25g	Saturates	......19g

20 mins   25–30 mins

SERVES 4

INGREDIENTS

6 tbsp butter

8 cups diced waxy potatoes

3 garlic cloves,crushed

1 tsp paprika

2 tomatoes, peeled, seeded, and diced

12 eggs

pepper

FILLING

8 oz/225 g baby spinach

1 tsp fennel seeds

4½ oz/125 g feta cheese, diced

4 tbsp unsweetened yogurt

1 Heat 2 tbsp of the butter in a skillet
and cook the potatoes over a low
heat, stirring constantly, for 7–10 minutes
until golden. Transfer to a bowl.

2 Add the garlic, paprika, and tomatoes
to the pan and cook for another
2 minutes.

3 Whisk the eggs together and season
with pepper. Pour the eggs into the
potatoes and mix well.

4 Cook the spinach in boiling water for
1 minute, until just wilted. Drain and
refresh under cold running water. Pat dry

with paper towels. Stir in the fennel seeds,
feta cheese, and yogurt.

5 Heat a quarter of the remaining
butter in a 6 inch/15 cm omelet pan.
Ladle a quarter of the egg and potato
mixture into the pan. Cook, turning once,
for 2 minutes, until set.

6 Transfer the omelet to a serving plate.
Spoon a quarter of the spinach
mixture on to one half of the omelet, then
fold the omelet in half over the filling.
Repeat to make 4 omelets.

VARIATION

Use any other cheese, such as
blue cheese, instead of the feta,
and blanched broccoli in place of
the baby spinach, if you prefer.

Spanish Tortilla

This classic Spanish dish is often served as part of an appetizer selection. A variety of cooked vegetables can be added to this recipe.

NUTRITIONAL INFORMATION

Calories 430   Sugars 6g
Protein ....16g   Fat 20g
Carbohydrate ...50g   Saturates 4g

10 mins   35 mins

SERVES 4

I N G R E D I E N T S

2 lb 4 oz/1 kg waxy potatoes, thinly sliced

4 tbsp vegetable oil

1 onion, sliced

2 garlic cloves, crushed

1 green bell pepper, seeded and diced

2 tomatoes, seeded and chopped

1 oz/25 g canned corn kernels, drained

6 large eggs, beaten

2 tbsp chopped parsley

salt and pepper

1 Parboil the potatoes in a pan of lightly salted boiling water for 5 minutes. Drain well.

2 Heat the oil in a large skillet. Add the potato and onions and sauté over a low heat, stirring constantly, for 5 minutes, until the potatoes have browned.

COOK'S TIP

Ensure that the handle of your pan is heatproof before placing it under the broiler and be sure to use an oven glove when removing it as it will be very hot.

3 Add the garlic, diced bell pepper, chopped tomato, and corn, and mix together well.

4 Pour in the eggs and add the chopped parsley. Season well with salt and pepper. Cook for 10–12 minutes, until the underside is cooked through.

5 Remove the skillet from the heat and continue to cook the tortilla under a preheated medium broiler for 5–7 minutes, or until the tortilla is set and the top is golden brown.

6 Cut the tortilla into wedges or cubes, depending on your preference, and transfer to serving dishes. Serve with salad. In Spain tortillas are served hot, cold, or warm.

Paprika Chips

These wafer-thin potato chips are great cooked over a barbecue grill and served with spicy vegetable kabobs.

NUTRITIONAL INFORMATION

Calories	149	Sugars	.......0.6g
Protein	.........2g	Fat	...........8g
Carbohydrate	...17g	Saturates	.......1g

🥧 5 mins   🕐 7 mins

SERVES 4

I N G R E D I E N T S

2 large potatoes

3 tbsp olive oil

½ tsp paprika

salt

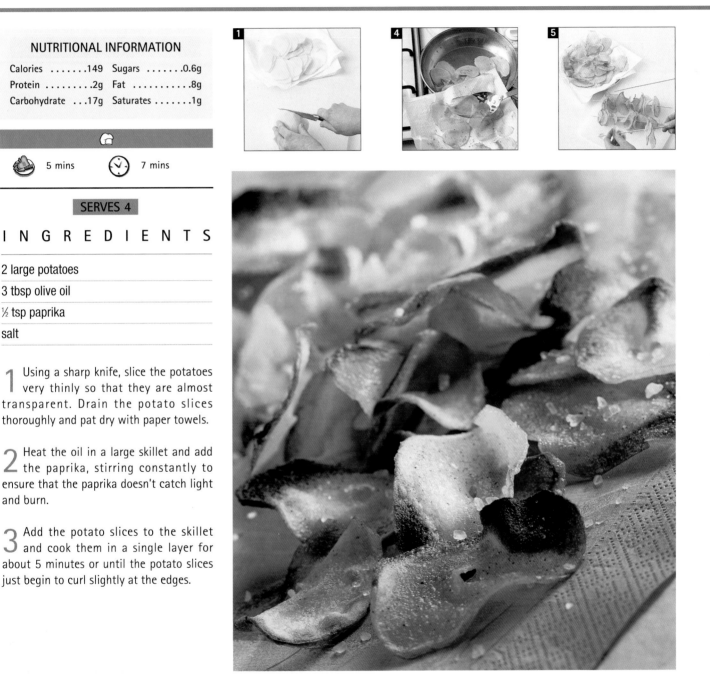

1 Using a sharp knife, slice the potatoes very thinly so that they are almost transparent. Drain the potato slices thoroughly and pat dry with paper towels.

2 Heat the oil in a large skillet and add the paprika, stirring constantly to ensure that the paprika doesn't catch light and burn.

3 Add the potato slices to the skillet and cook them in a single layer for about 5 minutes or until the potato slices just begin to curl slightly at the edges.

VARIATION

You could use curry powder or any other spice to flavor the chips instead of the paprika, if you prefer.

4 Remove the potato slices from the pan using a slotted spoon and transfer them to paper towels to drain thoroughly.

5 Thread the potato slices on to several wooden kabob skewers.

6 Sprinkle the potato slices with a little salt and cook over a medium hot barbecue grill or under a medium broiler, turning frequently, for 10 minutes, until the potato slices begin to go crisp. Sprinkle with a little more salt, if preferred, and serve immediately.

Creamy Stuffed Mushrooms

These oven-baked mushrooms are covered with a creamy potato and mushroom filling topped with melted cheese.

NUTRITIONAL INFORMATION

Calories 214   Sugars 1g
Protein . . . . .5g   Fat 17g
Carbohydrate . . . .11g   Saturates 11g

🥔 40 mins   🕐 40 mins

SERVES 4

INGREDIENTS

1 oz/25 g dried ceps

1½ cups diced mealy potatoes

2 tbsp butter, melted

4 tbsp heavy cream

2 tbsp chopped fresh chives

8 large open cup mushrooms

¼ cup grated Emmenthal cheese

⅔ cup vegetable bouillon

salt and pepper

fresh chives, to garnish

1 Place the dried ceps in a small bowl. Add sufficient boiling water to cover and let soak for 20 minutes.

2 Meanwhile, cook the potatoes in a medium pan of lightly salted boiling water for 10 minutes, until cooked through and tender. Drain well and mash until smooth.

3 Drain the soaked ceps and then chop them finely. Mix them into the mashed potato.

4 Thoroughly blend the butter, cream, and chives together and pour the mixture into the ceps and potato mixture, mixing well. Season to taste with salt and pepper.

5 Remove the stems from the open cup mushrooms. Chop the stems and stir them into the potato mixture. Spoon the mixture into the open cup mushrooms and sprinkle the cheese over the top.

6 Arrange the filled mushrooms in a shallow ovenproof dish and pour in the vegetable bouillon.

7 Cover the dish and cook in a preheated oven, 425°F/220°C, for 20 minutes. Remove the lid and cook for 5 minutes until golden.

8 Garnish the mushrooms with fresh chives and serve at once.

VARIATION

Use fresh mushrooms instead of the dried ceps, if preferred, and stir a mixture of chopped nuts into the mushroom stuffing mixture for extra crunch.

Potato & Mushroom Bake

Use any mixture of mushrooms to hand for this creamy layered bake. It can be served straight from the dish in which it is cooked.

NUTRITIONAL INFORMATION

Calories 304	Sugars 2g	
Protein 4g	Fat 24g	
Carbohydrate ...20g	Saturates 15g	

15 mins

1 hour

SERVES 4

INGREDIENTS

2 tbsp butter

1 lb 2 oz/500 g waxy potatoes, thinly sliced

2 cups sliced mixed mushrooms

1 tbsp chopped rosemary

4 tbsp chopped chives

2 garlic cloves, crushed

⅔ cup heavy cream

salt and pepper

snipped chives, to garnish

1 Grease a shallow round ovenproof dish with butter.

2 Parboil the sliced potatoes in a pan of boiling water for 10 minutes. Drain well. Layer a quarter of the potatoes in the base of the dish.

3 Arrange one-quarter of the mushrooms on top of the potatoes and sprinkle with one-quarter of the rosemary, chives, and garlic. Continue making layers in the same order, finishing with a layer of potatoes on top.

4 Pour the cream over the top of the potatoes. Season to taste with salt and pepper.

5 Cook in a preheated oven, 375°F/190°C, for about 45 minutes, or until the bake is golden brown and piping hot.

6 Garnish with snipped chives and serve at once straight from the dish.

COOK'S TIP

For a special occasion, the bake may be made in a lined cake pan and then turned out to serve.

Potato-Filled Naan Breads

This is a filling Indian sandwich. Spicy potatoes fill the naan breads, which are served with a cool cucumber raita and lime pickle.

NUTRITIONAL INFORMATION

Calories 244	Sugars 7g	
Protein 8g	Fat 8g	
Carbohydrate ...37g	Saturates 1g	

10 MINS   25 MINS

SERVES 4

INGREDIENTS

1½ cups scrubbed, and diced waxy potatoes

1 tbsp vegetable oil

1 onion, chopped

2 garlic cloves, crushed

1 tsp ground cumin

1 tsp ground coriander

½ tsp chili powder

1 tbsp tomato paste

3 tbsp vegetable bouillon

2¾ oz/75 g baby spinach, shredded

4 small or 2 large naan breads

lime pickle, to serve

RAITA

⅔ cup lowfat unsweetened yogurt

4 tbsp diced cucumber

1 tbsp chopped mint

1 Cook the diced potatoes in a pan of boiling water for 10 minutes. Drain thoroughly.

2 Heat the vegetable oil in a separate pan and cook the onion and garlic for 3 minutes, stirring. Add the spices and cook for a further 2 minutes.

3 Stir in the potatoes, tomato paste, vegetable bouillon, and spinach. Cook for 5 minutes until the potatoes are tender.

4 Warm the naan breads in a preheated oven, 300°F/150°C, for about 2 minutes.

5 To make the raita, mix the yogurt, cucumber, and mint together in a small bowl.

6 Remove the naan breads from the oven. Using a sharp knife, cut a pocket in the side of each naan bread. Spoon the spicy potato mixture into each pocket.

7 Serve the filled naan breads at once, accompanied by the raita and lime pickle.

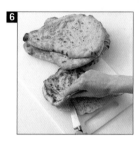

COOK'S TIP

To give the raita a much stronger flavor, make it in advance and leave to chill in the refrigerator until ready to serve.

Potato & Spinach Triangles

These small pasties are made with crisp phyllo pastry and filled with a tasty spinach and potato mixture flavored with chili and tomato.

NUTRITIONAL INFORMATION

Calories 514	Sugars 4g	
Protein 9g	Fat 37g	
Carbohydrate . . .37g	Saturates 8g	

🥔 🥔 🥔

🍲 25 mins   🕐 35 mins

SERVES 4

INGREDIENTS

2 tbsp butter, melted, plus extra
for greasing

1½ cups finely diced waxy potatoes

1 lb 2 oz/500 g baby spinach

1 tomato, seeded and chopped

¼ tsp chili powder

½ tsp lemon juice

8 oz/225 g phyllo pastry, thawed if frozen

salt and pepper

crisp salad, to serve

LEMON MAYONNAISE

⅔ cup mayonnaise

2 tsp lemon juice

zest of 1 lemon

1 Lightly grease a baking sheet with a little butter.

2 Cook the potatoes in a pan of lightly salted boiling water for 10 minutes, or until cooked through. Drain thoroughly and place in a mixing bowl.

3 Meanwhile, put the spinach in a pan with 2 tablespoonfuls of water. Cover and cook over a low heat for 2 minutes, until wilted. Drain the spinach thoroughly, squeezing out excess moisture, and add to the potato.

4 Stir in the chopped tomato, chili powder, and lemon juice. Season to taste with salt and pepper.

5 Lightly brush 8 sheets of phyllo pastry with melted butter. Spread out 4 of the sheets and lay the other 4 on top of each. Cut them into rectangles about 8 x 4 inches/20 x 10 cm.

6 Spoon the potato and spinach mixture on to one end of each rectangle. Fold a corner of the pastry over the filling, fold the pointed end back over the pastry strip, then fold over the remaining pastry to form a triangle.

7 Place the triangles on the baking sheet and bake in a preheated oven, 190°C/375°F/Gas Mark 5, for 20 minutes, or until golden brown.

8 To make the mayonnaise, mix the mayonnaise, lemon juice, and lemon zest together in a small bowl. Serve the potato and spinach triangles warm or cold with the lemon mayonnaise and a crisp salad.

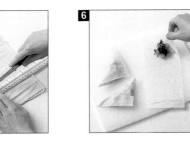

Spicy Garbanzo Snack

You can use fresh garbanzo beans, soaked overnight, for this popular Indian snack, but the canned variety is just as flavorsome.

NUTRITIONAL INFORMATION

Calories	190	Sugars	.........4g
Protein	.........9g	Fat	...........3g
Carbohydrate	...34g	Saturates	.....0.3g

5 mins   10 mins

SERVES 4

INGREDIENTS

14 oz/400 g can garbanzo beans, drained

1 lb/450g potatoes

1 medium onion

2 tbsp tamarind paste

6 tbsp water

1 tsp chili powder

2 tsp sugar

1 tsp salt

TO GARNISH

1 tomato, sliced

2 fresh green chilies, chopped

fresh cilantro leaves

1 Place the garbanzo beans in a bowl.

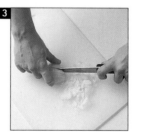

2 Using a sharp knife, cut the potatoes into dice.

3 Place the potatoes in a pan of water and boil until cooked through. Test by inserting the tip of a knife into the potatoes—they should feel soft and tender. Set the potatoes aside.

4 Using a sharp knife, finely chop the onion. Set aside until required.

5 Mix together the tamarind paste and water. Add the chili powder, sugar, and salt and mix again. Pour the mixture over the garbanzo beans.

6 Add the onion and the diced potatoes, and stir to mix. Season to taste.

7 Transfer to a serving bowl and garnish with tomatoes, chilies, and fresh cilantro leaves.

COOK'S TIP

Garbanzo beans have a nutty flavor and slightly crunchy texture. Indian cooks also grind these to make a flour called gram or besan, which is used to make breads, thicken sauces, and to make batters for deep-fried dishes.

Crispy Potato Skins

Use the potato flesh in this recipe for another meal, so make slightly more than you need. They make a delicious appetizer and are ideal for a barbecue.

NUTRITIONAL INFORMATION

Calories . . . . . . .395 Sugars 2g
Protein . . . . .12g Fat 20g
Carbohydrate . . .44g Saturates 9g

🧊 2 mins   🕐 1 hr 15 mins

SERVES 4

I N G R E D I E N T S

8 small baking potatoes, scrubbed

4 tbsp butter, melted

salt and pepper

O P T I O N A L   T O P P I N G

6 scallions, sliced

1¾ oz/50 g Gruyère cheese, grated

1¾ oz/50 g salami, cut into thin strips

1 Preheat the oven to 400°F/200°C. Prick the potatoes with a fork and bake for 1 hour or until tender.

2 Cut the potatoes in half and scoop out the flesh, leaving about ¼ inch/5 mm potato flesh lining the skin.

3 Brush the insides of the potato with melted butter.

4 Place the skins, cut-side down, over medium hot coals and barbecue (or broil) for 10–15 minutes.

5 Turn the potato skins over and barbecue (or broil) for a further 5 minutes or until they are crispy. Take care that they do not burn.

6 Season the potato skins with salt and pepper to taste and serve while they are still warm.

7 If wished, the skins can be filled with a variety of toppings. Barbecue (or broil) the potato skins as above for about 10 minutes, then turn cut-side up and sprinkle with slices of scallion, grated cheese, and chopped salami. Barbecue (or broil) for a further 5 minutes until the cheese begins to melt. Serve hot.

COOK'S TIP
Potato skins can be served on their own but they are delicious served with a dip. Try a spicy tomato or hummus dip.

Potatoes with Goat Cheese

This makes a luscious side dish to serve with meat, or a satisfying vegetarian main course. Goat cheese is a traditional food of Mexico.

NUTRITIONAL INFORMATION

Calories ......725 Sugars 4g
Protein ....30g Fat 43g
Carbohydrate ...56g Saturates 28g

20 mins   10 mins

SERVES 4

INGREDIENTS

2 lb 12 oz/1.25 kg baking potatoes, peeled and cut into chunks

pinch of salt

pinch of sugar

1 cup vegetable or chicken bouillon

3 garlic cloves, finely chopped

¾ cup crème fraîche

a few shakes of bottled chipotle salsa, or 1 dried chipotle, reconstituted, seeded and thinly sliced

8 oz/225 g goat cheese, sliced

1½ cups mozzarella or Cheddar cheese, grated

scant ⅔ cup Parmesan or pecorino cheese, grated

salt

1 Put the potatoes in a pan of water with the salt and sugar. Bring to a boil and cook for about 10 minutes until they are half cooked.

2 Combine the crème fraîche with the stock, garlic, and chipotle salsa.

3 Arrange half the potatoes in a casserole. Pour half the crème fraîche sauce over the potatoes and cover with

the goat cheese. Top with the remaining potatoes and the sauce.

4 Sprinkle with the grated mozzarella or Cheddar cheese, then with either the grated Parmesan or pecorino.

5 Bake in a preheated oven at 350°F/180°C for about 25 minutes, or until the potatoes are tender and the cheese topping is lightly golden and crisped in places. Serve at once.

Smoked Fish & Potato Pâté

This smoked fish pâté is given a tart fruity flavor by the gooseberries, which complement the fish perfectly.

NUTRITIONAL INFORMATION

Calories	418	Sugars	.........4g
Protein	.........18g	Fat	..........25g
Carbohydrate	...32g	Saturates	......6g

🥄 20 mins   🕐 10 mins

SERVES 4

INGREDIENTS

3⅔ cups diced mealy potatoes,

10½ oz/300 g smoked mackerel, skinned and flaked

2¾ oz/75 g cooked gooseberries

2 tsp lemon juice

2 tbsp lowfat crème fraîche

1 tbsp capers

1 gherkin, chopped

1 tbsp chopped dill pickle

1 tbsp chopped fresh dill

salt and pepper

lemon wedges, to garnish

toast or warm crusty bread, to serve

1 Cook the diced potatoes in a pan of boiling water for 10 minutes until tender, then drain well.

2 Place the cooked potatoes in a food processor or blender.

3 Add the skinned and flaked smoked mackerel and process for 30 seconds until fairly smooth. Alternatively, place the ingredients in a bowl and mash together with a fork.

4 Add the cooked gooseberries, lemon juice, and crème fraîche to the fish

and potato mixture. Blend for another 10 seconds or mash well.

5 Stir in the capers, chopped gherkin, dill pickle, and chopped fresh dill. Season well with salt and pepper.

6 Turn the fish pâté into a serving dish. Garnish with lemon wedges and serve with slices of toast or warm crusty bread cut into chunks or slices.

COOK'S TIP

Use stewed, canned, or bottled cooked gooseberries for convenience and to save time, or when fresh gooseberries are out of season.

Potato Kibbeh

Kibbeh is a Middle Eastern dish, traditionally made with cracked wheat, lamb, and spices. Serve with sesame sauce, salad, and warm bread.

NUTRITIONAL INFORMATION

Calories	600	Sugars	.........4g
Protein	........20g	Fat	..........35g
Carbohydrate	...53g	Saturates	.......8g

10 mins, plus 30 mins soaking time   20 mins

SERVES 4

INGREDIENTS

6 oz/175 g bulgar wheat

2 cups diced mealy potatoes

2 small eggs

2 tbsp butter, melted

pinch of ground cumin

pinch of ground coriander

pinch of grated nutmeg

salt and pepper

vegetable oil, for deep-frying

STUFFING

6 oz/175 g minced lamb

1 small onion, chopped

1 tbsp pine nuts

25 g/1 oz dried apricots, chopped

pinch of grated nutmeg

pinch of ground cinnamon

1 tbsp chopped fresh cilantro

2 tbsp lamb bouillon

1 Put the bulgar wheat in a bowl and cover with boiling water. Soak for 30 minutes until the water has been absorbed and the bulgar wheat has swollen.

2 Meanwhile, cook the diced potatoes in a pan of boiling water for 10 minutes or until cooked through. Drain and mash until smooth.

3 Add the bulgar wheat to the mashed potato with the eggs, the melted butter, the ground cumin, and coriander, and the grated nutmeg. Mix well and season with salt and pepper.

4 To make the stuffing, dry fry the lamb for 5 minutes. Add the onion and cook for another 2–3 minutes. Add the remaining stuffing ingredients and cook for 5 minutes until the lamb stock has been absorbed. Let the mixture cool slightly, then divide into 8 portions. Roll each one into a ball.

5 Divide the potato mixture into 8 portions and flatten each into a round. Place a portion of stuffing in the center of each round. Shape the coating around the stuffing to encase it completely.

6 In a large pan, heat the oil to 350°F-375°F/180°C-190°C or until a cube of bread browns in 30 seconds, and cook the kibbeh for 5–7 minutes until golden brown. Drain well and serve at once.

Fish Balls with Tomato Sauce

These spicy potato and fish balls are served with a rich tomato sauce.
They may be made in advance and fried just before eating.

NUTRITIONAL INFORMATION

Calories . . . . . . .438 Sugars 4g
Protein . . . . .18g Fat 32g
Carbohydrate . . .23g Saturates 8g

🥮 🥮 🥮

🍞 5 mins   🕐 40 mins

SERVES 4

I N G R E D I E N T S

2⅔ cups diced mealy potatoes

8 oz/225 g smoked fish fillets, such as cod,
  skinned

3 tbsp butter

2 eggs, beaten

1 tbsp chopped fresh dill

½ tsp cayenne pepper

vegetable oil, for deep-frying

salt and pepper

dill sprigs, to garnish

S A U C E

1¼ cups strained tomatoes

1 tbsp tomato paste

2 tbsp chopped fresh dill

⅔ cup fish bouillon

1 Cook the diced potatoes in a pan of boiling water for 10 minutes or until cooked. Drain well, then add the butter to the potato and mash until smooth. Season well with salt and pepper.

2 Meanwhile, poach the fish in boiling water for 10 minutes, turning once. Drain and mash the fish. Stir it into the potato mixture and let cool.

3 While the potato and fish mixture is cooling, make the sauce. Put the strained tomatoes, tomato paste, dill, and bouillon in a pan and bring to a boil. Reduce the heat, then cover the pan and simmer for 20 minutes until thickened.

4 Add the eggs, dill, and cayenne pepper to the potato and fish mixture and beat until well mixed.

5 In a large pan, heat the oil to 350°F–375°F/180°C-190°C, or until a cube of bread browns in 30 seconds. Drop dessertspoons of the potato mixture into the oil and cook for 3–4 minutes until golden brown. Drain on paper towels.

6 Garnish the potato and fish balls with fresh dill sprigs and serve with the tomato sauce.

VARIATION

Smoked fish is used for extra flavor, but white fish fillets or ground shrimp may be used, if preferred.

Salmon Crêpes

These pancakes are based on the latke, a thin, crisp crêpe. Here they are served with smoked salmon and sour cream for a little taste of luxury.

NUTRITIONAL INFORMATION

Calories	142	Sugars	.......1.0g
Protein	........6.8g	Fat	..........7.8g
Carbohydrate	..11.9g	Saturates	.....2.8g

🕔 0 mins   🕐 0 mins

SERVES 4

I N G R E D I E N T S

2¼ cups grated mealy potatoes

2 scallions, chopped

2 tbsp self-rising flour

2 eggs, beaten

2 tbsp vegetable oil

salt and pepper

fresh chives, to garnish

T O P P I N G

⅔ cup sour cream

4½ oz/125 g smoked salmon

1 Rinse the grated potatoes under cold running water. Drain and pat dry on paper towels. Transfer to a mixing bowl.

2 Mix the chopped scallions, flour, and eggs into the potatoes and season well with salt and pepper.

3 Heat 1 tablespoon of the oil in a skillet. Drop about 4 tablespoonfuls of the mixture into the pan and spread each one with the back of a spoon to form a round (the mixture should make 16 crêpes). Cook for 5–7 minutes, turning once, until golden. Drain well.

4 Heat the remaining oil and cook the remaining mixture in batches.

5 Top the crêpes with the sour cream and smoked salmon. Garnish with fresh chives and serve hot.

VARIATION

These crêpes are equally delicious topped with prosciutto or any other dry-cured ham instead of the smoked salmon.

Tuna Fishcakes

This makes a satisfying and quick midweek supper.

🍞 🍞 🍞

5 mins   1 hr 10 mins

SERVES 4

I N G R E D I E N T S

8 oz potatoes, cubed

1 tbsp olive oil

1 large shallot, finely chopped

1 garlic clove, finely chopped

1 tsp thyme leaves

14 oz/400 g canned tuna in olive oil, drained

grated zest ½ lemon

1 tbsp chopped fresh parsley

2–3 tbsp all-purpose flour

1 egg, lightly beaten

4 oz/115 g fresh bread crumbs

vegetable oil, for shallow frying

salt and pepper

Q U I C K   T O M A T O   S A U C E

2 tbsp olive oil

14 oz/400 g canned chopped tomatoes

1 garlic clove, crushed

1 tsp sugar

grated zest 1 lemon

1 tbsp chopped fresh basil

salt and pepper

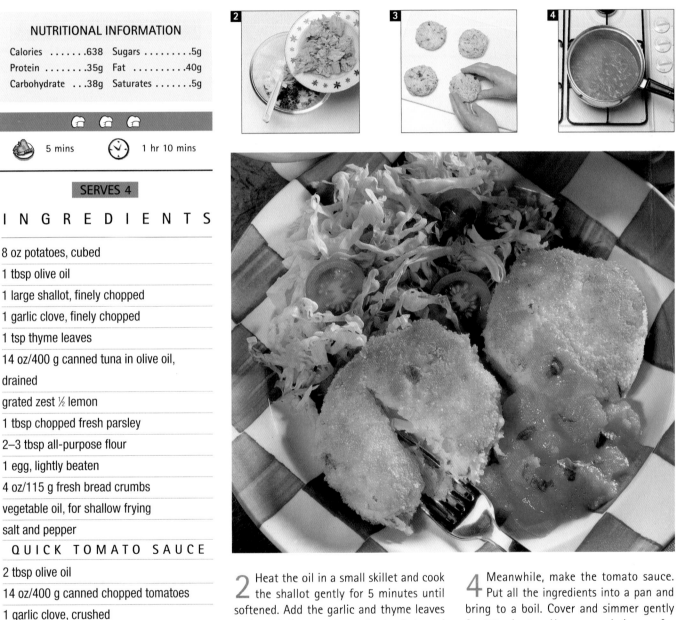

1 For the tuna fishcakes, cook the potatoes in plenty of boiling salted water for 12–15 minutes until tender. Mash, leaving a few lumps, and set aside.

2 Heat the oil in a small skillet and cook the shallot gently for 5 minutes until softened. Add the garlic and thyme leaves and cook for another minute. Let cool slightly, then add to the potatoes with the tuna, lemon zest, parsley, and seasoning. Mix together well, but leave some texture.

3 Form the mixture into 6–8 cakes. Dip the cakes first in the flour, then the egg, and finally the bread crumbs to coat. Refrigerate for 30 minutes.

4 Meanwhile, make the tomato sauce. Put all the ingredients into a pan and bring to a boil. Cover and simmer gently for 30 minutes. Uncover and simmer for another 15 minutes until thickened.

5 Heat enough oil in a skillet to generously cover the bottom. When hot, add the chilled fishcakes in batches and cook for 3–4 minutes each side until golden and crisp. Drain on paper towels while you cook the remaining fishcakes. Serve hot with the tomato sauce.

Salt Cod Hash

As well as being a simple supper dish, this would make a delicious addition to a brunch menu.

NUTRITIONAL INFORMATION

Calories	857	Sugars	.........5g
Protein	.......58g	Fat	..........36g
Carbohydrate	...82g	Saturates	......10g

5 mins, plus 50 hrs soaking/salting time

30 mins

SERVES 4

INGREDIENTS

1 oz/25 g sea salt

1 lb 10 oz/750 g fresh boneless cod fillet

4 eggs

3 tbsp olive oil, plus extra for drizzling

8 slices bacon, chopped

generous 4 cups main crop potatoes, diced

8 garlic cloves

8 thick slices good-quality white bread

2 plum tomatoes, skinned and chopped

2 tsp red wine vinegar

2 tbsp chopped fresh parsley, plus extra to garnish

salt and pepper

lemon wedges, to garnish

1 Sprinkle the salt over both sides of the cod fillet. Place in a shallow dish, cover and refrigerate for 48 hours. When ready to cook, remove the cod from the refrigerator and rinse under cold water. Let soak in cold water for 2 hours, then drain well.

2 Bring a large pan of water to a boil and add the fish. Remove from the heat and let stand for 10 minutes. Drain the fish on paper towels and flake the flesh. Set aside. Discard the soaking water.

3 Bring a pan of water to a boil. Add the eggs and simmer for 7–9 minutes from when the water returns to a boil—7 minutes for a slightly soft center, 9 for a firm center. Drain, then plunge the eggs into cold water. Shell the eggs and roughly chop. Set aside.

4 Heat the oil in a large skillet and add the bacon. Cook over a medium heat for 4–5 minutes until crisp and brown. Remove with a slotted spoon and drain on kitchen paper. Put the potatoes and garlic in the pan and cook over a medium heat for 8–10 minutes until crisp and golden. Meanwhile, toast the bread on both sides. Drizzle the bread with olive oil and set aside.

5 Add the plum tomatoes, bacon, fish, vinegar, and reserved chopped egg to the potatoes and garlic. Cook for 2 minutes. Stir in the parsley and season. Put the toast onto serving plates and top with the hash. Garnish with parsley and lemon wedges.

Fish Pasties

This is a seafood variation of a classic pasty. The addition of leek, tarragon, and cheese gives a delicious mixture of flavors and textures.

5–10 mins, plus 30 mins chilling time | 35 mins

SERVES 4

INGREDIENTS

DOUGH

4 cups self-rising flour

pinch salt

1¼ cups butter, diced

1 egg, lightly beaten

FILLING

¼ cup butter

1 small leek, diced

1 small onion, finely chopped

1 carrot, diced

1½ cups diced potatoes

12 oz/350 g firm white fish cut into 1 inch/2.5 cm pieces

4 tsp white wine vinegar

¼ cup Cheddar cheese, grated

1 tsp chopped fresh tarragon

salt and pepper

mixed salad leaves and tomatoes, to serve

1 In a large bowl, sift together the flour and salt. Add the butter and rub in with your fingertips until the mixture resembles coarse bread crumbs. Add about 3 tablespoons cold water to form a dough. Knead briefly until smooth. Cover with plastic wrap and chill for 30 minutes.

2 Meanwhile make the filling. Melt half the butter in a large skillet and add the leek, onion, and carrot. Cook gently for 7–8 minutes until the vegetables are softened. Remove from the heat, then put to one side and let the mixture cool slightly.

3 Put the vegetable mixture into a large mixing bowl and add the potato, fish, vinegar, remaining butter, cheese, tarragon, and seasoning. Set aside.

4 Remove the dough from the refrigerator and roll out thinly. Using a cutter, press out four 7½ inch/19 cm disks.

Alternatively, use a small plate of a similar size. Divide the filling between the 4 disks. Moisten the edges of the circles and fold over. Pinch to seal. Crimp the edges and place the pasties on a lightly greased baking sheet. Brush generously with the beaten egg, avoiding the base of the pasties to prevent them sticking to the sheet.

5 Bake in a preheated oven at 400°F/200°C for 15 minutes. Remove from the oven and brush again with the egg glaze. Return to the oven for another 20 minutes. Serve hot or cold with a salad of mixed leaves and tomatoes.

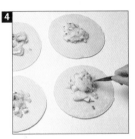

Thai Potato Crab Cakes

These small crab cakes are based on a traditional Thai recipe. They make a delicious snack when served with this sweet and sour cucumber sauce.

NUTRITIONAL INFORMATION

Calories 254   Sugars 9g
Protein . . . . .12g   Fat 6g
Carbohydrate . . .40g   Saturates 1g

🍲 10 mins   🕐 30 mins

SERVES 4

INGREDIENTS

2⅔ cups diced mealy potatoes

6 oz/175 g white crab meat, drained
   if canned

4 scallions, chopped

1 tsp light soy sauce

½ tsp sesame oil

1 tsp chopped lemon grass

1 tsp lime juice

3 tbsp all-purpose flour

2 tbsp vegetable oil

salt and pepper

SAUCE

4 tbsp finely chopped cucumber

2 tbsp clear honey

1 tbsp garlic wine vinegar

½ tsp light soy sauce

1 chopped red chili

TO GARNISH

1 red chili sliced

cucumber slices

1 Cook the diced potatoes in a pan of boiling water for 10 minutes until cooked through. Drain well and mash.

2 Mix the crab meat into the potato with the scallions, soy sauce, sesame oil, lemon grass, lime juice, and flour. Season with salt and pepper.

3 Divide the potato mixture into 8 portions of equal size and shape them into small rounds, using floured hands.

4 Heat the oil in a wok or skillet and cook the cakes, four at a time, for 5–7 minutes, turning once. Keep warm and repeat with the remaining crab cakes.

5 Meanwhile, make the sauce. In a small serving bowl, mix the chopped cucumber, honey, vinegar, soy sauce, and chopped red chili.

6 Garnish the cakes with the sliced red chili and cucumber slices and serve with the sauce.

Shrimp Rostis

These crisp little vegetable and shrimp cakes make an ideal light lunch or supper, accompanied with a salad.

NUTRITIONAL INFORMATION

Calories	445	Sugars	.........9g
Protein	........19g	Fat	..........29g
Carbohydrate	...29g	Saturates	.......4g

10 mins   1 hr

SERVES 4

INGREDIENTS

12 oz/350 g potatoes

12 oz/350 g celery root

1 carrot

1 small onion

8 oz/225 g cooked shelled shrimp, thawed if frozen and well-drained on paper towels

¼ cup all-purpose flour

1 egg, lightly beaten

vegetable oil, for deep-frying

salt and pepper

CHERRY TOMATO SALSA

8 oz/225 g mixed cherry tomatoes such as baby plum, yellow, orange, quartered

1 small mango, finely diced

1 red chili, seeded and finely chopped

1 small red onion, finely chopped

1 tbsp chopped cilantro

1 tbsp chopped fresh chives

2 tbsp olive oil

2 tsp lemon juice

salt and pepper

1 For the salsa, mix together the tomatoes, mango, chili, red onion, cilantro, chives, olive oil, lemon juice, and seasoning. Set aside for the flavors to infuse.

2 Using a food processor or the fine blade of a box grater, finely grate the potatoes, celery root, carrot, and onion. Mix together with the shrimp, flour, and egg. Season well and set aside.

3 Divide the shrimp mixture into 8 equal pieces. Press each into a greased 4 inch/10 cm cutter (if you have only 1 cutter, simply shape the rostis individually).

4 In a large skillet, heat a shallow layer of oil. When hot, transfer the vegetable cakes, still in the cutters, to the skillet, in 4 batches if necessary (preheat oven to keep them warm). When the oil sizzles underneath, remove the cutter. Cook gently, pressing down with a palette knife, for 6–8 minutes on each side, until browned and the vegetables are tender. Drain on paper towels and keep warm. Serve hot with the tomato salsa.

Spicy Fish & Potato Fritters

You need mealy, old potatoes for making these tasty fritters. Any white fish of your choice may be used.

NUTRITIONAL INFORMATION

Calories ....349 Sugars 4g
Protein ....31g Fat 8g
Carbohydrate ...41g Saturates 1g

15 mins   25 mins

SERVES 4

INGREDIENTS

1 lb 2 oz/500 g potatoes, peeled and cut into even-size pieces

1 lb 2 oz/500 g white fish fillets, such as cod or haddock, skinned and boned

6 scallions, sliced

1 fresh green chili, seeded

2 garlic cloves, peeled

1 tsp salt

1 tbsp medium or hot curry paste

2 eggs, beaten

5½ oz/150 g fresh white bread crumbs

vegetable oil, for shallow frying

mango chutney, to serve

TO GARNISH

cilantro sprigs and lime wedges

  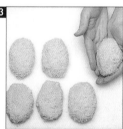

1 Cook the potatoes in a pan of boiling, salted water until tender. Drain well, then return the potatoes to the pan and place over a medium heat for a few moments to dry off. Cool slightly, then place in a food processor with the fish, scallions, chili, garlic, salt, and curry paste. Process until the ingredients are very finely chopped and blended.

2 Turn out the potato mixture into a bowl and mix in 2 tablespoons of beaten egg and 55 g/2 oz of the bread crumbs. Place the remaining beaten egg and bread crumbs in separate dishes.

3 Divide the potato mixture into eight equal portions and, using a spoon to help you (the mixture is quite soft), dip each potato portion first in the beaten egg and then coat it in the bread crumbs. When each portion is evenly coated, carefully shape it into an oval.

4 Heat enough oil in a large skillet for shallow frying. When the oil has reached the required temperature, cook the fritters over medium heat for 3–4 minutes, turning frequently, until golden brown and cooked through.

5 Drain on paper towels and garnish with lime wedges and fresh cilantro sprigs. Serve the fritters hot, with some mango chutney.

Chicken & Almond Rissoles

Potatoes and chicken are combined to make tasty rissoles rolled in chopped almonds, then served with stir-fried vegetables.

NUTRITIONAL INFORMATION

Calories 161   Sugars 3g
Protein . . . . .12g   Fat 9g
Carbohydrate . . . .8g   Saturates 1g

🔒 🔒 🔒

🍲 35 mins   🕐 20 mins

SERVES 4

I N G R E D I E N T S

4½ oz/125 g par-boiled potatoes

1 carrot

4½ oz/125 g cooked chicken meat

1 garlic clove, crushed

½ tsp dried tarragon or thyme

generous pinch of ground allspice or ground coriander seeds

1 egg yolk, or ½ egg, beaten

about ¼ cup slivered almonds

salt and pepper

STIR-FRIED VEGETABLES

1 celery stalk

2 scallions, trimmed

1 tbsp oil

8 baby corn cobs

about 10–12 snow peas or sugar snap peas, trimmed

2 tsp balsamic vinegar

salt and pepper

2 Add the egg and bind the ingredients together. Divide in half and shape into sausages. Chop the almonds and then evenly coat each rissole in the nuts. Place the rissoles in a greased ovenproof dish and cook in a preheated oven, 200°C/400°F/Gas Mark 6, for about 20 minutes until browned.

3 To prepare the stir-fried vegetables, cut the celery and scallions on the diagonal into narrow slices. Heat the oil in a skillet and toss in the vegetables. Cook over a high heat for 1–2 minutes, then add the corn cobs and peas, and cook for 2–3 minutes. Finally, add the balsamic vinegar and season well with salt and pepper.

4 Place the rissoles on to a platter and add the stir-fried vegetables.

1 Grate the boiled potatoes and raw carrots coarsely into a bowl. Chop finely or grind the chicken. Add to the vegetables with the garlic, herbs, and spices and plenty of salt and pepper.

Chicken & Herb Fritters

These fritters are delicious served with salad greens, a fresh vegetable salsa or a chili sauce dip.

NUTRITIONAL INFORMATION

Calories 333   Sugars 1g
Protein . . . . .16g   Fat 23g
Carbohydrate . . .17g   Saturates 5g

5 mins   10–15 mins

SERVES 4

INGREDIENTS

2 cups mashed potato, with butter added

1⅓ cups chopped, cooked chicken

⅔ cups cooked ham, finely chopped

1 tbsp mixed herbs

2 eggs, lightly beaten

1 tbsp milk

fresh brown bread crumbs, to coat

oil, for shallow frying

salt and pepper

sprig of fresh parsley, to garnish

salad greens, to serve

COOK'S TIP

A mixture of chopped fresh tarragon and parsley makes a fresh and flavorsome addition to these tasty fritters.

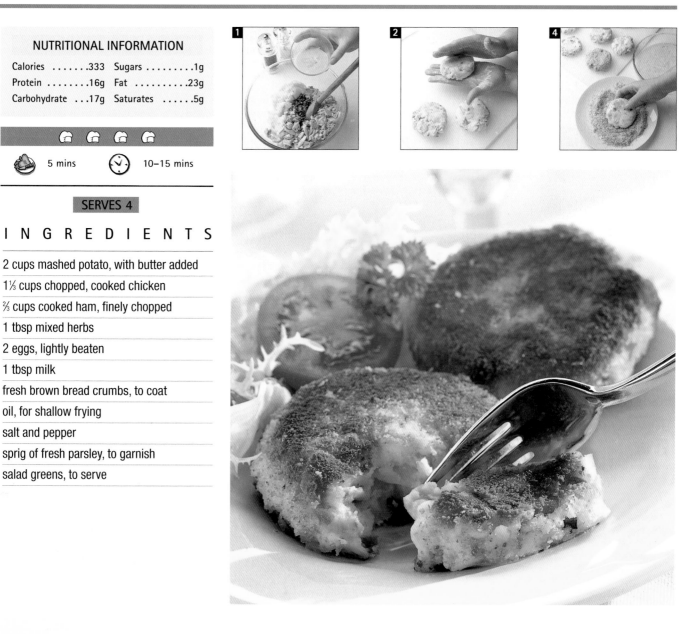

1 In a large bowl, blend the potato, chicken, ham, herbs, and one of the eggs, and season well.

2 Shape the mixture into small balls or flat pancakes.

3 Add a little milk to the second egg and mix together.

4 Place the bread crumbs on a plate. Dip the balls in the egg and milk mixture, then roll in the bread crumbs to coat them completely.

5 Heat the oil in a large skillet and cook the fritters, turning once, until they are golden brown on both sides. Garnish with a sprig of fresh parsley and serve at once with fresh salad greens.

Chicken & Cheese Jackets

Use the breasts from a roasted chicken to make these delicious potatoes and serve as a light lunch or supper dish.

NUTRITIONAL INFORMATION

Calories 417	Sugars 4g
Protein 28g	Fat 10g
Carbohydrate . . .57g	Saturates 5g

🕒 10 mins   ⏱ 50 mins

SERVES 4

I N G R E D I E N T S

4 large baking potatoes

8 oz/225 g cooked, boneless chicken breasts

4 scallions

1 cup lowfat soft cheese or Quark

pepper

1 Scrub the potatoes and pat dry with absorbent paper towels.

2 Prick the potatoes all over with a fork. Bake in a preheated oven, 400°F/200°C, for about 50 minutes until tender.

3 Using a sharp knife, dice the chicken and trim and thickly slice the scallions. Place the chicken and scallions in a bowl.

4 Add the lowfat soft cheese or Quark to the chicken and scallions and stir well to combine.

5 Cut a cross through the top of each potato and pull slightly apart. Spoon the chicken filling into the potatoes and sprinkle with pepper.

6 Serve the chicken and cheese jackets immediately with coleslaw, green salad or a mixed salad.

COOK'S TIP

Look for Quark in the chilled section. It is a lowfat, white, fresh curd cheese made from cow's milk with a delicate, slightly sour flavor.

Meatballs in Spicy Sauce

Serve these with bread to mop up the sauce, or make half as much mixture again, and roll into larger balls. Serve with rice and vegetables.

NUTRITIONAL INFORMATION

Calories 95   Sugars 2.7g
Protein ....4.5g   Fat 5.8g
Carbohydrate ...6.6g   Saturates 2.3g

🧀 🧀

🥔 00 mins   🕐 00 mins

SERVES 4

INGREDIENTS

1½ diced mealy potatoes

8 oz/225 g ground beef or lamb

1 onion, finely chopped

1 tbsp chopped fresh cilantro

1 celery stalk, finely chopped

2 garlic cloves, crushed

2 tbsp butter

1 tbsp vegetable oil

salt and pepper

chopped fresh cilantro, to garnish

SAUCE

1 tbsp vegetable oil

1 onion, finely chopped

2 tsp soft brown sugar

14 oz/400 g canned chopped tomatoes

1 green chili, chopped

1 tsp paprika

⅔ cup vegetable bouillon

2 tsp cornstarch

COOK'S TIP

Make the potato and meatballs in advance and chill or freeze them for later use. Make sure you defrost them thoroughly before cooking.

1 Cook the diced potatoes in a pan of boiling water for 25 minutes until cooked through. Drain well and transfer to a large mixing bowl. Mash until smooth.

2 Add the ground beef or lamb, onion, cilantro, celery and garlic and mix together well.

3 Bring the mixture together with your hands and roll it into 20 small balls.

4 To make the sauce, heat the oil in a pan and sauté the chopped onion for 5 minutes. Add the remaining sauce ingredients and bring to a boil, stirring. Lower the heat and simmer for about 20 minutes.

5 Meanwhile, heat the butter and oil for the potato and meat balls in a skillet. Add the balls in batches and cook for 10–15 minutes until browned, turning frequently. Keep warm whilst cooking the remainder. Serve the potato and meatballs in a warm shallow ovenproof dish with the sauce poured around them and garnished with cilantro.

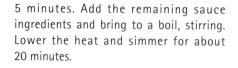

Croquettes with Ham

These may be served plain as an accompaniment, or with vegetables or salami and a cheese sauce as an appetizer.

NUTRITIONAL INFORMATION

Calories . . . . . . .792 Sugars 8g
Protein . . . . .28g Fat 54g
Carbohydrate . . .53g Saturates 21g

5 mins   30 mins

SERVES 4

I N G R E D I E N T S

2½ diced mealy potatoes

1½ cups milk

2 tbsp butter

4 scallions, chopped

¾ cup Cheddar cheese

¾ cup chopped smoked ham

1 celery stalk, diced

1 egg, beaten

½ cup all-purpose flour

vegetable oil, for deep frying

salt and pepper

C O A T I N G

2 eggs, beaten

4½ oz/125 g fresh whole-wheat
    bread crumbs

S A U C E

2 tbsp butter

¼ cup all-purpose flour

⅔ cup milk

⅔ cup vegetable bouillon

¾ cup Cheddar cheese, grated

1 tsp Dijon mustard

1 tbsp chopped cilantro

1 Place the potatoes in a pan with the milk and bring to a boil. Reduce to a simmer until the liquid has been absorbed and the potatoes are cooked.

2 Add the butter and mash the potatoes. Stir in the scallions, cheese, ham, celery, egg and flour. Season and leave to cool.

3 To make the coating, whisk the eggs in a bowl. Put the bread crumbs in a separate bowl.

4 Shape the potato mixture into 8 balls. First dip them in the egg, then in the bread crumbs.

5 To make the sauce, melt the butter in a small pan. Add the flour and cook for 1 minute. Remove from the heat and stir in the milk, stock, cheese, mustard, and cilantro. Bring to a boil, stirring until thickened. Reduce the heat and keep the sauce warm, stirring occasionally.

6 In a deep fat fryer, heat the oil to 180°C–190°C/350°F–375°F and fry the croquettes for 5 minutes until golden. Drain well and serve with the sauce.

Noodles with Cheese Sauce

Potatoes are used to make a pasta dough which is cut into thin noodles and boiled. These are served with a creamy bacon and mushroom sauce.

NUTRITIONAL INFORMATION

Calories 213   Sugars 1.6g
Protein . . . . .5.3g   Fat 13.5g
Carbohydrate . .18.7g   Saturates 7.4g

5 mins   20 mins

SERVES 4

INGREDIENTS

1 lb/450 g mealy potatoes, diced

2 cups all-purpose flour

1 egg, beaten

1 tbsp milk

salt and pepper

parsley sprig, to garnish

SAUCE

1 tbsp vegetable oil

1 onion, chopped

1 garlic clove, crushed

4½ oz/125 g open cup mushrooms, sliced

3 smoked bacon slices, chopped

scant ⅔ cup fresh grated Parmesan cheese

1¼ cups heavy cream

2 tbsp chopped fresh parsley

1 Cook the diced potatoes in a pan of boiling water for 10 minutes until cooked through. Drain well. Mash the potatoes until smooth, then beat in the flour, egg, and milk. Season with salt and pepper to taste and bring together to form a stiff paste.

2 On a lightly floured surface, roll out the paste to form a thin sausage shape. Cut the sausage into 2.5 cm/1 inch lengths. Bring a large pan of salted water to a boil, then drop in the dough pieces and cook for 3–4 minutes. They will rise to the top when cooked.

3 To make the sauce, heat the oil in a pan and sauté the onion and garlic for 2 minutes. Add the mushrooms and bacon and cook for 5 minutes. Stir in the cheese, cream and parsley and season.

4 Drain the noodles and transfer to a warm pasta bowl. Spoon the sauce over the top and toss to mix. Garnish with a parsley sprig and serve.

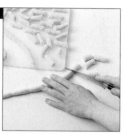

COOK'S TIP

Make the dough in advance, then wrap and store the noodles in the refrigerator for up to 24 hours.

Colcannon

This is an old Irish recipe, usually served with a piece of bacon, but it is equally delicious with a vegetarian entrée.

NUTRITIONAL INFORMATION

Calories 102   Sugars 4g
Protein . . . . .4g   Fat 4g
Carbohydrate . . .14g   Saturates 2g

🍲 20 mins   🕙 20 mins

SERVES 4

I N G R E D I E N T S

8 oz/225 g green cabbage, shredded

5 tbsp milk

1½ cup diced mealy potatoes

1 large leek, chopped

pinch of grated nutmeg

1 tbsp butter, melted

salt and pepper

1 Cook the shredded cabbage in a pan of boiling salted water for 7–10 minutes. Drain thoroughly and set aside.

2 Meanwhile, in a separate pan, bring the milk to a boil and add the potatoes and leek. Reduce the heat and simmer for 15–20 minutes, or until they are cooked through.

3 Stir in the grated nutmeg and thoroughly mash the potatoes and leek together.

4 Add the drained cabbage to the mashed potato and leek mixture and mix well.

5 Spoon the mixture into a warmed serving dish, making a hollow in the centre with the back of a spoon.

6 Pour the melted butter into the hollow and serve the colcannon immediately.

COOK'S TIP

There are many different varieties of cabbage, which produce hearts at varying times of year, so you can be sure of being able to make this delicious cabbage dish all year round.

Candied Sweet Potatoes

A taste of the Caribbean is introduced in this recipe, where sweet potatoes are cooked with sugar and lime with a dash of brandy.

NUTRITIONAL INFORMATION

Calories 348   Sugars 21g
Protein ....3g   Fat 9g
Carbohydrate ...67g   Saturates 6g

15 mins   25 mins

SERVES 4

INGREDIENTS

1½ lb/675 g sweet potatoes, sliced

3 tbsp butter

1 tbsp lime juice

½ cup soft dark brown sugar

1 tbsp brandy

grated zest of 1 lime

lime wedges, to garnish

1 Cook the sweet potatoes in a pan of boiling water for about 5 minutes. Test that the potatoes have softened by pricking with a fork. Remove the sweet potatoes with a perforated spoon and drain thoroughly.

2 Melt the butter in a large skillet. Add the lime juice and brown sugar and heat gently, stirring, to dissolve the sugar.

3 Stir the sweet potatoes and the brandy into the sugar and lime juice mixture. Cook over a low heat for about 10 minutes or until the potato slices are cooked through.

4 Sprinkle the lime zest over the top of the sweet potatoes and mix well.

5 Transfer the candied sweet potatoes to a serving plate. Garnish with lime wedges and serve at once.

COOK'S TIP

Sweet potatoes have a pinkish skin and either white, yellow or orange flesh. It doesn't matter which type is used for this dish.

Fried Potatoes & Onions

Fried potatoes are a classic favourite; here they are given extra flavor by cooking them in butter with onion, garlic and herbs.

NUTRITIONAL INFORMATION

Calories 140   Sugars 1.2g
Protein ....1.8g   Fat 8.8g
Carbohydrate ..14.1g   Saturates 5.7g

5 mins   40 mins

SERVES 4

INGREDIENTS

2 lb/900 g waxy potatoes, cut into cubes

½ cup butter

1 red onion, cut into 8 pieces

2 garlic cloves, crushed

1 tsp lemon juice

2 tbsp chopped fresh thyme

salt and pepper

1 Cook the cubed potatoes in a pan of boiling water for 10 minutes. Drain them thoroughly.

2 Melt the butter in a large, heavy-based skillet and add the red onion wedges, garlic and lemon juice. Cook for 2–3 minutes, stirring.

3 Add the potatoes to the pan and mix well to coat in the butter mixture.

4 Reduce the heat, then cover the skillet and cook for 25–30 minutes or until the potatoes are golden and tender.

5 Sprinkle the chopped thyme over the top of the potatoes and season with salt and pepper to taste.

6 Serve immediately as a side dish to accompany broiled meats or fish.

COOK'S TIP

Onions are used in a multitude of dishes to which they add their pungent flavor. The beautifully coloured purple-red onions used here have a mild, slightly sweet flavor as well as looking extremely attractive. Because of their mild taste, they are equally good eaten raw in salads .

Caramelized New Potatoes

This simple recipe is best served with a plainly cooked entrée, because it is fairly sweet and has delicious juices.

NUTRITIONAL INFORMATION

Calories	289	Sugars	........18g
Protein	.........3g	Fat	..........13g
Carbohydrate	...43g	Saturates	.......8g

5 mins   20 mins

SERVES 4

I N G R E D I E N T S

1½ lb/675 g new potatoes, scrubbed

4 tbsp dark brown sugar

5 tbsp butter

1 tbsp orange juice

1 tbsp chopped fresh parsley or cilantro

salt and pepper

orange zest curls, to garnish

1 Cook the new potatoes in a pan of boiling water for 10 minutes, or until almost tender. Drain thoroughly.

2 Melt the brown sugar in a large, heavy-based skillet over a low heat, stirring constantly.

3 Add the butter and orange juice to the pan, stirring the mixture constantly as the butter melts.

4 Add the potatoes to the orange and butter mixture and continue to cook, turning the potatoes frequently until they are completely coated in the caramel.

5 Sprinkle the chopped parsley or cilantro over the potatoes and season according to taste with salt and pepper.

6 Transfer the caramelized new potatoes to a serving dish and garnish with the orange zest. Serve immediately.

VARIATION

Lemon or lime juices may be used instead of the orange juice, if preferred. In addition, garnish the finished dish with pared lemon or lime zest, if preferred.

Spanish Potatoes

This type of dish is usually served as part of Spanish *tapas*, and is delicious with salad or a simply cooked entrée.

NUTRITIONAL INFORMATION

Calories	176	Sugars	.........9g
Protein	.........5g	Fat	...........6g
Carbohydrate	...27g	Saturates	.......1g

20 mins   35 mins

SERVES 4

INGREDIENTS

2 tbsp olive oil

1 lb 2 oz/500 g small new potatoes, halved

1 onion, halved and sliced

1 green bell pepper, seeded and
   cut into strips

1 tsp chili powder

1 tsp prepared mustard

1¼ cups strained tomatoes

1¼ cups vegetable bouillon

salt and pepper

chopped parsley, to garnish

1 Heat the olive oil in a large heavy-based skillet. Add the halved new potatoes and the sliced onion and cook, stirring frequently, for 4–5 minutes, until the onion slices are soft and translucent.

2 Add the green bell pepper strips, chili powder, and mustard to the pan and cook for another 2–3 minutes.

3 Stir the strained tomatoes and the vegetable bouillon into the pan and bring to a boil. Reduce the heat and simmer for about 25 minutes, or until the potatoes are tender.

4 Transfer the potatoes to a warmed serving dish. Sprinkle the parsley over the top and serve immediately. Alternatively, leave the Spanish potatoes to cool completely and serve cold, at room temperature.

COOK'S TIP

In Spain, tapas are traditionally served with a glass of chilled sherry or some other aperitif.

Spicy Indian Potatoes

Indian cooking has many variations of spicy potatoes. In this recipe, spinach is added for both color and flavor.

NUTRITIONAL INFORMATION

Calories 65	Sugars 1.9g
Protein 2.5g	Fat 3.4g
Carbohydrate . . .6.5g	Saturates 0.4g

🕑 10 mins ⏱ 40 mins

SERVES 4

INGREDIENTS

½ tsp coriander seeds

1 tsp cumin seeds

4 tbsp vegetable oil

2 cardamom pods

1 tsp fresh ginger root, grated

1 red chili, chopped

1 onion, chopped

2 garlic cloves, crushed

1 lb/450 g new potatoes, quartered

⅔ cup vegetable bouillon

1½ lb/675 g spinach, chopped

4 tbsp unsweetened yogurt

salt

VARIATION

Use frozen spinach instead of fresh spinach, if you prefer. Defrost the frozen spinach and drain it thoroughly before adding it to the dish, otherwise it will turn soggy.

1 Grind the coriander and cumin seeds using a pestle and mortar.

2 Heat the oil in a skillet. Add the ground coriander and cumin seeds to the pan together with the cardamom pods and ginger and cook for about 2 minutes.

3 Add the chopped chili, onion, and garlic to the pan. Cook for another 2 minutes, stirring frequently.

4 Add the potatoes to the pan together with the vegetable bouillon. Cook gently for 30 minutes or until the potatoes are cooked through, stirring occasionally.

5 Add the spinach to the pan and cook for another 5 minutes.

6 Remove the pan from the heat and stir in the yogurt. Season with salt and pepper to taste. Transfer the potatoes and spinach to a serving dish and serve.

Potatoes in Red Wine

This is a rich recipe which is best served with plain dark meats, such as beef or game, to complement the flavor.

NUTRITIONAL INFORMATION

Calories 116   Sugars 1.4g
Protein . . . . .1.5g   Fat 8.7g
Carbohydrate . . .7.0g   Saturates 5.7g

5 mins   40 mins

SERVES 4

INGREDIENTS

½ cup butter

1 lb/450 g new potatoes, halved

¾ cup red wine

6 tbsp beef bouillon

8 shallots, halved

4½ oz/125 g oyster mushrooms

1 tbsp chopped fresh sage or cilantro

salt and pepper

sage leaves or cilantro sprigs, to garnish

1 Melt the butter in a heavy-based skillet and add the halved potatoes. Cook gently for about 5 minutes, stirring constantly.

2 Add the red wine, beef bouillon, and halved shallots. Season to taste with salt and pepper and then simmer for 30 minutes.

3 Stir in the mushrooms and chopped sage or cilantro and cook for another 5 minutes.

4 Turn the potatoes and mushrooms into a warm serving dish. Garnish with fresh sage leaves or cilantro sprigs and serve at once.

VARIATION

If oyster mushrooms are unavailable, other mushrooms, such as large open cup mushrooms, can be used instead.

Gingered Potatoes

This is a simple, spicy dish which is ideal with a plain main course. The cashew nuts and celery add extra crunch.

NUTRITIONAL INFORMATION

Calories ....325 Sugars 1g
Protein ....5g Fat 21g
Carbohydrate ...30g Saturates 9g

20 mins   30 mins

SERVES 4

INGREDIENTS

1½ lb/675 g waxy potatoes, cubed

2 tbsp vegetable oil

4 tsp grated fresh ginger root

1 fresh green chili, chopped

1 celery stalk, chopped

¼ cup/25 g cashew nuts

a few strands of saffron

3 tbsp boiling water

5 tbsp butter

celery leaves, to garnish

1 Cook the potatoes in a pan of boiling water for 10 minutes, then drain them thoroughly.

2 Heat the oil in a heavy-based skillet and add the potatoes. Cook over a medium heat, stirring constantly, for 3–4 minutes.

3 Add the grated ginger, chili, celery, and cashew nuts and cook for 1 minute.

4 Meanwhile, place the saffron strands in a small bowl. Add the boiling water and let soak for 5 minutes.

5 Add the butter to the pan, then lower the heat and stir in the saffron mixture. Cook over a low heat for 10 minutes, or until the potatoes are tender.

6 Transfer to a warm serving dish. Garnish the gingered potatoes with the celery leaves and serve at once.

COOK'S TIP

Use a non-stick, heavy-based skillet as the potato mixture is fairly dry and may stick to an ordinary pan.

Thai Potato Stir-Fry

In this sweet and sour dish, tender vegetables are simply stir-fried with spices and coconut milk, and flavored with lime.

NUTRITIONAL INFORMATION

Calories	138	Sugars	.........5g
Protein	.........2g	Fat	...........6g
Carbohydrate	...20g	Saturates	.......1g

10 mins   20 mins

SERVES 4

INGREDIENTS

2lb/900 g waxy potatoes

2 tbsp vegetable oil

1 yellow bell pepper, seeded and diced

1 red bell pepper, seeded and diced

1 carrot, cut into thin strips

1 zucchini, cut into thin strips

2 garlic cloves, crushed

1 red chili, sliced

1 bunch scallions, halved lengthwise

½ cup coconut milk

1 tsp chopped lemon grass

2 tsp lime juice

finely grated zest of 1 lime

1 tbsp chopped fresh cilantro

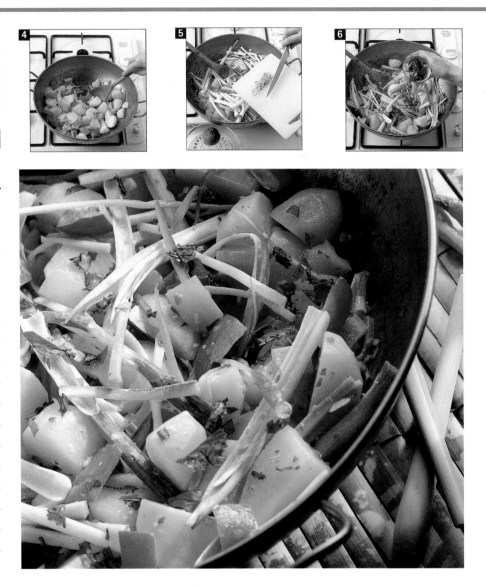

1 Using a sharp knife, cut the potatoes into small dice.

2 Bring a large pan of water to the boil and cook the diced potatoes for 5 minutes. Drain thoroughly.

3 Heat the vegetable oil in a wok or large skillet, swirling the oil around the base of the wok until it is really hot.

4 Add the potatoes, diced bell peppers, carrot, zucchini, garlic, and chili to the wok, and stir-fry the vegetables for 2–3 minutes.

5 Stir in the scallions, coconut milk, chopped lemon grass, and lime juice, and stir-fry the mixture for a further 5 minutes.

6 Add the lime zest and cilantro and stir-fry for 1 minute. Serve hot.

COOK'S TIP

Check that the potatoes are not overcooked in step 2, otherwise the potato pieces will disintegrate when they are stir-fried in the wok.

Cheese & Potato Slices

This recipe takes a while to prepare, but it is well worth the effort.
The golden potato slices coated in bread crumbs and cheese are

NUTRITIONAL INFORMATION

Calories ....560 Sugars 3g
Protein ....19g Fat 31g
Carbohydrate ...55g Saturates 7g

10 mins   40 mins

SERVES 4

INGREDIENTS

2 lb/900 g large waxy potatoes, unpeeled
and thickly sliced

1 cup fresh white bread crumbs

½ cup grated Parmesan cheese

1½ tsp chili powder

2 eggs, beaten

oil, for deep frying

chili powder, for dusting (optional)

1 Cook the sliced potatoes in a pan of boiling water for about 10–15 minutes, or until the potatoes are just tender. Drain thoroughly.

2 Mix the bread crumbs, cheese, and chili powder together in a bowl, then transfer to a shallow dish. Pour the beaten eggs into a separate shallow dish.

3 Dip the potato slices first in egg and then roll them in the bread crumbs to coat completely.

4 Heat the oil in a large pan to 350°F/180°C, or until a cube of bread browns in 30 seconds. Cook the cheese and potato slices, in several batches, for 4–5 minutes or until a golden brown color.

5 Remove the cheese and potato slices from the oil with a slotted spoon and drain thoroughly on paper towels. Keep the cheese and potato slices warm while you cook the remaining batches.

6 Transfer the cheese and potato slices to warm individual serving plates. Dust lightly with chili powder, if using, and serve immediately.

COOK'S TIP
The cheese and potato slices may be coated in the breadcrumb mixture in advance and then stored in the refrigerator until ready to use.

Broiled Potatoes with Lime

This dish is ideal with broiled or barbecued foods, as the potatoes themselves may be cooked by either method.

NUTRITIONAL INFORMATION

Calories 253   Sugars 0.7g
Protein . . . . .1.8g   Fat 22.2g
Carbohydrate . .12.4g   Saturates 5.8g

🍞 🍞

🥔 2 mins   🕐 15–20 mins

SERVES 4

I N G R E D I E N T S

1 lb/450 g potatoes, unpeeled and scrubbed

3 tbsp butter, melted

2 tbsp chopped fresh thyme

paprika, for dusting

L I M E   M A Y O N N A I S E

⅔ cup mayonnaise

2 tsp lime juice

finely grated zest of 1 lime

1 garlic clove, crushed

pinch of paprika

salt and pepper

1 Cut the potatoes into ½ inch/1 cm thick slices.

2 Cook the potatoes in a pan of boiling water for 5–7 minutes—they should still be quite firm. Remove the potatoes with a perforated spoon and drain thoroughly.

3 Line a broiler pan with aluminum foil, then place the potato slices on top of the foil.

4 Brush the potatoes with the melted butter and sprinkle the chopped thyme on top. Season to taste with salt and pepper.

5 Cook the potatoes under a preheated medium broiler for 10 minutes, turning them over once.

6 Meanwhile, make the lime mayonnaise. Combine the mayonnaise, lime juice, lime zest, garlic, paprika, and salt and pepper to taste, in a bowl.

7 Dust the hot potato slices with a little paprika and serve with the lime mayonnaise.

COOK'S TIP

For an impressive side dish, thread the potato slices on to skewers and cook over a medium hot barbecue grill.

Trio of Potato Purées

These small molds filled with layers of flavored potato look very impressive. They are ideal with fish or roast meats.

NUTRITIONAL INFORMATION

Calories 170   Sugars 5g
Protein . . . . .7g   Fat 6g
Carbohydrate . . .24g   Saturates 3g

15 mins   1¼ hours

SERVES 4

INGREDIENTS

1 tbsp butter, plus extra for greasing

10½ oz /300 g mealy potatoes, chopped

4½ oz/125 g rutabaga, chopped

1 carrot, chopped

1 lb/450 g spinach

1 tbsp skim milk

¼ cup all-purpose flour

1 egg

½ tsp ground cinnamon

1 tbsp orange juice

¼ tsp grated nutmeg

salt and pepper

carrot thin sticks, to garnish

1 Lightly grease four ⅔ cup/150 ml ramekins with butter.

2 Cook the potatoes in a pan of boiling water for 10 minutes. In separate pans cook the rutabaga and carrot in boiling water for 10 minutes. Blanch the spinach in boiling water for 5 minutes. Drain the vegetables. Add the milk and butter to the potatoes and mash until smooth. Stir in the flour and egg.

3 Divide the potato mixture into 3 bowls. Spoon the rutabaga into one bowl and mix well. Spoon the carrot into the second bowl and mix well. Spoon the spinach into the third bowl and mix well.

4 Add the cinnamon to the rutabaga and potato mixture and season to taste. Stir the orange juice into the carrot and potato mixture. Stir the nutmeg into the spinach and potato mixture.

5 Spoon a layer of the rutabaga and potato mixture into each of the ramekins and smooth over the top. Cover each with a layer of spinach and potato mixture, then top with the carrot and potato mixture. Cover the ramekins with foil and place in a roasting pan. Half-fill the pan with boiling water and cook in a preheated oven, 350°F/180°C, for 40 minutes or until set.

6 Turn out on to serving plates. Garnish with the carrot sticks and serve immediately.

Spicy Potato Fries

These home-made fries are flavored with spices and cooked in the oven.
Serve with Lime Mayonnaise (see page 123).

NUTRITIONAL INFORMATION

Calories	328	Sugars	.........2g
Protein	.........5g	Fat	...........11g
Carbohydrate	...56g	Saturates	.......7g

35 mins   40 mins

SERVES 4

INGREDIENTS

4 large waxy potatoes

2 sweet potatoes

4 tbsp butter, melted

½ tsp chili powder

1 tsp garam masala

salt

1 Cut the potatoes and sweet potatoes into slices about ½ inch/1 cm thick, then cut them into fries.

2 Place the potatoes in a large bowl of cold salted water. Let soak for 20 minutes.

3 Remove the potato slices with a slotted spoon and drain thoroughly. Pat with paper towels until completely dry.

COOK'S TIP

Rinsing the potatoes in cold water before cooking removes the starch, thus preventing them from sticking together. Soaking the potatoes in a bowl of cold salted water actually makes the cooked fries crisper.

4 Pour the melted butter on to a baking sheet. Transfer the potato slices to the baking sheet.

5 Sprinkle with the chili powder and garam masala, turning the potato slices to coat them with the mixture.

6 Cook the chips in a preheated oven, 400°F/200°C, turning frequently, for 40 minutes, until they are browned and cooked through.

7 Drain the chips on paper towels to remove the excess oil and then serve at once.

Italian Potato Wedges

These oven-cooked potato wedges use classic pizza ingredients and are delicious served with plain meats, such as pork or lamb.

NUTRITIONAL INFORMATION

Calories 115   Sugars 4g
Protein . . . . .6g   Fat 5g
Carbohydrate . . .13g   Saturates 3g

15 mins   35 mins

SERVES 4

INGREDIENTS

2 large waxy potatoes, unpeeled

4 large ripe tomatoes, peeled and seeded

⅔ cup vegetable bouillon

2 tbsp tomato paste

1 small yellow bell pepper, cut into strips

4½ oz/125 g white mushrooms, quartered

1 tbsp chopped fresh basil

½ cup grated cheese

salt and pepper

1 Cut each of the potatoes into 8 equal wedges. Parboil the potatoes in a pan of boiling water for 15 minutes. Drain well and place in a shallow ovenproof dish.

2 Chop the tomatoes and add to the dish. Mix together the vegetable bouillon and tomato paste, then pour the mixture over the potatoes and tomatoes.

3 Add the yellow bell pepper strips, quartered mushrooms, and chopped basil. Season well with salt and pepper.

4 Sprinkle the grated cheese over the top and cook in a preheated oven, 375°F/190°C, for 15–20 minutes until the topping is golden brown. Serve at once.

Saffron-Flavored Potatoes

Saffron is made from the dried stigma of the crocus and is native to Greece. It is very expensive, but only a very small amount is needed.

NUTRITIONAL INFORMATION

Calories ....197 Sugars 4g
Protein ....4g Fat 6g
Carbohydrate ...30g Saturates 1g

25 mins   40 mins

SERVES 4

I N G R E D I E N T S

1 tsp saffron strands

6 tbsp boiling water

1 1/2 lb/675 g waxy potatoes, unpeeled and cut into wedges

1 red onion, cut into 8 wedges

2 garlic cloves, crushed

1 tbsp white wine vinegar

2 tbsp olive oil

1 tbsp whole-grain mustard

5 tbsp vegetable bouillon

5 tbsp dry white wine

2 tsp chopped rosemary

salt and pepper

1 Place the saffron strands in a small bowl and pour over the boiling water. Set aside to soak for about 10 minutes.

2 Place the potatoes in a roasting pan, together with the red onion wedges and crushed garlic.

3 Add the vinegar, oil, mustard, vegetable bouillon, white wine, rosemary, and saffron water to the potatoes and onion in the pan. Season to taste with salt and pepper.

4 Cover the roasting pan with aluminum foil and bake in a preheated oven, 400°F/200°C, for about 30 minutes.

5 Remove the foil and cook the potatoes for another 10 minutes until crisp, browned, and cooked through. Serve them hot.

COOK'S TIP

Turmeric may be used instead of saffron to provide the yellow color in this recipe. However, it is worth using saffron, if possible, for the lovely nutty flavor it gives a dish.

Chili Roast Potatoes

Small new potatoes are scrubbed and boiled in their skins, then coated in a chili mixture and roasted to perfection in the oven.

NUTRITIONAL INFORMATION

Calories ....178 Sugars 2g
Protein ....2g Fat 11g
Carbohydrate ...18g Saturates 1g

5–10 mins   30 mins

SERVES 4

INGREDIENTS

500 g/1 lb 2 oz small new potatoes, scrubbed

²⁄₃ cup vegetable oil

1 tsp chili powder

½ tsp caraway seeds

1 tsp salt

1 tbsp chopped basil

1 Cook the potatoes in a pan of boiling water for 10 minutes, then drain them thoroughly.

2 Pour a little of the oil into a shallow roasting pan to coat the base. Heat the oil in a preheated oven, 400°F/200°C, for 10 minutes. Add the potatoes to the pan and brush them with the hot oil.

3 In a small bowl, mix together the chili powder, caraway seeds, and salt. Sprinkle the mixture over the potatoes, turning to coat them all over.

4 Add the remaining oil to the pan and roast in the oven for about 15 minutes, or until the potatoes are cooked through.

5 Using a slotted spoon, remove the potatoes from the the oil, draining them well, and transfer them to a warmed serving dish. Sprinkle the chopped basil over the top and serve immediately.

VARIATION

Use any other spice of your choice, such as curry powder or paprika, for a variation in flavor.

Parmesan Potatoes

This is a very simple way to jazz up roast potatoes. Serve them in the same way as roast potatoes with roasted meats or fish.

NUTRITIONAL INFORMATION

Calories 307	Sugars 2g
Protein 11g	Fat 14g
Carbohydrate . . .37g	Saturates 6g

🍲 🍲

⏲ 15 mins   🕐 1 HR 5 MINS

SERVES 4

I N G R E D I E N T S

3 lb/1.3 kg potatoes

scant ⅔ cup Parmesan cheese, grated

pinch of grated nutmeg

1 tbsp chopped fresh parsley

4 smoked bacon slices, cut into strips

vegetable oil, for roasting

salt

1 Cut the potatoes in half lengthwise and cook them in a pan of boiling salted water for 10 minutes. Drain them thoroughly.

2 Mix the grated Parmesan cheese, nutmeg, and parsley together in a shallow bowl.

3 Roll the potato pieces in the cheese mixture to coat them completely. Shake off any excess.

4 Pour a little oil into a roasting pan and heat it in a preheated oven, 400°F/200°C, for 10 minutes. Remove from the oven and place the potatoes into the pan. Return the pan to the oven and cook for 30 minutes, turning once.

5 Remove from the oven and sprinkle the bacon on top of the potatoes. Return to the oven for 15 minutes or until the potatoes and bacon are cooked. Drain off any excess fat and serve.

VARIATION

If you prefer, use slices of salami or prosciutto instead of the bacon, adding it to the dish 5 minutes before the end of the cooking time.

Potatoes Dauphinois

This is a classic potato dish of layered potatoes, cream, garlic, onion, and cheese. Serve with pies, bakes, and casseroles.

NUTRITIONAL INFORMATION

Calories 580	Sugars 5g
Protein 10g	Fat 46g
Carbohydrate ...34g	Saturates 28g

25 mins   1½ HOURS

SERVES 4

INGREDIENTS

1 tbsp butter

1½ lb/675 g waxy potatoes, sliced

2 garlic cloves, crushed

1 red onion, sliced

¾ cup grated Swiss cheese

1¼ cups heavy cream

salt and pepper

1 Lightly grease a 4 cup/1 liter shallow ovenproof dish with the butter.

2 Arrange a single layer of potato slices in the base of the prepared dish.

3 Top the potato slices with half the garlic, half the sliced red onion, and one-third of the grated Swiss cheese. Season to taste with a little salt and pepper to taste.

4 Repeat the layers in exactly the same order, finishing with a layer of potatoes topped with grated cheese.

5 Pour the cream over the top of the potatoes and cook in a preheated oven, 350°F/180°C, for 1½ hours, or until the potatoes are cooked through and the top is browned and crispy. Serve at once, straight from the dish.

COOK'S TIP

There are many versions of this classic potato dish, but the different recipes always contain heavy cream, making it a rich and very filling side dish or accompaniment. This recipe must be cooked in a shallow dish to ensure there is plenty of crispy topping.

Pommes Anna

This is a classic potato dish, which may be left to cook unattended while the remainder of the meal is being prepared, so it is ideal with stews.

NUTRITIONAL INFORMATION

Calories	237	Sugars	.........1g
Protein	.........4g	Fat	..........13g
Carbohydrate	...29g	Saturates	.......8g

15 mins   2 HOURS

SERVES 4

I N G R E D I E N T S

5 tbsp butter, melted

1½ lb/675 g waxy potatoes

4 tbsp chopped mixed herbs

salt and pepper

chopped fresh herbs, to garnish

1 Brush a shallow 4 cup/1 liter ovenproof dish with a little of the melted butter.

2 Slice the potatoes thinly and pat dry with paper towels.

3 Arrange a layer of potato slices in the prepared dish until the base is covered. Brush with a little butter and sprinkle with a quarter of the chopped mixed herbs. Season to taste.

4 Continue layering the potato slices, brushing each layer with melted butter and sprinkling with herbs, until they are all used up.

5 Brush the top layer of potato slices with butter. Cover the dish and cook in a preheated oven, 190°C/375°F, for 1½ hours.

6 Turn out on to a warm ovenproof platter and return to the oven for another 25–30 minutes, until golden brown. Serve at once, garnished with fresh herbs.

COOK'S TIP

Make sure that the potatoes are sliced very thinly so that they are almost transparent. This will ensure that they cook thoroughly.

Potatoes with Almonds

This oven-cooked dish has a subtle, creamy almond flavor and a pale yellow color as a result of being cooked with turmeric.

NUTRITIONAL INFORMATION

Calories	.531	Sugars	.6g
Protein	.7g	Fat	.46g
Carbohydrate	.24g	Saturates	.23g

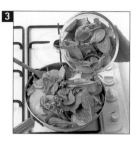

5 mins   40–45 mins

SERVES 4

INGREDIENTS

1lb 5oz/600 g potatoes, unpeeled and sliced

1 tbsp vegetable oil

1 red onion, halved and sliced

1 garlic clove, crushed

½ cup almond slivers

½ tsp turmeric

4½ oz/125 g arugula leaves

1¼ cups heavy cream

salt and pepper

1 Cook the sliced potatoes in a pan of boiling water for 10 minutes. Drain them thoroughly.

2 Heat the vegetable oil in a heavy-based skillet. Add the onion and garlic and cook over a medium heat, stirring frequently, for 3–4 minutes.

3 Add the almonds, turmeric, and potato slices to the skillet and cook, stirring constantly, for 2–3 minutes. Stir in the arugula leaves.

4 Transfer the potato and almond mixture to a shallow ovenproof dish. Pour the heavy cream over the top and season with salt and pepper.

5 Cook in a preheated oven, 375°F/190°C, for 20 minutes, or until the potatoes are cooked through. Transfer to a warmed serving dish and serve them immediately.

Casseroled Potatoes

This potato dish is cooked in the oven with leeks and wine. It is very quick and simple to make.

NUTRITIONAL INFORMATION

Calories	187	Sugars	.........2g
Protein	.........4g	Fat	..........3g
Carbohydrate	...31g	Saturates	......2g

🕿 🕿

🥔 10 mins ⏲ 50 mins

SERVES 4

INGREDIENTS

1½ lb/675 g waxy potatoes, cut into chunks

1 tbsp butter

2 leeks, sliced

⅔ cup dry white wine

⅔ cup vegetable bouillon

1 tbsp lemon juice

2 tbsp chopped mixed fresh herbs

salt and pepper

TO GARNISH

grated lemon zest

mixed fresh herbs optional

1 Cook the potato chunks in a pan of boiling water for 5 minutes. Drain them thoroughly.

2 Meanwhile, melt the butter in a skillet and sauté the leeks for 5 minutes or until they have softened.

3 Spoon the partly cooked potatoes and leeks into an ovenproof dish.

4 In a measuring jug, mix together the wine, vegetable bouillon, lemon juice, and chopped mixed herbs. Season to taste with salt and pepper, then pour the mixture over the potatoes.

5 Cook in a preheated oven, 375°F/ 190°C, for 35 minutes or until the potatoes are tender.

6 Garnish the potato casserole with lemon zest and fresh herbs (if using) and serve as an accompaniment to meat casseroles or roast meat.

COOK'S TIP

Cover the ovenproof dish halfway through cooking if the leeks start to brown on the top.

Cheese Crumble-Topped Mash

To liven up mashed potato top it with a crumble mixture flavored with herbs, mustard, and onion, which turns crunchy on baking.

NUTRITIONAL INFORMATION

Calories 131	Sugars 1.4g	
Protein 3.8g	Fat 5.7g	
Carbohydrate . .17.3g	Saturates 3.4g	

5 mins   20–25 mins

SERVES 4

I N G R E D I E N T S

generous 5 cups diced mealy potatoes

2 tbsp butter

2 tbsp milk

½ cup grated sharp cheese or blue cheese

C R U M B L Y   T O P P I N G

3 tbsp butter

1 onion, cut into chunks

1 garlic clove, crushed

1 tbsp whole-grain mustard

3 cups fresh whole-wheat bread crumbs

2 tbsp chopped fresh parsley

salt and pepper

1 Cook the potatoes in a pan of boiling water for 10 minutes or until they are cooked through.

2 Meanwhile, make the crumbly topping. Melt the butter in a skillet. Add the onion, garlic, and mustard and cook gently for 5 minutes until the onion chunks have softened, stirring constantly.

3 Put the bread crumbs in a mixing bowl and stir in the fried onion. Season to taste with salt and pepper.

4 Drain the potatoes thoroughly and place them in a mixing bowl. Add the butter and milk, then mash until smooth. Stir in the grated cheese while the potato is still hot.

5 Spoon the mashed potato into a shallow ovenproof dish and sprinkle with the crumbly topping.

6 Cook in a preheated oven, 400°F/200°C, for 10–15 minutes until the crumbly topping is golden brown and crunchy. Serve immediately.

COOK'S TIP

For extra crunch, add freshly cooked vegetables, such as celery and bell peppers, to the mashed potato in step 4.

Carrot & Potato Soufflé

Hot soufflés have a reputation for being difficult to make, but this one is both simple and impressive. Make sure you serve it as soon as it is ready.

NUTRITIONAL INFORMATION

Calories 294   Sugars 6g
Protein . . . . .10g   Fat 9g
Carbohydrate . . .46g   Saturates 4g

15 mins   40 mins

SERVES 4

I N G R E D I E N T S

2 tbsp butter, melted

4 tbsp fresh whole-wheat bread crumbs

3 mealy potatoes, baked in their skins

2 carrots, grated

2 eggs, separated

2 tbsp orange juice

¼ tsp grated nutmeg

salt and pepper

carrot curls, to garnish

1 Brush the inside of a 3¾ cup/900 ml soufflé dish with butter. Sprinkle three-quarters of the bread crumbs over the base and sides.

2 Cut the baked potatoes in half and scoop the flesh into a mixing bowl.

3 Add the carrot, egg yolks, orange juice, and nutmeg to the potato flesh. Season to taste with salt and pepper.

4 In a separate bowl, whisk the egg whites until soft peaks form, then gently fold into the potato mixture with a metal spoon until well incorporated.

5 Gently spoon the potato and carrot mixture into the prepared soufflé dish. Sprinkle the remaining bread crumbs over the top of the mixture.

6 Cook in a preheated oven, 400°F/200°C, for 40 minutes, until risen and golden. Do not open the oven door during the cooking time, otherwise the soufflé will sink. Serve at once, garnished with carrot curls.

COOK'S TIP

To bake the potatoes, prick the skins and cook in a preheated oven, 375°F/190°C, for about 1 hour.

Potatoes En Papillotes

New potatoes are perfect for this recipe. The potatoes and vegetables are wrapped in waxed paper and sealed, then steamed in the oven.

NUTRITIONAL INFORMATION

Calories . . . . .85 Sugars 4g
Protein . . . . .2g Fat 0.5g
Carbohydrate . . .15g Saturates 0.1g

10 mins · 35 mins

SERVES 4

INGREDIENTS

1 lb/450 g small new potatoes

1 carrot, cut into thin sticks

1 fennel bulb, sliced

2¾ oz/75 g green beans

1 yellow bell pepper, cut into strips

16 tbsp dry white wine

4 rosemary sprigs

salt and pepper

rosemary sprigs, to garnish

1 Cut 4 squares of waxed paper measuring about 10 inches/25 cm in size.

2 Divide the vegetables equally between the 4 paper squares, placing them in the center.

3 Bring the edges of the paper together and scrunch them together to encase the vegetables, leaving the top open.

4 Place the parcels in a shallow roasting pan and spoon 4 tablespoons of white wine into each parcel. Add a rosemary sprig and season.

5 Fold the top of each parcel over to seal it. Cook in a preheated oven, 375°F/190°C, for 30–35 minutes or until the vegetables are tender.

6 Transfer the sealed parcels to 4 individual serving plates and garnish with rosemary sprigs.

7 Open the parcels at the table for the full aroma of the vegetables to be appreciated.

COOK'S TIP

If small new potatoes are unavailable, use larger potatoes which have been halved or quartered to ensure that they cook through in the specified cooking time.

Spicy Potatoes & Onions

Masala aloo are potatoes cooked in a spicy mixture called baghaar. Semi-dry when cooked, they make an excellent accompaniment to almost any curry.

NUTRITIONAL INFORMATION

Calories 313   Sugars 5g
Protein . . . . .2g   Fat 25g
Carbohydrate . . .21g   Saturates 3g

10–15 mins   10 mins

SERVES 4

INGREDIENTS

6 tbsp vegetable oil

2 medium-sized onions, finely chopped

1 tsp finely chopped fresh ginger root

1 tsp crushed garlic

1 tsp chili powder

1½ tsp ground cumin

1½ tsp ground coriander

1 tsp salt

400 g/14 oz canned new potatoes

1 tbsp lemon juice

BAGHAAR

3 tbsp oil

3 dried red chilies

½ tsp onion seeds

½ tsp mustard seeds

½ tsp fenugreek seeds

TO GARNISH

fresh cilantro leaves

1 green chili, finely chopped

cumin, ground coriander, salt, and potatoes and stir-fry for about 1 minute. Remove the pan from the heat and set aside until required.

1 Heat the oil in a large, heavy-based pan. Add the onions and cook, stirring, until golden brown. Reduce the heat, add the ginger, garlic, chili powder, ground

2 Drain the water from the potatoes. Add the potatoes to the onion and spice mixture and heat through. Sprinkle in the lemon juice and mix well.

3 To make the baghaar, heat the oil in a separate pan. Add the red chilies, onion seeds, mustard seeds, and fenugreek seeds and cook until the seeds turn a shade darker. Remove the pan from the heat and pour the baghaar over the potatoes.

4 Garnish with cilantro leaves and chilies, then serve.

Cheese & Potato Pie

This really is a great side dish, perfect for serving with main meals cooked in the oven.

NUTRITIONAL INFORMATION

Calories ....295 Sugars 5g
Protein ....13g Fat 17g
Carbohydrate ...24g Saturates 11g

20 mins   1½ HOURS

SERVES 4

INGREDIENTS

1 lb 2 oz/500 g potatoes

1 leek, sliced

3 garlic cloves, crushed

½ cup grated Cheddar cheese

½ cup grated mozzarella cheese

⅓ cup grated Parmesan cheese

2 tbsp chopped fresh parsley

⅔ cup light cream

⅔ cup milk

salt and pepper

chopped fresh flat leaf parsley, to garnish

1 Cook the potatoes in a pan of boiling salted water for 10 minutes. Drain well.

2 Cut the potatoes into thin slices. Arrange a layer of potatoes in the base of an ovenproof dish. Layer with a little of the leek, garlic, cheeses, and parsley. Season to taste.

3 Repeat the layers until all of the ingredients have been used, finishing with a layer of cheese. Mix the cream and milk together and season with salt and pepper to taste. Pour over the potato layers.

4 Cook in a preheated oven, 325°F/160°C, for 1–1¼ hours, or until the cheese is golden brown and bubbling and the potatoes are cooked right through and tender.

5 Garnish with chopped fresh flatleaf parsley and serve immediately.

COOK'S TIP

Potatoes make a very good basis for a vegetable accompaniment. They are a good source of complex carbohydrate and contain a number of vitamins. From the point of view of flavor, they combine well with a vast range of other ingredients.

Spiced Potatoes & Spinach

This is a classic Indian accompaniment for many different curries or plainer main vegetable dishes. It is very quick to cook.

NUTRITIONAL INFORMATION

Calories 176	Sugars 4g
Protein 6g	Fat 9g
Carbohydrate ...18g	Saturates 1g

10 mins   20 mins

SERVES 4

INGREDIENTS

3 tbsp vegetable oil

1 red onion, sliced

2 garlic cloves, crushed

½ tsp chili powder

2 tsp ground coriander

1 tsp ground cumin

⅔ cup vegetable bouillon

1¾ cups potatoes, diced

1 lb 2 oz/500 g baby spinach

1 red chili, sliced

salt and pepper

1 Heat the oil in a heavy-based skillet. Add the onion and garlic and sauté over a medium heat, stirring occasionally, for 2–3 minutes.

2 Stir in the chili powder, ground coriander, and cumin, and cook, stirring constantly, for another 30 seconds.

3 Add the vegetable bouillon, diced potatoes, and spinach, and bring to a boil. Reduce the heat, cover the skillet, and simmer for about 10 minutes, or until the potatoes are cooked right through and tender.

4 Uncover and season to taste with salt and pepper, then add the chili and cook for another 2–3 minutes. Transfer to a warmed serving dish and serve immediately.

COOK'S TIP

Besides adding extra color to a dish, red onions have a sweeter, less pungent flavor than other varieties.

Souffléd Cheesy Potato Fries

These small potato chunks are mixed in a creamy cheese sauce and fried in oil until deliciously golden brown.

NUTRITIONAL INFORMATION

Calories 614	Sugars 2g
Protein 12g	Fat 46g
Carbohydrate . . .40g	Saturates 18g

🥔 20 mins   🕐 25 mins

SERVES 4

INGREDIENTS

2 lb/900 g potatoes, cut into chunks

⅔ cup heavy cream

¾ cup grated Swiss cheese

pinch of cayenne pepper

2 egg whites

vegetable oil, for deep-frying

salt and pepper

chopped flat leaf parsley and grated
   cheese, to garnish

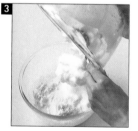

1 Cook the potatoes in a pan of lightly salted boiling water for about 10 minutes. Drain thoroughly and pat dry with absorbent paper towels. Set aside until required.

2 Mix the heavy cream and Swiss cheese in a large bowl. Stir in the cayenne pepper and season with salt and pepper to taste.

3 Whisk the egg whites until stiff peaks form. Gently fold into the cheese mixture until fully incorporated.

4 Add the cooked potatoes, turning to coat thoroughly in the mixture.

5 In a deep pan, heat the oil to 350°F/180°C or until a cube of bread browns in 30 seconds. Remove the potatoes from the cheese mixture with a slotted spoon and cook in the oil, in batches if necessary, for 3–4 minutes, or until golden.

6 Transfer the potatoes to a warmed serving dish and garnish with parsley and grated cheese. Serve immediately.

VARIATION

Add other flavorings, such as grated nutmeg or curry powder, to the cream and cheese.

Pesto Potatoes

Pesto sauce is more commonly used as a pasta sauce but is delicious served over potatoes as well.

NUTRITIONAL INFORMATION

Calories 531	Sugars 3g	
Protein 13g	Fat 38g	
Carbohydrate . . .36g	Saturates 8g	

15 mins   15 mins

SERVES 4

INGREDIENTS

2 lb/900 g small new potatoes

2¾ oz/75 g fresh basil

2 tbsp pine nuts

3 garlic cloves, crushed

½ cup olive oil

¾ cup freshly grated Parmesan cheese
   and pecorino cheese, mixed

salt and pepper

fresh basil sprigs, to garnish

1 Cook the potatoes in a pan of salted boiling water for 15 minutes or until tender. Drain well, transfer to a warm serving dish, and keep warm until required.

2 Meanwhile, put the basil, pine nuts, garlic, and a little salt and pepper to taste in a food processor. Blend for 30 seconds, adding the oil gradually, until the mixture is smooth.

3 Remove the mixture from the food processor and place in a mixing bowl. Stir in the grated Parmesan and pecorino cheeses and mix together.

4 Spoon the pesto sauce over the potatoes and mix well. Garnish with fresh basil sprigs and serve immediately.

Mini Vegetable Puff Pastries

These are ideal with a more formal meal as they take a little time to prepare and look really impressive.

NUTRITIONAL INFORMATION

Calories 210   Sugars 2.3g
Protein . . . . .3.8g   Fat 12.9g
Carbohydrate . .20.8g   Saturates 1.7g

15 mins   25 mins

SERVES 4

I N G R E D I E N T S

PASTRY

1 lb/450 g puff pastry

1 egg, beaten

FILLING

8 oz/225 g sweet potatoes, cubed

3½ oz/100 g baby asparagus spears

2 tbsp butter

1 leek, sliced

2 small open cup mushrooms, sliced

1 tsp lime juice

1 tsp chopped thyme

pinch of dried mustard

salt and pepper

  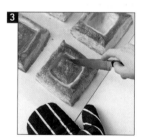

1 Cut the pastry into 4 equal pieces. Roll each piece out on a lightly floured surface to form a 5 inch/12 cm square. Place the pieces on a dampened baking sheet and score a smaller 2.5 inch/6 cm square inside.

2 Brush with beaten egg and cook in a preheated oven, 400°F/200°C, for 20 minutes or until risen and golden brown.

3 While the pastry is cooking, start the filling. Cook the sweet potato in a pan of boiling water for 15 minutes, then drain well. Blanch the asparagus in a pan of

boiling water for 10 minutes or until tender. Drain and reserve.

4 Remove the pastry squares from the oven. Cut out the central square of pastry and lift out. Reserve.

5 Melt the butter or margarine in a pan and sauté the leek and mushrooms for 2–3 minutes. Add the lime juice, thyme, and mustard and season well. Stir in the sweet potatoes and asparagus. Spoon into the pastry cases. Top with the reserved pastry squares and serve immediately.

COOK'S TIP

Use a colorful selection of any vegetables you have at hand for this recipe.

Bombay Potatoes

Although virtually unknown in India, this dish is a very popular item on Indian restaurant menus in other parts of the world.

NUTRITIONAL INFORMATION

Calories	307	Sugars	. . . . .9g
Protein	. . . . .9g	Fat	. . . . .9g
Carbohydrate	. . .51g	Saturates	. . . . . . .5g

5 mins

1 hr 10 mins

SERVES 4

INGREDIENTS

2 lb 4 oz/1 kg waxy potatoes

2 tbsp vegetable ghee

1 tsp panch poran spice mix

3 tsp ground turmeric

2 tbsp tomato paste

1¼ cups unsweetened yogurt

salt

chopped cilantro, to garnish

1 Put the whole potatoes into a large pan of salted cold water. Bring to a boil, then simmer until the potatoes are just cooked, but not tender; the time depends on the size of the potato, but an average-sized one should take about 15 minutes.

COOK'S TIP

Panch poran spice mix can be bought from Asian or Indian grocery stores, or make your own from equal quantities of cumin seeds, fennel seeds, mustard seeds, nigella seeds, and fenugreek seeds.

2 Heat the ghee in a pan over a medium heat and add the panch poran, turmeric, tomato paste, yogurt, and salt. Bring to a boil and simmer, uncovered, for 5 minutes.

3 Drain the potatoes and cut each one into 4 pieces. Add the potatoes to the pan, then cover and cook briefly. Transfer to an ovenproof casserole. Cook in a preheated oven, 350°F/180°C, for about 40 minutes, or until the potatoes are tender and the sauce has thickened a little.

4 Sprinkle with chopped cilantro and serve immediately.

Potato Salad

You can use leftover cold potatoes, cut into bite-size pieces, for this salad, but tiny new potatoes are best for maximum flavor.

NUTRITIONAL INFORMATION

Calories 275   Sugars 8g
Protein ....5g   Fat 13g
Carbohydrate ...38g   Saturates 2g

20 mins   10–15 mins

SERVES 4

INGREDIENTS

1 lb 9 oz/700 g tiny new potatoes

8 scallions

1 hard-cooked egg, optional

1 cup lowfat mayonnaise

1 tsp paprika

salt and pepper

TO GARNISH

2 tbsp fresh chives, snipped

pinch of paprika

1 Bring a large pan of lightly salted water to the boil. Add the potatoes to the pan and cook for 10–15 minutes or until they are just tender.

2 Drain the potatoes in a colander and rinse them under cold running water until they are completely cold. Drain them again thoroughly. Transfer the potatoes to a mixing bowl and set aside until required.

3 Trim and slice the scallions thinly on the diagonal.

4 Chop the hard-cooked egg (if using).

5 Mix together the mayonnaise, paprika, and salt and pepper to taste in a bowl until well blended. Pour the mixture over the potatoes.

6 Add the sliced scallions and chopped egg (if using) to the potatoes and toss together.

7 Transfer the potato salad to a serving bowl. Sprinkle with snipped chives and a pinch of paprika. Cover and let chill in the refrigerator until required.

COOK'S TIP

To make a lighter dressing, use a mixture of half mayonnaise and half unsweetened yogurt.

Potatoes Lyonnaise

In this classic French recipe, sliced potatoes are cooked with onions to make a delicious accompaniment to a main meal.

NUTRITIONAL INFORMATION

Calories	277	Sugars	.........4g
Protein	.........5g	Fat	..........12g
Carbohydrate	...40g	Saturates	.......4g

10 mins   25 mins

SERVES 6

I N G R E D I E N T S

2 lb 12 oz/1.25 kg potatoes

4 tbsp olive oil

2 tbsp butter

2 onions, sliced

2–3 garlic cloves, crushed (optional)

salt and pepper

chopped fresh parsley, to garnish

1 Slice the potatoes into 5 mm/¼ inch slices. Put in a large pan of lightly salted water and bring to a boil. Cover and simmer gently for about 10–12 minutes, until just tender. Avoid boiling too rapidly or the potatoes will break up and lose their shape. When cooked, drain well.

COOK'S TIP

If the potatoes blacken slightly as they are boiling, add a spoonful of lemon juice to the cooking water.

2 While the potatoes are cooking, heat the oil and butter in a very large skillet. Add the onions and garlic, if using, and fry over a medium heat, stirring frequently, until the onions are softened.

3 Add the cooked potato slices to the skillet and cook with the onions and garlic, carefully stirring occasionally, for about 5–8 minutes until the potatoes are well browned.

4 Season to taste with salt and pepper. Sprinkle over the chopped parsley to serve. If wished, transfer the potatoes and onions to a large ovenproof dish and keep warm in a low oven until ready to serve.

Three-Way Potato Salad

Small new potatoes, served warm in a delicious dressing. The nutritional information is for the potato salad with the curry dressing only.

NUTRITIONAL INFORMATION

Calories	310	Sugars 12g
Protein	.........6g	Fat 19g
Carbohydrate	...31g	Saturates 4g

10–20 mins   20 mins

SERVES 4

INGREDIENTS

1 lb 2 oz/500 g new potatoes (for each dressing)

herbs, to garnish

LIGHT CURRY DRESSING

1 tbsp vegetable oil

1 tbsp medium curry paste

1 small onion, chopped

1 tbsp mango chutney, chopped

6 tbsp unsweetened yogurt

3 tbsp light cream

2 tbsp mayonnaise

salt and pepper

1 tbsp light cream, to garnish

VINAIGRETTE DRESSING

6 tbsp hazelnut oil

3 tbsp cider vinegar

1 tsp whole-grain mustard

1 tsp superfine sugar

few basil leaves, torn

PARSLEY CREAM

⅔ cup sour cream

3 tbsp light mayonnaise

4 scallions, finely chopped

1 tbsp chopped fresh parsley

1 To make the Light Curry Dressing, heat the vegetable oil in a pan. Add the curry paste and onion and cook, stirring frequently, until the onion is soft. Remove from the heat and set aside to cool slightly.

2 Mix together the mango chutney, yogurt, cream, and mayonnaise. Add the curry mixture and blend together. Season with salt and pepper.

3 To make the Vinaigrette Dressing, whisk the oil, vinegar, mustard, sugar, and basil together in a small jug or bowl. Season with salt and pepper.

4 To make the Parsley Cream, combine the mayonnaise, sour cream, scallions, and parsley, mixing well. Season with salt and pepper.

5 Cook the potatoes in lightly salted boiling water until just tender. Drain well and let cool for 5 minutes, then add the chosen dressing, tossing to coat. Serve, garnished with fresh herbs, spooning a little light cream on to the potatoes if you have used the curry dressing.

Potatoes in Creamed Coconut

A colorful way to serve potatoes which is quick and easy to make.
Serve it with spicy meat curries with a salad on the side.

🕙 10 mins   🕐 15 mins

SERVES 4

I N G R E D I E N T S

1 lb 5 oz/600 g potatoes

1 onion, thinly sliced

2 red bird-eye chilies, finely chopped

½ tsp salt

½ tsp ground black pepper

½ cup creamed coconut

1½ cups vegetable or chicken bouillon

fresh cilantro or basil, chopped,
    to garnish

1 Peel the potatoes thinly. Use a sharp knife to cut into ¾ inch/2 cm chunks.

2 Place the potatoes in a pan with the onion, chilies, salt, pepper, and creamed coconut. Stir in the bouillon.

3 Bring to a boil, stirring, then lower the heat and cover. Simmer gently, stirring occasionally, until the potatoes are tender.

4 Adjust the seasoning to taste, then sprinkle with chopped cilantro or basil. Serve immediately while hot.

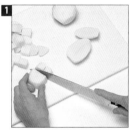

COOK'S TIP

If the potatoes are
thin-skinned, or a new variety,
simply wash or scrub to remove
any dirt and cook with the skins on.
This adds extra dietary fiber and
nutrients to the finished dish, and cuts
down on the preparation time. Baby
new potatoes can be cooked whole.

Potatoes in Green Sauce

These earthy potatoes are delicious either as a side dish with simmered or braised meat, or as a vegetarian main course.

NUTRITIONAL INFORMATION

Calories 61   Sugars 1.4g
Protein . . . . .2g   Fat 1.4g
Carbohydrate . .10.6g   Saturates 0.2g

5 mins   25 mins

SERVES 5

INGREDIENTS

2 lb 4 oz/1 kg small waxy potatoes

1 onion, halved and unpeeled

8 garlic cloves, unpeeled

1 fresh green chili

8 tomatillos, outer husks removed, or small tart tomatoes

scant 1 cup chicken, meat, or vegetable bouillon, preferably homemade

½ tsp ground cumin

1 sprig fresh thyme or generous pinch dried

1 sprig fresh oregano or generous pinch dried

2 tbsp vegetable or extra-virgin olive oil

1 zucchini, roughly chopped

1 bunch fresh cilantro, chopped

salt

1 Put the potatoes in a pan of salted water. Bring to a boil and cook for about 15 minutes or until almost tender. Do not over-cook them. Drain and set aside.

2 Meanwhile, lightly char the onion, garlic, chili, and tomatillos or tomatoes in a heavy-based, ungreased skillet. Set aside, and when cool enough to handle, peel and chop the onion, garlic, and chili; chop the tomatillos or tomatoes. Put in a blender or food processor with half the bouillon and process to form a purée. Add the cumin, thyme, and oregano.

3 Heat the oil in the heavy-based skillet. Add the purée and cook for 5 minutes, stirring, to reduce slightly and concentrate the flavors.

4 Add the potatoes and zucchini to the purée and pour in the rest of the stock. Add approximately half the cilantro and cook for a further 5 minutes or until the zucchini are tender.

5 Transfer to a serving bowl and serve sprinkled with the remaining chopped cilantro to garnish.

Chinese Potato Sticks

These potato sticks are a variation of the great Western favorite, flavored with soy sauce and chili.

NUTRITIONAL INFORMATION

Calories 326   Sugars 1g
Protein . . . . .4g   Fat 22g
Carbohydrate . . .29g   Saturates 3g

10 mins   15 mins

SERVES 4

INGREDIENTS

1 lb 7 oz/650 g medium potatoes

8 tbsp vegetable oil

1 fresh red chili, halved

1 small onion, quartered

2 garlic cloves, halved

2 tbsp soy sauce

pinch of salt

1 tsp wine vinegar

1 tbsp coarse sea salt

pinch of chili powder

1 Peel the potatoes and cut into thin slices along their length. Cut the slices into very thin sticks.

2 Bring a pan of water to a boil and blanch the potato sticks for 2 minutes. Drain and rinse under cold water, then drain well again. Pat the potato sticks thoroughly dry with paper towels.

3 Heat the oil in a preheated wok until it is almost smoking. Add the chili, onion, and garlic and stir-fry for 30 seconds. Remove and discard the chili, onion, and garlic.

4 Add the potato sticks to the oil and fry for 3–4 minutes, or until golden.

5 Add the soy sauce, salt, and vinegar to the wok. Reduce the heat and cook for 1 minute, or until the potatoes are crisp.

6 Remove the potatoes with a slotted spoon and leave to drain on paper towels.

7 Transfer the potato sticks to a serving dish. Sprinkle with the sea salt and chili powder and serve.

VARIATION

Sprinkle other flavorings over the cooked potato sticks, such as curry powder, or serve with a chili dip.

Spicy Sweet Potato Slices

Serve these as an accompaniment to other barbecue grill dishes or with a spicy dip as an appetizer while the main dishes are being cooked.

NUTRITIONAL INFORMATION

Calories	178	Sugars	.......0.8g
Protein	.........2g	Fat	...........6g
Carbohydrate	...32g	Saturates	.....0.7g

10 mins   25 mins

SERVES 4

INGREDIENTS

1 lb/450 g sweet potatoes, unpeeled

2 tbsp sunflower oil

1 tsp chili sauce

salt and pepper

1 Bring a large pan of water to a boil. Add the sweet potatoes and parboil them for 10 minutes. Drain thoroughly and transfer to a chopping board.

2 Peel the potatoes and cut them into thick slices.

3 Mix together the sunflower oil, chili sauce, and salt and pepper to taste in a small bowl.

COOK'S TIP

For a simple spicy dip, combine ²/₃ cup sour cream with ¹/₂ teaspoon of sugar, ¹/₂ teaspoon of Dijon mustard, and salt and pepper to taste. Chill until required.

4 Brush the spicy mixture liberally over one side of the potatoes. Place the potatoes, oil side down, over medium hot coals and grill for 5–6 minutes.

5 Lightly brush the tops of the potatoes with the oil, then turn them over and

grill for another 5 minutes or until crisp and golden.

6 Transfer the potatoes to a warm serving dish and serve at once.

Grilled Potato Wedges

Serve this tasty potato dish with grilled kabobs, bean burgers, or vegetarian sausages.

NUTRITIONAL INFORMATION

Calories	257	Sugars	.........1g
Protein	.........3g	Fat	..........16g
Carbohydrate	...26g	Saturates	.......5g

🥔 10 mins   🕐 30–35 mins

SERVES 4

INGREDIENTS

3 large baking potatoes, scrubbed

4 tbsp olive oil

2 tbsp butter

2 garlic cloves, chopped

1 tbsp chopped fresh rosemary

1 tbsp chopped fresh parsley

1 tbsp chopped fresh thyme

salt and pepper

1 Bring a large pan of water to a boil. Add the potatoes and parboil them for 10 minutes. Drain the potatoes and refresh under cold water, then drain them again thoroughly.

2 Transfer the potatoes to a cutting board. When the potatoes are cold enough to handle, cut them into thick wedges, but do not peel.

3 Heat the oil and butter in a small pan together with the garlic. Cook gently until the garlic begins to brown, then remove the pan from the heat.

4 Stir the herbs and salt and pepper to taste into the mixture in the pan.

5 Brush the herb mixture all over the potato wedges.

6 Grill the potatoes over hot coals for 10–15 minutes, brushing liberally with any of the remaining herb and butter mixture, or until the potato wedges are just tender.

7 Transfer the garlic potato wedges to a warm serving plate and serve as an appetizer or as a side dish.

COOK'S TIP

You may find it easier to grill these potatoes in a hinged rack or in a specially designed roasting pan.

Vegetarian & Vegan Suppers

The potato has become a valued staple of the vegetarian

diet, yet anyone who thought this would make for dull

eating will be pleasantly surprised by

the rich variety of dishes in this chapter.

In addition to traditional hearty bakes

and hotpots, there are also influences

from around the world in dishes such as Bean Curd &

Vegetable Stir-fry from China, and Potato & Cauliflower

Curry from India. They all make exciting

eating at any time of year.

Mixed Bean Soup

This is a really hearty soup, filled with color, flavor, and goodness, which may be adapted to any vegetables that you have at hand.

NUTRITIONAL INFORMATION

Calories 190	Sugars 9g
Protein 10g	Fat 4g
Carbohydrate ...30g	Saturates 0.5g

10 mins   40 mins

SERVES 4

INGREDIENTS

1 tbsp vegetable oil

1 red onion, halved and sliced

⅔ cup diced potatoes

1 carrot, diced

1 leek, sliced

1 green chili, sliced

3 garlic cloves, crushed

1 tsp ground coriander

1 tsp chili powder

4 cups vegetable bouillon

1 lb/450 g mixed canned beans, such as
   red kidney beans, borlotti beans,
   black-eye peas, or lima beans, drained

salt and pepper

2 tbsp chopped cilantro, to garnish

1 Heat the vegetable oil in a large pan. Add the onion, potato, carrot, and leek and sauté, stirring constantly, for about2 minutes, until the vegetables are slightly softened.

2 Add the sliced chili and crushed garlic and cook for a further 1 minute.

3 Stir in the ground coriander, chili powder, and vegetable stock.

4 Bring the soup to a boil. Reduce the heat and cook for 20 minutes, or until the vegetables are tender.

5 Stir in the beans. Season well with salt and pepper and cook, stirring occasionally, for a further 10 minutes.

6 Transfer the soup to a warm tureen or individual bowls. Garnish with chopped cilantro and serve.

COOK'S TIP

Serve this soup with slices of warm corn bread or a cheese loaf.

Potato & Mushroom Hash

This is a quick one-pan dish which is ideal for a snack. Packed with color and flavor it is very versatile, as you can add other vegetables.

NUTRITIONAL INFORMATION

Calories 182   Sugars 6g
Protein ....5g   Fat 4g
Carbohydrate ...34g   Saturates 0.5g

5 mins   30 mins

SERVES 4

INGREDIENTS

1½ lb/675 g potatoes, cubed

1 tbsp olive oil

2 garlic cloves, crushed

1 green bell pepper, seeded and cubed

1 yellow bell pepper, seeded and cubed

3 tomatoes, diced

1 cup white mushrooms, halved

1 tbsp Worcestershire sauce

2 tbsp chopped basil

salt and pepper

basil sprigs, to garnish

warm crusty bread, to serve

1 Cook the potatoes in a pan of boiling salted water for 7–8 minutes. Drain well and reserve.

2 Heat the olive oil in a large, heavy-based skillet. Add the potatoes and cook, stirring constantly, for 8–10 minutes, until browned.

3 Add the garlic and bell peppers and cook, stirring frequently, for 2–3 minutes.

4 Stir in the tomatoes and mushrooms and cook, stirring frequently, for 5–6 minutes.

5 Stir in the Worcestershire sauce and basil and season to taste with salt and pepper. Transfer to a warm serving dish. Garnish with basil sprigs and serve with warm crusty bread.

COOK'S TIP

Most brands of Worcestershire sauce contain anchovies, so if you are vegetarian, check the label to make sure you choose a vegetarian variety.

Curry Pasties

These pasties, which are suitable for vegans, are a delicious combination of vegetables and spices. They can be eaten either hot or cold.

NUTRITIONAL INFORMATION

Calories ....455 Sugars 5g
Protein ....8g Fat 27g
Carbohydrate ...48g Saturates 5g

1 hour   1 hour

SERVES 4

INGREDIENTS

2 cups all-purpose whole-wheat flour

⅓ cup vegetarian margarine,
   cut into small pieces

4 tbsp water

2 tbsp oil

8 oz/225 g diced root vegetables, such as
   potatoes, carrots, and parsnips

1 small onion, chopped

2 garlic cloves, finely chopped

½ tsp curry powder

½ tsp ground turmeric

½ tsp ground cumin

½ tsp whole-grain mustard

5 tbsp vegetable bouillon

soy milk, to glaze

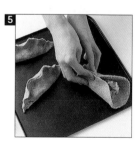

1 Place the flour in a mixing bowl and rub in the margarine with your fingertips until the mixture resembles bread crumbs. Stir in the water and bring together to form a soft dough. Wrap and let chill in the refrigerator for 30 minutes.

2 To make the filling, heat the oil in a large pan. Add the diced root vegetables, chopped onion, and garlic, and cook, stirring occasionally, for 2 minutes. Stir in all of the spices, turning the vegetables to coat them thoroughly. Cook the vegetables, stirring constantly, for another minute.

3 Add the bouillon to the pan and bring to a boil. Cover and simmer, stirring occasionally, for about 20 minutes, until the vegetables are tender and the liquid has been absorbed. Let cool.

4 Divide the dough into 4 portions. Roll each portion into a 6 inch/15 cm round. Place the filling on one half of each round.

5 Brush the edges of each round with soy milk, then fold over and press the edges together to seal. Place on a baking sheet. Bake in a preheated oven, 400°F/200°C , for 25–30 minutes until golden brown.

Potato & Vegetable Curry

Very little meat is eaten in India, and the Indian diet is mainly vegetarian.
This potato curry with added vegetables makes a substantial entrée.

NUTRITIONAL INFORMATION

Calories	301	Sugars	. . . . .10g
Protein	. . . . .9g	Fat	. . . . .12g
Carbohydrate	. . .41g	Saturates	. . . . . . .1g

5 mins   45 mins

SERVES 4

I N G R E D I E N T S

4 tbsp vegetable oil

1½/675 g lb waxy potatoes, cut into large chunks

2 onions, quartered

3 garlic cloves, crushed

1 tsp garam masala

½ tsp turmeric

½ tsp ground cumin

½ tsp ground coriander

2 tsp grated fresh ginger root

1 fresh red chili, chopped

8 oz/225 g cauliflower florets

4 tomatoes, peeled and quartered

¾ cup frozen peas

2 tbsp chopped (cilantro)

1¼ cups vegetable bouillon

shredded cilantro, to garnish

COOK'S TIP

Using a large, heavy-based pan or skillet for this recipe ensures that the potatoes are cooked thoroughly.

1 Heat the vegetable oil in a large heavy-based pan or skillet. Add the potato chunks, onion, and garlic and cook over a low heat, stirring frequently, for 2–3 minutes.

2 Add the garam masala, turmeric, ground cumin, ground coriander, grated ginger, and chopped chili to the pan, mixing the spices into the vegetables. Cook over a low heat, stirring constantly, for 1 minute.

3 Add the cauliflower florets, tomatoes, peas, chopped cilantro, and vegetable bouillon to the curry mixture.

4 Cook the potato curry over a low heat for 30–40 minutes, or until the potatoes are tender and completely cooked through.

5 Garnish the potato curry with fresh cilantro and serve with plain boiled rice or warm Indian bread.

Bubble & Squeak

Bubble and squeak is best known as fried mashed potato and leftover greens served as an accompaniment.

NUTRITIONAL INFORMATION

Calories . . . . .301 Sugars 5g
Protein . . . . .11g Fat 18g
Carbohydrate . . .24g Saturates 2g

15 mins   40 mins

SERVES 4

INGREDIENTS

2⅔ cups mealy diced potatoes

8 oz/225 g Savoy cabbage, shredded

5 tbsp vegetable oil

2 leeks, chopped

1 garlic clove, crushed

8 oz/225 g smoked bean curd, cubed

salt and pepper

shredded cooked leek, to garnish

1 Cook the diced potatoes in a pan of lightly salted boiling water for 10 minutes, until tender. Drain and mash the potatoes.

2 Meanwhile, in a separate pan, blanch the cabbage in boiling water for 5 minutes. Drain well and add to the potato.

COOK'S TIP

This vegetarian version is a perfect main meal, as the smoked bean curd cubes added to the basic bubble and squeak mixture make it very substantial and nourishing.

3 Heat the oil in a heavy-based skillet. Add the leeks and garlic and cook gently for 2–3 minutes. Stir into the potato and cabbage mixture.

4 Add the smoked bean curd and season well with salt and pepper. Cook over a medium heat for 10 minutes.

5 Carefully turn the whole mixture over and continue to cook over a medium heat for another 5–7 minutes, until crispy underneath. Serve immediately, garnished with shredded leek.

Baked Potatoes with Salsa

Once cooked, the flesh is flavored with avocado and piled back into the shell with a salad garnish. It is then served with a hot tomato salsa.

NUTRITIONAL INFORMATION

Calories 71	Sugars 1.4g	
Protein 2.3g	Fat 2.7g	
Carbohydrate . .10.0g	Saturates 0.5g	

10 mins   1 hour

SERVES 4

INGREDIENTS

4 baking potatoes

1 large ripe avocado

1 tsp lemon juice

6 oz/175 g smoked bean curd, diced

2 garlic cloves, crushed

1 onion, chopped finely

1 tomato, chopped finely

4½ oz/125 g mixed salad leaves

fresh cilantro sprigs, to garnish

SALSA

2 ripe tomatoes, seeded and diced

1 tbsp chopped cilantro

1 shallot, diced finely

1 green chili, diced

1 tbsp lemon juice

salt and pepper

1 Scrub the potatoes and prick the skins with a fork. Rub a little salt into the skins and place them on a baking sheet.

2 Cook in a preheated oven, 375°F/190°C, for 1 hour or until cooked through and the skins are crisp.

3 Cut the potatoes in half lengthwise and scoop the flesh into a bowl, leaving a thin layer of potato inside the shells.

4 Halve and stone the avocado. Using a spoon, scoop out the avocado flesh and add to the bowl containing the potato. Stir in the lemon juice and mash the mixture together with a fork. Mix in the bean curd, garlic, onion, and tomato. Spoon the mixture into one half of the potato shells.

5 Arrange the salad leaves on top of the guacamole mixture and place the other half of the potato shell on top.

6 To make the salsa, mix the tomatoes, cilantro, shallots, chili, lemon juice, and salt and pepper to taste in a bowl. Garnish the potatoes with sprigs of fresh cilantro and serve with the salsa.

Green Bean & Potato Curry

You can use fresh or canned green beans for this semi-dry vegetable curry, served with an Oil-dressed dhaal for flavor and color.

NUTRITIONAL INFORMATION

Calories . . . . . . .690 Sugars 4g
Protein . . . . .3g Fat 69g
Carbohydrate . . .16g Saturates 7g

15 mins   30 mins

SERVES 4

I N G R E D I E N T S

1¼ cups vegetable oil

1 tsp white cumin seeds

1 tsp mustard and onion seeds

4 dried red chilies

3 fresh tomatoes, sliced

1 tsp salt

1 tsp finely chopped fresh ginger root

1 tsp fresh garlic, crushed

1 tsp chili powder

7 oz/200 g green beans

2⅔ cups diced potatoes

1¼ cups water

1 tbsp chopped fresh cilantro

2 green chilies, finely chopped

boiled rice, to serve

1 Heat the vegetable oil in a large, heavy-based pan.

2 Add the white cumin seeds, mustard and onion seeds, and dried red chilies to the pan, stirring well.

3 Add the tomatoes to the pan and cook the mixture for 3-5 minutes.

4 Mix together the salt, ginger, garlic, and chili powder, and spoon into the pan. Blend the whole mixture together.

5 Add the green beans and potatoes to the pan and cook for about 5 minutes.

6 Add the water to the pan, then reduce the heat and leave to simmer for 10-15 minutes, stirring occasionally.

7 Garnish the green bean and potato curry with chopped cilantro leaves and green chilies, and serve hot with cooked rice.

COOK'S TIP

Mustard seeds are often fried in oil or ghee to bring out their flavor before being combined with other ingredients.

Vegetable Kabobs

These kabobs, made from a spicy vegetable mixture, are delightfully easy to make and taste delicious.

NUTRITIONAL INFORMATION

Calories 268   Sugars 1g
Protein . . . . .2g   Fat 25g
Carbohydrate . . . .9g   Saturates 3g

20 mins   25–30 mins

MAKES 12

INGREDIENTS

3½ cups potatoes, sliced

1 onion, sliced

½ medium cauliflower, cut into small florets

scant ½ cup peas

1 tbsp spinach paste

2–3 green chilies

1 tbsp fresh cilantro leaves

1 tsp finely chopped fresh ginger root

1 tsp crushed garlic

1 tsp ground coriander

1 pinch turmeric

1 tsp salt

1 cup bread crumbs

1¼ cups vegetable oil

fresh chili strips, to garnish

1 Place the potatoes, onion, and cauliflower florets in a pan of water and bring to a boil. Reduce the heat and simmer until the potatoes are cooked through. Remove the vegetables from the pan with a slotted spoon and drain thoroughly. Set aside.

2 Add the peas and spinach paste to the vegetables and mix, mashing down thoroughly with a fork.

3 Using a sharp knife, finely chop the green chilies and cilantro leaves.

4 Mix the chilies and cilantro leaves with the ginger, garlic, ground coriander, turmeric, and salt.

5 Blend the spice mixture into the vegetables, mixing with a fork to make a paste.

6 Scatter the bread crumbs on to a large plate.

7 Break off 10–12 small balls from the spice paste. Flatten them with the palm of your hand to make flat, round shapes.

8 Dip each kabob in the bread crumbs, coating well.

9 Heat the oil in a heavy-based skillet and cook the kabobs, in batches, until golden brown, turning occasionally. Transfer to serving plates and garnish with fresh chili strips. Serve hot.

Vegetable Curry

This colorful and interesting mixture of vegetables, cooked in a spicy sauce, is excellent served with rice and naan bread.

NUTRITIONAL INFORMATION

Calories 421	Sugars 20g
Protein 12g	Fat 24g
Carbohydrate . . .42g	Saturates 3g

15 mins   45 mins

SERVES 4

INGREDIENTS

8 oz/225 g turnips or rutabaga, peeled

1 eggplant, leaf end trimmed

12 oz/350 g new potatoes

8 oz/225 g cauliflower

8 oz/225 g white mushrooms

1 large onion

8 oz/225 g carrots

6 tbsp vegetable ghee or oil

2 garlic cloves, crushed

4 tsp finely chopped fresh ginger root

1–2 fresh green chilies, seeded
  and chopped

1 tbsp paprika

2 tsp ground coriander

1 tbsp mild or medium curry powder
  or paste

1¾ cups vegetable bouillon

14 oz/400 g canned chopped tomatoes

1 green bell pepper, seeded and sliced

1 tbsp cornstarch

⅔ cup coconut milk

2–3 tbsp ground almonds

salt

fresh cilantro sprigs, to garnish

1 Cut the turnips or rutabaga, eggplant, and potatoes into ½ inch/1 cm cubes. Divide the cauliflower into small florets. Leave the mushrooms whole, or slice thickly if preferred. Peel and slice the onion and carrots.

2 Heat the ghee or oil in a large pan. Add the onion, turnip or rutabaga, potato, and cauliflower, and cook over a low heat, stirring frequently, for 3 minutes.

3 Add the garlic, ginger, chilies, paprika, ground coriander, and curry powder or paste and cook, stirring, for 1 minute.

4 Add the bouillon, tomatoes, eggplant, and mushrooms, and season with salt. Cover and simmer, stirring occasionally, for about 30 minutes, or until tender. Add the green bell pepper and carrots, then cover and cook for another 5 minutes.

5 Blend the cornstarch with the coconut milk to a smooth paste and stir into the mixture. Add the ground almonds and simmer, stirring constantly, for 2 minutes. Season if necessary. Transfer the curry to serving plates and serve hot, garnished with sprigs of fresh cilantro.

Stuffed Rice Crêpes

Dosas (crêpes) are widely eaten in southern India. The rice and urid dhal need to soak and ferment, so prepare well in advance.

NUTRITIONAL INFORMATION

Calories 748	Sugars 1g
Protein 10g	Fat 47g
Carbohydrate ...76g	Saturates 5g

6¼ hours   40–45 mins

SERVES 4

INGREDIENTS

1 cup rice and ¼ cup urid dhal, or 1¾ cups ground rice and ½ cup urid dhal flour (ata)

2–2½ cups water

1 tsp salt

4 tbsp vegetable oil

FILLING

generous 5 cups diced potatoes

3 fresh green chilies, chopped

½ tsp turmeric

1 tsp salt

⅔ cup vegetable oil

1 tsp mixed mustard and onion seeds

3 dried chilies

4 curry leaves

2 tbsp lemon juice

2 Heat about 1 tbsp of oil in a large, non-stick skillet. Using a ladle, spoon the batter into the skillet. Tilt the skillet to spread the mixture over the base. Cover and cook over a medium heat for about 2 minutes. Remove the lid and turn the dosa over very carefully. Pour a little oil around the edge, then cover and cook for another 2 minutes. Repeat with the remaining batter.

3 To make the filling, cook the potatoes in a pan of boiling water. Add the chilies, turmeric, and salt, and cook until the potatoes are just soft. Drain and mash lightly with a fork.

4 Heat the vegetable oil in a pan and cook the mustard and onion seeds, dried red chilies, and curry leaves, stirring constantly, for about 1 minute. Pour the spice mixture over the mashed potatoes, then sprinkle over the lemon juice and mix well. Spoon the potato filling on one half of each of the dosas and fold the other half over it. Transfer to a warmed serving dish and serve hot.

1 To make the dosas, soak the rice and urid dhal for 3 hours. Grind the rice and urid dhal to a smooth consistency, adding water if necessary. Set aside for a further 3 hours to ferment. Alternatively, if you are using ground rice and urid dhal flour (ata), mix together in a bowl. Add the water and salt and stir until a batter is formed.

Potato Curry

Served hot with pooris, this curry makes an excellent brunch with mango chutney as the perfect accompaniment.

NUTRITIONAL INFORMATION

Calories	390	Sugars	.......0.7g
Protein	.........2g	Fat	.........34g
Carbohydrate	...19g	Saturates	.......4g

🥔 10 mins   🕐 25 mins

SERVES 4

INGREDIENTS

3 medium potatoes

5 fl oz/150 ml vegetable oil

1 tsp onion seeds

½ tsp fennel seeds

4 curry leaves

1 tsp ground cumin

1 tsp ground coriander

1 tsp chili powder

pinch of turmeric

1 tsp salt

1½ tsp dried mango powder

1 Peel and rinse the potatoes. Using a sharp knife, cut each potato into 6 slices.

2 Cook the potato slices in a pan of boiling water until just cooked, but not mushy (test by piercing with a sharp knife or a skewer). Drain and set aside until required.

3 Heat the vegetable oil in a separate, heavy-bottomed pan over a moderate heat. Reduce the heat and add the onion seeds, fennel seeds, and curry leaves and stir thoroughly.

4 Remove the pan from the heat and add the ground cumin, coriander, chili powder, turmeric, salt, and dried mango powder, stirring well to combine.

5 Return the pan to a low heat and cook the mixture, stirring constantly, for about 1 minute.

6 Pour this mixture over the cooked potatoes, mix together and stir-fry over a low heat for about 5 minutes.

7 Transfer the potato curry to serving dishes and serve immediately.

COOK'S TIP

Traditionally, semolina dessert is served to follow Potato Curry.

Indian Potatoes & Peas

This quick and easy-to-prepare Indian dish can be served either as an accompaniment or on its own with chapatis.

NUTRITIONAL INFORMATION

Calories ....434 Sugars 6g
Protein ....5g Fat 35g
Carbohydrate ...28g Saturates 4g

🕑 15 mins   🕐 25 mins

SERVES 4

INGREDIENTS

⅔ cup vegetable oil

3 medium onions, sliced

1 tsp crushed garlic

1 tsp finely chopped fresh ginger root

1 tsp chili powder

½ tsp turmeric

1 tsp salt

2 fresh green chilies, finely chopped

1¼ cups water

1½ lb/675 g potatoes

1 cup peas

TO GARNISH

fresh cilantro leaves and chopped red chilies

1 Heat the vegetable oil in a large, heavy-based skillet.

2 Add the onions to the skillet and cook, stirring occasionally, until the onions are golden brown.

3 Mix together the garlic, ginger, chili powder, turmeric, salt, and fresh green chilies. Add the spice mixture to the onions in the pan.

4 Stir in ⅔ cup of the water, then cover and cook until the onions are cooked right through.

5 Meanwhile, cut the potatoes into six slices each, using a sharp knife.

6 Add the potato slices to the mixture in the pan and cook for 5 minutes.

7 Add the peas and the remaining water to the pan, then cover and cook for 7–10 minutes.

8 Transfer the potatoes and peas to serving plates and serve, garnished with fresh cilantro leaves.

COOK'S TIP

Turmeric is an aromatic root which is dried and ground to produce the distinctive bright yellow-orange powder used in many Indian dishes. It has a warm, aromatic smell and a full, somewhat musty taste.

Garbanzo Bean Curry

This curry is very popular in India. There are many different ways of cooking garbanzo beans, but this is probably one of the most delicious.

NUTRITIONAL INFORMATION

Calories 114   Sugars 1.9g
Protein . . . . .2.9g   Fat 7.3g
Carbohydrate . .10.1g   Saturates 0.7g

5-10 mins   15 mins

SERVES 4

INGREDIENTS

6 tbsp vegetable oil

2 onions, sliced

1 tsp finely chopped fresh ginger root

1 tsp ground cumin

1 tsp ground coriander

1 tsp fresh garlic, crushed

1 tsp chili powder

2 fresh green chilies

1 tbsp fresh cilantro leaves

⅔ cup water

10½ oz/300 g potato

14 oz/400 g canned garbanzo beans, drained

1 tbsp lemon juice

1 Heat the oil in a large pan.

2 Add the onions to the pan and cook, stirring occasionally, until golden brown.

3 Reduce the heat, then add the ginger, ground cumin, ground coriander, garlic, chili powder, fresh green chilies, and fresh cilantro leaves to the pan and cook for 2 minutes.

4 Add the water to the mixture in the pan and stir to mix.

5 Using a sharp knife, cut the potato into small dice.

6 Add the potatoes and the drained garbanzo beans to the mixture in the pan. Cover and leave to simmer, stirring occasionally, for 5–7 minutes.

7 Sprinkle the lemon juice over the curry.

8 Transfer the garbanzo bean curry to serving dishes. Serve the curry hot with chapati, if you wish.

COOK'S TIP

Using canned garbanzo beans saves time, but you can use dried garbanzo beans if you prefer. Soak them overnight, then boil them for 15–20 minutes or until soft.

Mixed Vegetables

This is one of my favorite vegetarian recipes. You can make it with any vegetables you choose, but I think the combination below is ideal.

NUTRITIONAL INFORMATION

Calories 669   Sugars 17g
Protein . . . . .7g   Fat 57g
Carbohydrate . . .36g   Saturates 8g

5 mins   45 mins

SERVES 4

INGREDIENTS

1¼ cups vegetable oil

1 tsp mustard seeds

1 tsp onion seeds

½ tsp white cumin seeds

3–4 curry leaves, chopped

1 lb/450 g onions, finely chopped

3 tomatoes, chopped

½ red and ½ green bell pepper, sliced

1 tsp finely chopped fresh ginger root

1 tsp fresh garlic, crushed

1 tsp chili powder

¼ tsp turmeric

1 tsp salt

2 cups water

1 lb/450 g potatoes, and cut into pieces

½ cauliflower, cut into small florets

4 carrots, sliced

3 green chilies, finely chopped

1 tbsp fresh cilantro leaves

1 tbsp lemon juice

1 Heat the oil in a large pan. Add the mustard, onion and white cumin seeds, and the curry leaves and cook until they turn a shade darker.

2 Add the onions to the pan and cook over a medium heat until golden brown.

3 Add the tomatoes and bell peppers and cook for about 5 minutes.

4 Add the ginger, garlic, chili powder, turmeric, and salt, and mix well.

5 Add 1¼ cups of the water. Cover and leave to simmer for 10–12 minutes, stirring occasionally.

6 Add the potatoes, cauliflower, carrots, green chilies, and cilantro leaves and cook for about 5 minutes.

7 Add the remaining ⅔ cup of water and the lemon juice, stirring to combine. Cover and let simmer for about 15 minutes, stirring occasionally.

8 Transfer the mixed vegetables to serving plates and serve immediately.

Potato & Cauliflower Curry

Potatoes and cauliflower go very well together. Served with a dhal and rice or bread, this dish makes a perfect vegetarian meal.

NUTRITIONAL INFORMATION

Calories ....426 Sugars 6g
Protein ....4g Fat 35g
Carbohydrate ...26g Saturates 4g

10 mins   25 mins

SERVES 4

INGREDIENTS

⅔ cup vegetable oil

½ tsp white cumin seeds

4 dried red chilies

2 onions, sliced

1 tsp finely chopped fresh root ginger

1 tsp crushed garlic

1 tsp chili powder

1 tsp salt

pinch of turmeric

1½ lb/675g potatoes, chopped

½ cauliflower, cut into small florets

2 green chilies, optional

1 tbsp fresh cilantro leaves

⅔ cup water

1 Heat the oil in a large, heavy-based pan. Add the white cumin seeds and dried red chilies to the pan, stirring to mix thoroughly.

2 Add the onions to the pan and cook over a medium heat, stirring occasionally, for about 5–8 minutes, until golden brown.

3 Mix the ginger, garlic, chili powder, salt, and turmeric together. Add the spice mixture to the onions and cook for about 2 minutes.

4 Add the potatoes and cauliflower to the pan and stir to coat thoroughly with the spice mixture. Reduce the heat and add the green chilies (if using), cilantro leaves, and water to the pan. Cover and simmer for about 10–15 minutes, until the vegetables are cooked through and tender.

5 Transfer the potato and cauliflower curry to warmed serving plates and serve immediately.

COOK'S TIP

Ground ginger is no substitute for the fresh root. It is less aromatic and flavorsome and cannot be used in sautéed dishes, as it burns easily at the high temperatures required.

Vegetable-Stuffed Paratas

This bread can be quite rich and is usually made for special occasions.
It can be eaten on its own or with a vegetable curry.

NUTRITIONAL INFORMATION

Calories . . . . .391 Sugars 2g
Protein . . . . .6g Fat 24g
Carbohydrate . . .40g Saturates 2.5g

🖐 🖐 🖐

🧊 25 mins   🕐 30–35 mins

SERVES 6

I N G R E D I E N T S

D O U G H

1¾ cups whole-wheat flour
(ata or chapati flour)

½ tsp salt

scant 1 cup water

3½ oz/100 g vegetable ghee

2 tbsp ghee, for frying

F I L L I N G

1½ lb/675 g potatoes

½ tsp turmeric

1 tsp garam masala

1 tsp finely chopped fresh ginger root

1 tbsp fresh cilantro leaves

3 green chilies, finely chopped

1 tsp salt

1 To make the paratas, mix the flour, salt, water, and ghee in a bowl to form a dough.

2 Divide the dough into 6–8 equal portions. Roll each portion out on to a floured counter. Brush the middle of the dough portions with ½ teaspoon of ghee. Fold the dough portions in half and roll into a pipelike shape, then flatten with the palms of your hands and roll around a finger to form a coil. Roll out again, using flour to dust when necessary, to form a round about 7 inches/18 cm in diameter.

3 Place the potatoes in a pan of boiling water and cook until soft enough to be mashed.

4 Blend the turmeric, garam masala, ginger, cilantro leaves, chilies, and salt together in a bowl.

5 Add the spice mixture to the mashed potato and mix well. Spread about 1 tablespoon of the spicy potato mixture on each dough portion and cover with another rolled-out piece of dough. Seal the edges well.

6 Heat 2 teaspoons of ghee in a heavy-based skillet. Place the paratas gently in the pan, in batches, and cook, turning and moving them about gently with a flat spoon, until golden.

7 Remove the paratas from the skillet and serve immediately.

Pakoras

Pakoras are eaten all over India. They are made in many different ways and with a variety of fillings. Sometimes they are served with yogurt.

NUTRITIONAL INFORMATION

Calories . . . . .331 Sugars 5g
Protein . . . . .9g Fat 22g
Carbohydrate . . .27g Saturates 3g

15 mins   15–20 mins

SERVES 4

INGREDIENTS

6 tbsp gram flour

½ tsp salt

1 tsp chili powder

1 tsp baking powder

1½ tsp white cumin seeds

1 tsp pomegranate seeds

1¼ cups water

1 tbsp finely chopped fresh cilantro leaves

vegetables of your choice: cauliflower cut
    into small florets, onions cut into rings,
    sliced potatoes, sliced eggplants,
    or fresh spinach leaves

vegetable oil

1 Sift the gram flour into a large mixing bowl. Add the salt, chili powder, baking powder, cumin, and pomegranate seeds, and blend together well. Pour in the water and beat thoroughly to form a smooth batter.

2 Add the cilantro and mix. Set the batter aside.

3 Dip the prepared vegetables of your choice into the batter, carefully shaking off any of the excess batter.

4 Heat enough oil to cover the pakoras in a deep, heavy-based pan. Place the battered vegetables of your choice in the oil and cook, in batches, turning once.

5 Repeat this process until all of the batter has been used up.

6 Transfer the battered vegetables to paper towels and drain thoroughly. Serve immediately.

COOK'S TIP

When cooking pakoras, it is important to use oil at the correct temperature. If the oil is too hot, the outside of the food will burn, as will the spices, before the inside is cooked. If the oil is too cool, the food will be soaked with oil before a crisp batter forms.

Potato & Lemon Casserole

This is based on a Moroccan dish in which potatoes are spiced with cilantro and cumin and cooked in a lemon sauce.

NUTRITIONAL INFORMATION

Calories 338	Sugars 8g	
Protein 5g	Fat 23g	
Carbohydrate ...29g	Saturates 2g	

15 mins   35 mins

SERVES 4

I N G R E D I E N T S

½ cup olive oil

2 red onions, cut into eight

3 garlic cloves, crushed

2 tsp ground cumin

2 tsp ground coriander

pinch of cayenne pepper

1 carrot, thickly sliced

2 small turnips, quartered

1 zucchini, sliced

1 lb 2 oz/500 g potatoes, thickly sliced

juice and zest of 2 large lemons

1¼ cups vegetable bouillon

2 tbsp chopped cilantro

salt and pepper

COOK'S TIP

Check the vegetables while they are cooking, as they may begin to stick to the pan. Add a little more boiling water or stock if necessary.

1 Heat the olive oil in a flameproof casserole. Add the onion and sauté over a medium heat, stirring frequently, for 3 minutes.

2 Add the garlic and cook for 30 seconds. Stir in the spices and cook, stirring constantly, for 1 minute.

3 Add the carrot, turnips, zucchini, and potatoes, and stir to coat in the oil.

4 Add the lemon juice and zest and the vegetable bouillon. Season to taste with salt and pepper. Cover and cook over a medium heat, stirring occasionally, for 20–30 minutes, until tender.

5 Remove the lid, then sprinkle in the chopped cilantro and stir well. Serve immediately.

Bean Curd Stir-Fry

This is a quick dish to prepare, making it ideal as a mid-week supper dish after a busy day at work!

NUTRITIONAL INFORMATION

Calories ....124 Sugars 2g
Protein ....6g Fat 6g
Carbohydrate ....11g Saturates 1g

5 mins   25 mins

SERVES 4

INGREDIENTS

1¼ cups potatoes, cubed

1 tbsp vegetable oil

1 red onion, sliced

8 oz/225 g firm bean curd, diced

2 zucchini, diced

8 canned artichoke hearts, halved

⅔ cup strained tomatoes

1 tbsp sweet chili sauce

1 tbsp soy sauce

1 tsp superfine sugar

2 tbsp chopped basil

salt and pepper

1 Cook the potatoes in a pan of boiling water for 10 minutes. Drain thoroughly and set aside until required.

2 Heat the vegetable oil in a wok or large skillet and sauté the red onion for 2 minutes until the onion has softened, stirring continuously.

3 Stir in the diced bean curd and zucchini and cook for 3–4 minutes until they begin to brown slightly.

4 Add the cooked potatoes to the wok or skillet, stirring to mix.

5 Stir in the artichoke hearts, strained tomatoes, sweet chili sauce, soy sauce, sugar, and basil.

6 Season to taste with salt and pepper and cook for another 5 minutes, stirring well.

7 Transfer the bean curd and vegetable stir-fry to serving dishes and serve immediately.

COOK'S TIP

Canned artichoke hearts should be drained thoroughly and rinsed before use because they often have salt added.

Jacket Potatoes with Beans

Baked jacket potatoes, topped with a tasty mixture of beans in a spicy sauce, provide a deliciously filling, high-fiber dish.

NUTRITIONAL INFORMATION

Calories 378	Sugars 9g
Protein 15g	Fat 9g
Carbohydrate ...64g	Saturates 1g

15 mins   1¼ hours

SERVES 6

INGREDIENTS

4lb/1.8 kg potatoes

4 tbsp vegetable ghee or oil

1 large onion, chopped

2 garlic cloves, crushed

1 tsp ground turmeric

1 tbsp cumin seeds

2 tbsp mild or medium curry paste

12 oz/350 g cherry tomatoes

14 oz/400 g canned black-eye peas, drained and rinsed

14 oz/400 g canned red kidney beans, drained and rinsed

1 tbsp lemon juice

2 tbsp tomato paste

⅔ cup water

2 tbsp chopped fresh mint or cilantro

salt and pepper

VARIATION

Instead of cutting the potatoes in half, cut a cross in each and squeeze gently to open out. Spoon some of the prepared filling into the cross and place any remaining filling to the side.

1 Scrub the potatoes and prick several times with a fork. Place in a preheated oven, 350°F/180°C, and then cook for 1–1¼ hours, or until the potatoes feel soft when gently squeezed.

2 About 20 minutes before the end of cooking time, prepare the topping. Heat the ghee or oil in a pan, then add the onion and cook over a low heat, stirring frequently, for 5 minutes. Add the garlic, turmeric, cumin seeds, and curry paste and cook gently for 1 minute.

3 Stir in the tomatoes, black-eye peas, red kidney beans, lemon juice, tomato paste, water, and chopped mint. Season to taste with salt and pepper, then cover and simmer over a low heat, stirring frequently, for 10 minutes.

4 When the potatoes are cooked, cut them in half and mash the flesh lightly with a fork. Spoon the prepared bean mixture on top. Place on warmed serving plates and serve immediately.

Yellow Curry

Potatoes are not highly regarded in Thai cooking, as rice is the traditional staple. This dish is an exception, with its creamy, golden coconut sauce.

NUTRITIONAL INFORMATION

Calories 160	Sugars 4g	
Protein 3g	Fat 10g	
Carbohydrate ...15g	Saturates 1g	

5 mins

15 hours

SERVES 4

INGREDIENTS

2 garlic cloves, finely chopped

3 cm/1¼ inch piece galangal, finely chopped

1 lemon grass stem,

finely chopped

1 tsp coriander seeds

3 tbsp vegetable oil

2 tsp Thai red curry paste

½ tsp turmeric

scant 1 cup coconut milk

9 oz/250 g potatoes, cubed

scant ½ cup vegetable bouillon

7 oz/200 g young spinach leaves

1 small onion, thinly sliced into rings

1 Place the garlic, galangal, lemon grass, and coriander seeds in a pestle and mortar and pound until a smooth paste forms.

2 Heat 2 tablespoons of the oil in a skillet or wok. Stir in the paste and cook for 30 seconds. Stir in the curry paste and turmeric, then add the coconut milk and bring to a boil.

3 Add the potatoes and bouillon. Return to a boil, then lower the heat and simmer, uncovered, for 10–12 minutes until the potatoes are almost tender.

4 Stir in the spinach and simmer until the leaves are wilted.

5 Meanwhile, cook the onions in the remaining oil until crisp. Place on top of the curry just before serving.

COOK'S TIP

Choose a firm, waxy potato for this dish, one that will keep its shape during cooking, in preference to a mealy variety which will break up easily once cooked.

Sweet Potato Cakes

Enticing little tasty mouthfuls of sweet potato, served hot and sizzling from the pan with a delicious fresh tomato sauce.

NUTRITIONAL INFORMATION

Calories	349	Sugars	.........9g
Protein	.........4g	Fat	..........24g
Carbohydrate	...32g	Saturates	.......3g

10–15 mins   15 mins

SERVES 4

I N G R E D I E N T S

1 lb 2 oz/500 g sweet potatoes

2 garlic cloves, crushed

1 small green chili, chopped

2 sprigs fresh cilantro, chopped

1 tbsp dark soy sauce

all-purpose flour, for shaping

vegetable oil, for frying

sesame seeds, for sprinkling

SOY-TOMATO SAUCE

2 tsp vegetable oil

1 garlic clove, finely chopped

1½ tsp fresh ginger root, finely chopped

3 tomatoes, skinned and chopped

2 tbsp dark soy sauce

1 tbsp lime juice

2 tbsp chopped fresh cilantro

1 Make the soy-tomato sauce. Heat the oil in a wok and cook the garlic and ginger for about 1 minute. Add the tomatoes and cook for another 2 minutes. Remove from the heat and stir in the soy sauce, lime, and cilantro. Set aside and keep warm.

2 Peel the sweet potatoes and grate finely (you can do this quickly with a food processor). Place the garlic, chili, and cilantro in a pestle and mortar and crush to a smooth paste. Stir in the soy sauce mix with the sweet potatoes.

3 Divide the mixture into 12 equal portions. Dip into flour and pat into a flat, round patty shape.

4 Heat a shallow layer of oil in a wide skillet. Fry the sweet potato cakes in batches over a high heat until golden, turning once.

5 Drain on paper towels and sprinkle with sesame seeds. Serve hot, with a spoonful of the soy-tomato sauce.

COOK'S TIP

Make sure that the potatoes are sliced very thinly so that they are almost transparent. This will ensure that they cook thoroughly.

Vegetable Savories

This chapter proves that meat does not have to be involved in a truly excellent main meal. In this section you will find dishes from all over the world, such as Potato & Spinach

Gnocchi from Italy, and Vegetable Pulao from India. Family favorites such as Nutty Harvest Loaf and Vegetable Hotpot have been included, while the needs of the dinner party have not been forgotten with the spectacular Potato & Three Cheese Soufflé. Whatever the occasion, you are sure to find something to satisfy the heartiest of appetites.

Sweet Potato & Leek Patties

Sweet potatoes have very dense flesh and a delicious, sweet, earthy taste, which contrasts well with the pungent flavor of the ginger.

NUTRITIONAL INFORMATION

Calories . . . . . . .403 Sugars 34g
Protein . . . . .8g Fat 12g
Carbohydrate . . .67g Saturates 2g

2 hours   40 mins

SERVES 4

INGREDIENTS

2 lb/900 g sweet potato

4 tsp sunflower oil

2 leeks, trimmed and finely chopped

1 garlic clove, crushed

2 tsp finely chopped fresh ginger root

7 oz /200 g canned corn kernels, drained

2 tbsp lowfat unsweetened yogurt

generous ½ cup whole-wheat flour

salt and pepper

GINGER SAUCE

2 tbsp white wine vinegar

2 tsp superfine sugar

1 red chili, seeded and chopped

1 inch/2.5 cm piece fresh ginger root, cut into thin strips

2 tbsp ginger wine

4 tbsp vegetable bouillon

1 tsp cornstarch

TO SERVE

lettuce leaves

1 scallion, shredded

1 Peel the potatoes. Cut into thick cubes and boil for 10–15 minutes. Drain well and mash. Let cool.

2 Heat 2 tsp of oil and fry the leeks, garlic and ginger for 2–3 minutes. Stir into the potato with the corn, unsweetened yogurt, and seasoning. Form into 8 patties and toss in the flour. Chill for 30 minutes. Place the patties on a preheated broiler rack and lightly brush with oil. Broil for 5 minutes, then turn over, brush with oil, and broil for another 5 minutes.

3 Place the vinegar, sugar, chili, and ginger in a pan and simmer for 5 minutes. Stir in the wine. Blend the bouillon and cornstarch and add to the sauce, stirring, until thickened. Serve the patties with lettuce and scallions, and the sauce.

Vegetable Ratatouille

Ratatouille is a classic dish of vegetables cooked in a tomato and herb sauce. Here it is topped with diced potatoes and cheese.

NUTRITIONAL INFORMATION

Calories 287	Sugars 13g
Protein 14g	Fat 4g
Carbohydrate ...53g	Saturates 2g

15 mins   45 mins

SERVES 4

INGREDIENTS

2 onions

1 garlic clove

1 red bell pepper

1 green bell pepper

1 eggplant

2 zucchini

1 lb 12 oz/800 g canned chopped tomatoes

1 bouquet garni

2 tbsp tomato paste

2 lb/900 g potatoes

¾ cup grated reduced-fat sharp
   Cheddar cheese

salt and pepper

2 tbsp snipped fresh chives, to garnish

1 Peel and finely chop the onions and garlic. Rinse, seed, and slice the bell peppers. Rinse, trim, and cut the eggplant into small dice. Rinse, trim, and thinly slice the zucchini.

2 Place the onion, garlic and bell peppers into a large pan. Add the tomatoes, and stir in the bouquet garni, tomato paste, and salt and pepper to taste. Bring to a boil, cover and simmer for 10 minutes, stirring halfway through. Stir in the prepared eggplant and zucchini and cook, uncovered, for a further 10 minutes, stirring occasionally.

3 Meanwhile, peel the potatoes and cut into 1 inch/ 2.5 cm cubes. Place the potatoes into another pan and cover with water. Bring to a boil and cook for 10–12 minutes until tender. Drain and set aside.

4 Transfer the vegetables onto a heatproof gratin dish. Arrange the cooked potatoes evenly over the vegetables.

5 Preheat the broiler to medium. Sprinkle grated cheese over the potatoes and place under the broiler for 5 minutes until golden, bubbling and hot. Serve garnished with snipped chives.

VARIATION

You can vary the vegetables in this dish depending on seasonal availability and personal preference. Try broccoli, carrots, or corn, if you prefer.

Potato & Pepperoni Pizza

Potatoes make a great pizza base and this recipe is well worth making, rather than using a store-bought base, both for texture and flavor.

NUTRITIONAL INFORMATION

Calories ...... .234 Sugars 5g
Protein .... .4g Fat .... .12g
Carbohydrate ...30g Saturates 1g

20 mins   45 mins

SERVES 4

INGREDIENTS

generous 5 cups diced mealy potatoes

1 tbsp butter

2 garlic cloves, crushed

2 tbsp mixed chopped fresh herbs

1 egg, beaten

6 tbsp strained tomatoes

2 tbsp tomato paste

1¾ oz/50 g pepperoni slices

1 green bell pepper, cut into strips

1 yellow bell pepper, cut into strips

2 large open cup mushrooms, sliced

1 oz/25 g pitted black olives,
        quartered

4½ oz/125 g mozzarella cheese, sliced

1 Grease and flour a 9 inch/23 cm pizza pan.

2 Cook the diced potatoes in a saucepan of boiling water for 10 minutes or until cooked through. Drain and mash until smooth. Transfer the mashed potato to a mixing bowl and stir in the butter, garlic, herbs, and egg.

3 Spread the mixture into the prepared pizza pan. Cook in a preheated oven, at 425°F/220°C, for 7–10 minutes or until the pizza base begins to set.

4 Mix the strained tomatoes and tomato paste together and spoon it over the pizza base, to within ½ inch/1 cm of the edge of the base.

5 Arrange the pepperoni, bell peppers, mushrooms, and olives on top of the strained tomatoes.

6 Scatter the mozzarella cheese on top of the pizza. Return to the oven for 20 minutes or until the base is cooked through and the cheese has melted on top. Serve hot.

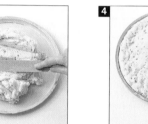

COOK'S TIP

This pizza base is softer in texture than a normal bread dough and is ideal served from the pan. Top with any of your favorite pizza ingredients that you have to hand.

Potato & Spinach Gnocchi

These small potato dumplings are flavored with spinach, cooked in boiling water and served with a simple tomato sauce.

NUTRITIONAL INFORMATION

Calories 315   Sugars 7g
Protein . . . . .8g   Fat 8g
Carbohydrate . . .56g   Saturates 1g

20 mins   30 mins

SERVES 4

I N G R E D I E N T S

1⅔ diced mealy potatoes

6 oz/175 g spinach

1 egg yolk

1 tsp olive oil

1 cup all-purpose flour

salt and pepper

spinach leaves, to garnish

S A U C E

1 tbsp olive oil

2 shallots, chopped

1 garlic clove, crushed

1¼ cups strained tomatoes

2 tsp soft light brown sugar

1 Cook the diced potatoes in a pan of boiling water for 10 minutes or until cooked through. Drain and mash the potatoes.

2 Meanwhile, in a separate pan, blanch the spinach in a little boiling water for 1–2 minutes. Drain the spinach and shred the leaves.

3 Transfer the mashed potato to a lightly floured cutting board and make a well in the center. Add the egg yolk, olive oil, spinach, and a little of the flour. Quickly mix the ingredients into the potato, adding more flour as you go, until you have a firm dough. Divide the mixture into very small dumplings.

4 Cook the gnocchi, in batches, in a saucepan of boiling salted water for about 5 minutes or until they rise to the surface.

5 Meanwhile, make the sauce. Put the oil, shallots, garlic, strained tomatoes, and sugar into a saucepan and cook over a low heat for 10–15 minutes or until the sauce has thickened.

6 Drain the gnocchi using a perforated spoon and transfer to warm serving dishes. Spoon the sauce over the gnocchi and garnish with the fresh spinach leaves.

VARIATION

Add chopped fresh herbs and cheese to the gnocchi dough instead of the spinach, if you prefer.

Potato-Topped Vegetables

This is a very colorful and nutritious dish, packed full of crunchy vegetables in a tasty white wine sauce.

NUTRITIONAL INFORMATION

Calories 413	Sugars 11g
Protein 19g	Fat 18g
Carbohydrate . . .41g	Saturates 11g

20 mins   1¼ hours

SERVES 4

I N G R E D I E N T S

1 carrot, diced

6 oz/175 g cauliflower florets

6 oz/175 g broccoli florets

1 fennel bulb, sliced

2¾ oz/75 g green beans, halved

2 tbsp butter

¼ cup all-purpose flour

⅔ cup vegetable bouillon

⅔ cup dry white wine

⅔ cup milk

6 oz/175 g crimini mushrooms, quartered

2 tbsp chopped sage

T O P P I N G

generous 5 cups diced mealy potatoes

2 tbsp butter

4 tbsp unsweetened yogurt

generous ⅔ cup freshly grated
        Parmesan cheese

1 tsp fennel seeds

salt and pepper

2 Melt the butter in a pan. Stir in the flour and cook for 1 minute. Remove from the heat and stir in the bouillon, wine, and milk. Return to the heat and bring to a boil, stirring until thickened. Stir in the reserved vegetables, mushrooms, and sage.

3 Meanwhile, make the topping. Cook the diced potatoes in a pan of boiling

water for 10–15 minutes. Drain and mash with the butter, yogurt, and half the Parmesan cheese. Stir in the fennel seeds.

4 Spoon the vegetable mixture into a 4 cup/1 liter pie dish. Spoon the potato over the top and sprinkle with the remaining cheese. Cook in a preheated oven, 375°F/190°C, for 30–35 minutes, or until golden. Serve hot.

1 Cook the carrot, cauliflower, broccoli, fennel, and beans in a large pan of boiling water for 10 minutes, until just tender. Drain the vegetables thoroughly and set aside.

Three Cheese Soufflé

This soufflé is very simple to make, yet it has a delicious flavor and melts in the mouth. Choose three alternative cheeses, if preferred.

NUTRITIONAL INFORMATION

Calories	447	Sugars	.........1g
Protein	........22g	Fat	..........23g
Carbohydrate	...41g	Saturates	......11g

10 mins   55 mins

SERVES 4

INGREDIENTS

2 tbsp butter

2 tsp all-purpose flour

2 lb/900 g mealy potatoes

8 eggs, separated

¼ cup grated Swiss cheese

¼ cup crumbled blue cheese

¼ cup grated sharp Cheddar cheese

salt and pepper

1 Butter a 10-cup/2.2 liter soufflé dish and dust with the flour. Set aside.

2 Cook the potatoes in a pan of boiling water until tender. Mash until very smooth and then transfer to a mixing bowl to cool.

3 Beat the egg yolks into the potato and stir in the Swiss cheese, blue cheese, and Cheddar, mixing well. Season to taste with salt and pepper.

4 Whisk the egg whites until standing in peaks, then gently fold them into the potato mixture with a metal spoon until fully incorporated.

5 Spoon the potato mixture into the prepared soufflé dish.

6 Cook in a preheated oven, 425°F/220°C, for 35–40 minutes, until risen and set. Serve immediately.

COOK'S TIP

Insert a fine skewer into the center of the soufflé; it should come out clean when the soufflé is fully cooked through.

Nutty Harvest Loaf

This attractive and nutritious loaf is also delicious. Served with a fresh tomato sauce, it can be eaten hot or cold with salad.

NUTRITIONAL INFORMATION

Calories 554	Sugars 12g
Protein 16g	Fat 37g
Carbohydrate . . .43g	Saturates 16g

🥔 20 mins   🕐 1 hr 20 mins

SERVES 4

INGREDIENTS

2 tbsp butter, plus extra for greasing

2⅔ cups diced mealy potatoes

1 onion, chopped

2 garlic cloves, crushed

4½ oz/125 g unsalted peanuts

1⅓ cups fresh white bread crumbs

1 egg, beaten

2 tbsp chopped fresh cilantro

⅔ cup vegetable bouillon

2¾ oz/75 g sliced mushrooms

1¾ oz/50 g sun-dried tomatoes, sliced

salt and pepper

SAUCE

⅔ cup crème fraîche

2 tsp tomato paste

2 tsp clear honey

2 tbsp chopped fresh cilantro

1 Grease a 1 lb/450 g loaf pan. Cook the potatoes in a pan of boiling water for 10 minutes, until cooked through. Drain well, then mash and set aside.

2 Melt half of the butter in a skillet. Add the onion and garlic and cook gently for 2–3 minutes, until soft. Finely chop the nuts or process them in a food processor for 30 seconds with the bread crumbs.

3 Mix the chopped nuts and bread crumbs into the potatoes with the egg, cilantro, and vegetable bouillon. Stir in the onion and garlic and mix well.

4 Melt the remaining butter in the skillet. Add the sliced mushrooms and cook for 2–3 minutes.

5 Press half of the potato mixture into the base of the loaf pan. Spoon the mushrooms on top and sprinkle with the sun-dried tomatoes. Spoon the remaining potato mixture on top and smooth the surface. Cover with aluminum foil and bake in a preheated oven, 350°F/190°C, for 1 hour, or until firm to the touch.

6 Meanwhile, mix the sauce ingredients together. Cut the nutty harvest loaf into slices and serve with the sauce.

Vegetable Cake

This is a savory version of a cheesecake with a layer of fried potatoes as a delicious base. Use frozen mixed vegetables for the topping, if you like.

NUTRITIONAL INFORMATION

Calories 502   Sugars 8g
Protein ....16g   Fat 31g
Carbohydrate ...41g   Saturates 14g

20 mins   45 mins

SERVES 4

INGREDIENTS

BASE

2 tbsp vegetable oil, plus extra for brushing

2lb 12 oz/1.25 kg large waxy potatoes, thinly sliced

TOPPING

1 tbsp vegetable oil

1 leek, chopped

1 zucchini, grated

1 red bell pepper, seeded and diced

1 green bell pepper, seeded and diced

1 carrot, grated

2 tsp chopped parsley

1 cup full-fat soft cheese

¼ cup grated sharp cheese

2 eggs, beaten

salt and pepper

shredded cooked leek, to garnish

salad, to serve

1 Brush a 8 inch/20 cm springform cake pan with oil.

2 To make the base, heat the oil in a skillet. Cook the potato slices until softened and browned. Drain on paper towels and place in the base of the pan.

3 To make the topping, heat the oil in a separate skillet. Add the leek and fry over a low heat, stirring frequently, for 3–4 minutes, until softened.

4 Add the zucchini, bell peppers, carrot, and parsley to the pan and cook over a low heat for 5–7 minutes, or until the vegetables have softened.

5 Meanwhile, beat the cheeses and eggs together in a bowl. Stir in the vegetables and season to taste with salt and pepper. Spoon the mixture evenly over the potato base.

6 Cook in a preheated oven, 375°F/190°C, for 20–25 minutes, until the cake is set.

7 Remove the vegetable cake from the pan and transfer to a warm serving plate. Garnish with shredded leek and serve with a crisp salad.

Potato Hash

This is a variation of beef hash, which was made with salt beef and leftovers and served to sea-going New Englanders.

NUTRITIONAL INFORMATION

Calories	302	Sugars	.........5g
Protein	........15g	Fat	..........10g
Carbohydrate	...40g	Saturates	.......4g

10 mins   30 mins

SERVES 4

INGREDIENTS

2 tbsp butter

1 red onion, halved and sliced

1 carrot, diced

1 oz/25 g green beans, halved

generous 5 cups diced waxy potatoes

½ cup all-purpose flour

1¼ cups vegetable bouillon

8 oz/225 g bean curd, diced

salt and pepper

chopped fresh parsley, to garnish

1 Melt the butter in a large, heavy-based skillet. Add the onion, carrot, green beans, and potatoes, and cook over a fairly low heat, stirring constantly, for about 5–7 minutes, or until the vegetables begin to turn golden brown.

2 Add the flour to the skillet and cook, stirring constantly, for 1 minute. Gradually pour in the bouillon, stirring constantly.

3 Reduce the heat to low and simmer for 15 minutes, or until the potatoes are tender.

4 Add the diced bean curd to the pan and cook for another 5 minutes. Season to taste with salt and pepper.

5 Sprinkle the chopped parsley over the top of the potato hash to garnish and then serve hot straight from the skillet.

COOK'S TIP

A traditional hash dish is always made from chopped fresh ingredients, such as bell peppers, onion, and celery.

Twice Baked Pesto Potatoes

This is an easy, but very filling meal. The potatoes are baked until fluffy, then mixed with a tasty pesto filling and baked again.

NUTRITIONAL INFORMATION

Calories	444	Sugars	.........3g
Protein	........10g	Fat	..........28g
Carbohydrate	...40g	Saturates	......13g

🕐 10 mins   🕐 1½ hours

SERVES 4

INGREDIENTS

4 baking potatoes

⅔ cup heavy cream

⅓ cup vegetable bouillon

1 tbsp lemon juice

2 garlic cloves, crushed

3 tbsp chopped basil

2 tbsp pine nuts

scant ½ cup freshly grated Parmesan cheese

salt and pepper

1 Scrub the potatoes well and prick the skins with a fork. Rub a little salt into the skins and place on a baking sheet.

2 Cook in a preheated oven, 375°F/190°C, for 1 hour, or until the potatoes are cooked through and the skins are crisp.

3 Remove the potatoes from the oven and cut them in half lengthwise. Using a spoon, scoop the potato flesh into a mixing bowl, leaving a thin shell of potato inside the skins. Mash the potato flesh with a fork.

4 Meanwhile, mix the cream and bouillon in a pan and simmer over a low heat for about 8–10 minutes, or until reduced by half.

5 Stir in the lemon juice, garlic, and chopped basil, and season to taste with salt and pepper. Stir the mixture into the mashed potato flesh, together with the pine nuts.

6 Spoon the mixture back into the potato shells and sprinkle the Parmesan cheese on top. Return the potatoes to the oven for 10 minutes, or until the cheese has browned. Serve.

VARIATION

Add full-fat soft cheese or thinly sliced mushrooms to the mashed potato flesh in step 5, if you prefer.

Pan Potato Cake

This tasty meal is made with sliced potatoes, bean curd, and vegetables cooked in the pan from which it is served.

NUTRITIONAL INFORMATION

Calories 452	Sugars 6g	
Protein 17g	Fat 28g	
Carbohydrate ...35g	Saturates 13g	

15 mins   30 mins

SERVES 4

INGREDIENTS

1½ lb/675 g waxy potatoes, unpeeled and sliced

1 carrot, diced

8 oz/225 g small broccoli florets

5 tbsp butter

2 tbsp vegetable oil

1 red onion, quartered

2 garlic cloves, crushed

6 oz/175 g bean curd, diced

2 tbsp chopped fresh sage

¾ cup grated sharp cheese

1 Cook the sliced potatoes in a large pan of boiling water for 10 minutes. Drain thoroughly.

2 Meanwhile, cook the carrot and broccoli florets in a separate pan of boiling water for 5 minutes. Drain with a slotted spoon.

3 Heat the butter and oil in a 9 inch/ 23 cm skillet. Add the onion and garlic and cook over a low heat for 2–3 minutes. Add half of the potatoes slices to the skillet, covering the base of the skillet.

4 Cover the potato slices with the carrot, broccoli, and the bean curd. Sprinkle with half of the sage and cover with the remaining potato slices. Sprinkle the grated cheese over the top.

5 Cook over a moderate heat for 8–10 minutes. Then place the pan under a preheated medium broiler for 2–3 minutes, or until the cheese melts and browns.

6 Garnish with the remaining sage and serve immediately.

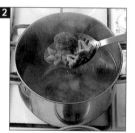

COOK'S TIP

Make sure that the mixture fills the whole width of your skillet to let the layers remain intact.

Cheese & Potato Layer Bake

This is a quick dish to prepare and it can be left to cook in the oven without needing any more attention.

NUTRITIONAL INFORMATION

Calories	766	Sugars	........14g
Protein	........44g	Fat	..........40g
Carbohydrate	...60g	Saturates	......23g

🧊 25 mins   🕐 45 mins

SERVES 4

I N G R E D I E N T S

2 lb/900 g unpeeled waxy potatoes, cut into wedges

2 tbsp butter

1 red onion, halved and sliced

2 garlic cloves, crushed

¼ cup all-purpose flour

2½ cups milk

14 oz/400 g canned artichoke hearts in brine, drained and halved

5½ oz/150 g frozen mixed vegetables, thawed

1¼ cups grated Swiss cheese

1¼ cups grated sharp cheese

½ cup crumbled Gorgonzola

⅓ cup freshly grated Parmesan cheese

8 oz/225 g bean curd, sliced

2 tbsp chopped fresh thyme

salt and pepper

fresh thyme sprigs, to garnish

1 Cook the potato wedges in a pan of boiling water for 10 minutes. Drain thoroughly.

2 Meanwhile, melt the butter in a pan. Add the sliced onion and garlic and cook over a low heat, stirring frequently, for 2–3 minutes.

3 Stir the flour into the pan and cook for 1 minute. Gradually add the milk and bring to a boil, stirring constantly.

4 Reduce the heat and add the artichoke hearts, mixed vegetables, half of each of the 4 cheeses, and the bean curd to the pan, mixing well. Stir in the chopped thyme and season with salt and pepper to taste.

5 Arrange a layer of parboiled potato wedges in the base of a shallow ovenproof dish. Spoon the vegetable mixture over the top and cover with the remaining potato wedges. Sprinkle the rest of the 4 cheeses over the top.

6 Cook in a preheated oven, 400°F/200°C for 30 minutes, or until the potatoes are cooked and the top is golden brown. Serve the bake garnished with fresh thyme sprigs.

Potato & Eggplant Gratin

Similar to a simple moussaka, this recipe is made up of layers of eggplant, tomato, and potato baked with a yogurt topping.

NUTRITIONAL INFORMATION

Calories 409   Sugars 17g
Protein ....28g   Fat 14g
Carbohydrate ...45g   Saturates 3g

25 mins   1¼ hours

SERVES 4

INGREDIENTS

1 lb 2 oz/500 g waxy potatoes, sliced

1 tbsp vegetable oil

1 onion, chopped

2 garlic cloves, crushed

1 lb 2 oz/500 g bean curd, diced

2 tbsp tomato paste

½ cup all-purpose flour

1¼ cups vegetable bouillon

2 large tomatoes, sliced

1 eggplant, sliced

2 tbsp chopped fresh thyme

scant 2 cups unsweetened yogurt

2 eggs, beaten

salt and pepper

salad, to serve

VARIATION

You can use marinated or smoked bean curd for extra flavor, if you wish.

1 Cook the sliced potatoes in a pan of boiling water for 10 minutes, until tender, but not breaking up. Drain and then set aside.

2 Heat the oil in a skillet. Add the onion and garlic and cook, stirring occasionally, for 2–3 minutes.

3 Add the bean curd, tomato paste, and flour, and cook for 1 minute. Gradually stir in the stock and bring to a boil, stirring. Reduce the heat and simmer for 10 minutes.

4 Arrange a layer of the potato slices in the base of a deep ovenproof dish.

Spoon the bean curd mixture evenly on top. Layer the sliced tomatoes, then the eggplant, and finally, the remaining potato slices, on top of the bean curd mixture, making sure that it is completely covered. Sprinkle with thyme.

5 Mix the yogurt and beaten eggs together in a bowl and season to taste with salt and pepper. Spoon the yogurt topping over the sliced potatoes to cover them completely.

6 Bake in a preheated oven, 375°F/190°C, for about 35–45 minutes or until the topping is browned. Serve with a crisp salad.

Spicy Potato & Nut Terrine

This delicious baked terrine has a base of mashed potato which is flavored with nuts, cheese, herbs, and spices.

NUTRITIONAL INFORMATION

Calories . . . . . . .1100 Sugars 13g
Protein . . . . .34g Fat 93g
Carbohydrate . . .31g Saturates 22g

15 mins   1½ hours

SERVES 4

INGREDIENTS

1⅓ cups mealy potatoes, diced

8 oz/225 g pecan nuts

8 oz/225 g unsalted cashew nuts

1 onion, finely chopped

2 garlic cloves, crushed

4½ oz/125 g diced open cup mushrooms

2 tbsp butter

2 tbsp chopped mixed herbs

1 tsp paprika

1 tsp ground cumin

1 tsp ground coriander

4 eggs, beaten

½ cup full-fat soft cheese

⅔ cup freshly grated Parmesan cheese

salt and pepper

SAUCE

3 large tomatoes, peeled, seeded, and chopped

2 tbsp tomato paste

5 tbsp red wine

1 tbsp red wine vinegar

pinch of superfine sugar

1 Lightly grease a 2-lb/1-kg loaf pan and line with baking parchment.

2 Cook the potatoes in a large pan of lightly salted boiling water for 10 minutes, or until cooked through. Drain and mash thoroughly.

3 Finely chop the pecan and cashew nuts or process in a food processor. Mix the nuts with the onion, garlic, and mushrooms. Melt the butter in a skillet and cook the nut mixture for 5–7 minutes. Add the herbs and spices. Stir in the eggs, cheeses, and potatoes, and season to taste with salt and pepper.

4 Spoon the mixture into the prepared loaf pan, pressing down firmly. Cook in a preheated oven, 375°F/190°C, for 1 hour, or until set.

5 To make the sauce, mix the tomatoes, tomato paste, wine, wine vinegar, and sugar in a pan and bring to a boil, stirring. Cook for 10 minutes, or until the tomatoes have reduced. Press the sauce through a strainer or process in a food processor for 30 seconds. Turn the terrine out of the pan on to a serving plate and cut into slices. Serve with the tomato sauce.

Potato & Tomato Calzone

These pizza dough Italian pasties are best served hot with a salad for a delicious lunch or supper dish.

NUTRITIONAL INFORMATION

Calories	524	Sugars	........8g
Protein	........17g	Fat	..........8g
Carbohydrate	..103g	Saturates	......2g

1½ hours   35 mins

SERVES 4

INGREDIENTS

DOUGH

4 cups white bread flour

1 tsp active dry yeast

1¼ cups vegetable bouillon

1 tbsp clear honey

1 tsp caraway seeds

skim milk, for glazing

FILLING

1 tbsp vegetable oil

1⅓ cups diced waxy potatoes

1 onion, halved and sliced

2 garlic cloves, crushed

1½ oz/40 g sun-dried tomatoes

2 tbsp chopped fresh basil

2 tbsp tomato paste

2 celery stalks, sliced

½ cup grated mozzarella cheese

1 To make the dough, sift the flour into a large mixing bowl and stir in the yeast. Make a well in the center of the mixture. Stir in the vegetable bouillon, honey, and caraway seeds, and bring the mixture together to form a dough.

2 Turn the dough out on to a lightly floured counter and knead for 8 minutes until smooth. Place the dough in a lightly oiled mixing bowl, then cover and leave to rise in a warm place for 1 hour or until it has doubled in size.

3 Meanwhile, make the filling. Heat the oil in a skillet and add all the remaining ingredients except for the cheese. Cook for about 5 minutes, stirring.

4 Divide the risen dough into 4 pieces. On a lightly floured counter, roll them out to form four 7 inch/ 18 cm circles. Spoon equal amounts of the filling on to one half of each circle. Sprinkle the cheese over the filling. Brush the edge of the dough with milk and fold the dough over to form 4 semi-circles, pressing to seal the edges.

5 Place on a non-stick baking sheet and brush with milk. Cook in a preheated oven, 425°F/220°C, for 30 minutes until golden and risen.

Potato-Topped Lentil Bake

A wonderful mixture of red lentils, bean curd, and vegetables is cooked beneath a crunchy potato topping for a really hearty meal.

10 mins   1½ hours

SERVES 4

INGREDIENTS

TOPPING

4 cups diced mealy potatoes

2 tbsp butter

1 tbsp milk

½ cup chopped pecan nuts

2 tbsp chopped thyme

thyme sprigs, to garnish

FILLING

1 cup red lentils

5 tbsp cup butter

1 leek, sliced

2 garlic cloves, crushed

1 celery stalk, chopped

4½ oz/125 g broccoli florets

6 oz/175 g smoked bean curd, cubed

2 tsp tomato paste

salt and pepper

1 To make the topping, cook the potatoes in a pan of boiling water for 10–15 minutes, or until cooked through. Drain well. Add the butter and milk and mash thoroughly. Stir in the pecan nuts and chopped thyme and set aside.

2 Cook the lentils in boiling water for 20–30 minutes, or until tender. Drain and set aside.

3 Melt the butter in a skillet. Add the leek, garlic, celery, and broccoli. Cook over a medium heat, stirring frequently, for 5 minutes, until softened. Add the

bean curd cubes. Stir in the lentils, together with the tomato paste. Season with salt and pepper to taste, then turn the mixture into the base of a shallow ovenproof dish.

4 Spoon the mashed potato on top of the lentil mixture, spreading to cover it completely.

5 Cook in a preheated oven, 400°F/ 200°C, for about 30–35 minutes, or until the topping is golden. Garnish with sprigs of fresh thyme and serve hot.

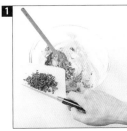

VARIATION

You can use almost any combination of your favorite vegetables in this dish.

Vegetable Pulao

This is a delicious way of cooking rice and vegetables together, and the saffron gives it a beautiful aroma. Serve this with any kabob.

NUTRITIONAL INFORMATION

Calories	557	Sugars	........9g
Protein	........11g	Fat	..........14g
Carbohydrate	..104g	Saturates	.......7g

20 mins   55 mins

SERVES 6

I N G R E D I E N T S

2 potatoes, each cut into 12 pieces

1 eggplant, cut into 6

2 carrots, sliced

1¾ oz/50 g green beans, chopped

4 tbsp vegetable ghee

2 onions, sliced

¾ cup unsweetened yogurt

2 tsp finely chopped fresh ginger root

2 tsp crushed garlic

2 tsp garam masala

2 tsp black cumin seeds

½ tsp turmeric

3 black cardamom pods

3 cinnamon sticks

2 tsp salt

1 tsp chili powder

½ tsp saffron strands

1¼ cups milk

3 cups basmati rice

5 tbsp lemon juice

T O   G A R N I S H

4 green chilies, chopped

cilantro leaves, chopped

1 Prepare the vegetables. Heat the ghee in a skillet. Add the potatoes, eggplant, carrots, and beans and cook, turning frequently, until softened. Remove from the pan and set aside.

2 Add the onions and cook, stirring frequently, until soft. Add the yogurt, ginger, garlic, garam masala, 1 teaspoon black cumin seeds, the turmeric, 1 cardamom pod, 1 cinnamon stick, 1 teaspoon salt, and the chili powder and cook for 3–5 minutes. Return the vegetables to the pan and cook for 4–5 minutes.

3 Put the saffron and milk in a pan and bring to the boil, stirring. Remove from the heat and set aside.

4 In a pan of boiling water, half-cook the rice with 1 teaspoon salt, 2 cinnamon sticks, 2 black cardamom pods, and 1 teaspoon black cumin seeds. Drain the rice, leaving half in the pan, while transferring the other half to a bowl. Pour the vegetable mixture on top of the rice in the pan. Pour half of the lemon juice and half of the saffron milk over the vegetables and rice, then cover with the remaining rice and pour the remaining lemon juice and saffron milk over the top. Garnish with chilies and cilantro, then return to the heat and cover. Cook over a low heat for about 20 minutes. Serve hot.

Vegetable Strudels

These strudels look really impressive and are perfect if friends are coming round or for a more formal dinner party dish.

NUTRITIONAL INFORMATION

Calories .... .485 Sugars 5g
Protein ....16g Fat 27g
Carbohydrate ...47g Saturates 5g

🡒 25 mins   🕐 30 mins

SERVES 4

INGREDIENTS

FILLING

2 tbsp vegetable oil

2 tbsp butter

¾ finely diced cup potatoes

1 leek, shredded

2 garlic cloves, crushed

1 tsp garam masala

½ tsp chili powder

½ tsp turmeric

1¾ oz/50 g okra, sliced

3½ oz/100 g sliced white mushrooms

2 tomatoes, diced

8 oz/225 g firm bean curd, diced

salt and pepper

FILLING

12 oz/350 g phyllo pastry

2 tbsp butter, melted

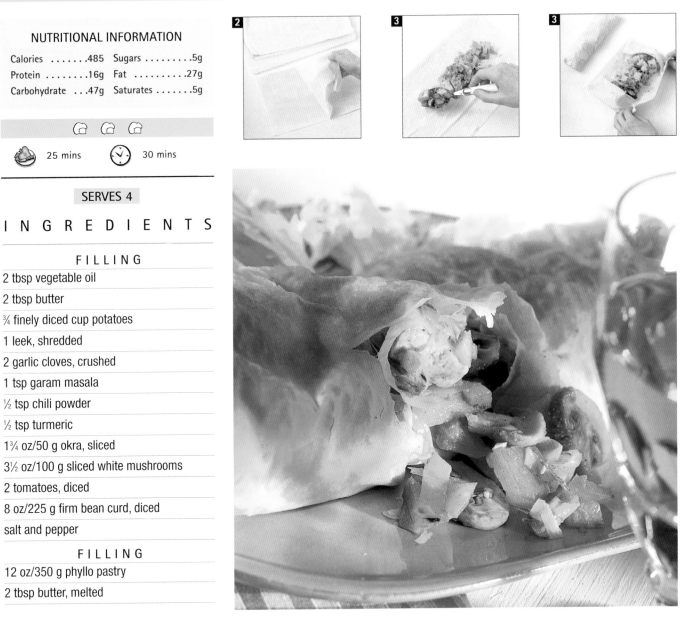

1 To make the filling, heat the oil and butter in a skillet. Add the potatoes and leek and cook, stirring constantly, for 2–3 minutes. Add the garlic and spices, okra, mushrooms, tomatoes, and bean curd, and season to taste with salt and pepper. Cook, stirring, for 5–7 minutes, or until the mixture is tender.

2 Lay the pastry out on a cutting board and brush each individual sheet with melted butter. Place 3 sheets on top of one another; repeat to make 4 stacks.

3 Spoon a quarter of the filling along the center of each stack and brush the edges with melted butter. Fold the short edges in and roll up lengthwise to form a cigar shape. Brush the outside with melted butter. Place the strudels on a greased baking sheet.

4 Cook in a preheated oven, 375°F/190°C, for 20 minutes, or until golden brown and crisp. Transfer to a warm serving dish and serve immediately.

Vegetable Hotpot

In this recipe, a variety of vegetables are cooked under a layer of potatoes, topped with cheese and cooked until golden brown.

NUTRITIONAL INFORMATION

Calories ....279 Sugars 12g
Protein ....10g Fat 11g
Carbohydrate ...34g Saturates 4g

25 mins 1 hour

SERVES 4

INGREDIENTS

1 lb 5 oz/600 g potatoes, thinly sliced

2 tbsp vegetable oil

1 red onion, halved and sliced

1 leek, sliced

2 garlic cloves, crushed

1 carrot, cut into chunks

3½ oz/100 g broccoli florets

3½ oz/100 g cauliflower florets

2 small turnips, quartered

¼ cup all-purpose flour

3 cups vegetable bouillon

⅔ cup dry hard cider

1 eating apple, cored and sliced

2 tbsp chopped sage

pinch of cayenne pepper

½ cup grated Cheddar cheese

salt and pepper

1 Cook the potato slices in a pan of boiling water for 10 minutes. Drain thoroughly and reserve.

2 Heat the oil in a flameproof casserole. Add the onion, leek, and garlic, and sauté, stirring occasionally, for 2–3 minutes. Add the remaining vegetables and cook, stirring constantly, for a further 3–4 minutes.

3 Stir in the flour and cook for 1 minute. Gradually add the stock and hard cider and bring to a boil. Add the apple, sage, and cayenne pepper, and season well. Remove from the heat and transfer the vegetables to an ovenproof dish.

4 Arrange the potato slices on top of the vegetable mixture to cover.

5 Sprinkle the cheese on top of the potato slices and cook in a preheated oven, 375°F/190°C, for 30–35 minutes or until the potato is golden brown and beginning to go crisp around the edges. Serve immediately.

Vegetable Biryani

The Biryani originated in the North of India, and was a dish reserved for festivals. The vegetables are marinated in a yogurt-based marinade.

NUTRITIONAL INFORMATION

Calories ....449 Sugars 18g

Protein ....12g Fat 12g

Carbohydrate ...79g Saturates 6g

2¼ hours   1 hr 5 mins

SERVES 4

INGREDIENTS

10½ oz/300 g potato, cubed

3½ oz/100 g baby carrots

1¾ oz/50 g okra, thickly sliced

2 celery stalks, sliced

2¾ oz/75 g baby white mushrooms, halved

1 eggplant, halved and sliced

1¼ cups unsweetened yogurt

1 tbsp grated fresh ginger root

2 large onions, grated

4 garlic cloves, crushed

1 tsp turmeric

1 tbsp curry powder

2 tbsp butter

2 onions, sliced

1¼ cups basmati rice

chopped fresh cilantro, to garnish

1 Cook the potato cubes, carrots, and okra in a pan of boiling salted water for 7–8 minutes. Drain well and place in a large bowl. Mix with the celery, mushrooms, and eggplant.

2 Mix the unsweetened yogurt, ginger, grated onions, garlic, turmeric, and curry powder, and spoon over the vegetables. Set aside in a cool place to marinate for at least 2 hours.

3 Heat the butter in a heavy-based skillet. Add the sliced onions and cook over a medium heat for 5–6 minutes, until golden brown. Remove a few onions from the pan and reserve for the garnish.

4 Cook the rice in a large pan of boiling water for 7 minutes. Drain thoroughly and set aside.

5 Add the marinated vegetables to the onions and cook for 10 minutes.

6 Put half of the rice in a 8¾ cup/2 liter casserole dish. Spoon the vegetables on top and cover with the remaining rice. Cover and cook in a preheated oven, 375°F/190°C, for 20–25 minutes, or until the rice is tender.

7 Spoon the biryani on to a serving plate. Garnish with the reserved onions and cilantro and serve.

Cauliflower Bake

The red of the tomatoes is a great contrast to the cauliflower and herbs, making this dish appealing to both the eye and the palate.

NUTRITIONAL INFORMATION

Calories 305   Sugars 9g
Protein . . . . .15g   Fat 14g
Carbohydrate . . .31g   Saturates 6g

10 mins   40 mins

SERVES 4

INGREDIENTS

1 lb 2 oz/500 g cauliflower florets

1 lb 5 oz/600 g potatoes, cubed

3½ oz/100 g cherry tomatoes

SAUCE

2 tbsp butter or margarine

1 leek, sliced

1 garlic clove, crushed

1 oz/25 g plain all-purpose flour

1¼ cups milk

¾ cup mixed grated cheese, such as
    Cheddar, Parmesan, and Swiss cheese

½ tsp paprika

2 tbsp chopped fresh flatleaf parsley

salt and pepper

chopped fresh parsley, to garnish

1 Cook the cauliflower in a pan of boiling water for 10 minutes. Drain well and reserve. Meanwhile, cook the potatoes in a pan of boiling water for 10 minutes, drain and reserve.

2 To make the sauce, melt the butter or margarine in a pan and sauté the leek and garlic for 1 minute. Stir in the flour and cook, stirring constantly, for 1 minute. Remove the pan from the heat and gradually stir in the milk, ½ cup of the cheese, the paprika, and the parsley. Return the pan to the heat and bring to a boil, stirring constantly. Season with salt and pepper to taste.

3 Spoon the cauliflower into a deep ovenproof dish. Add the cherry tomatoes and top with the potatoes. Pour the sauce over the potatoes and sprinkle on the remaining cheese.

4 Cook in a preheated oven, 350°F/180°C, for 20 minutes, or until the vegetables are cooked through and the cheese is golden brown and bubbling. Garnish and serve immediately.

VARIATION

This dish could be made with broccoli instead of the cauliflower as an alternative.

Gnocchi & Tomato Sauce

Freshly made potato gnocchi are delicious, especially when they are topped with a fragrant tomato sauce.

NUTRITIONAL INFORMATION

Calories 216	Sugars 5g	
Protein 5g	Fat 6g	
Carbohydrate . . .39g	Saturates 1g	

30 mins

45 mins

SERVES 4

INGREDIENTS

12 oz/350 g mealy potatoes, halved

scant 3 cups self-rising flour, plus extra for rolling out

2 tsp dried oregano

2 tbsp oil

1 large onion, chopped

2 garlic cloves, chopped

14 oz/400 g canned chopped tomatoes

½ vegetable bouillon cube dissolved in generous ⅓ cup boiling water

2 tbsp basil, shredded, plus whole leaves to garnish

salt and pepper

Parmesan cheese, freshly grated, to serve

1 Bring a large saucepan of water to a boil. Add the potatoes and cook for 12–15 minutes or until tender. Drain and let cool.

2 Peel and then mash the potatoes with the salt and pepper, sifted flour, and oregano. Mix together with your hands to form a dough.

3 Heat the oil in a pan. Add the onions and garlic and cook for 3–4 minutes.

Add the tomatoes and stock and cook, uncovered, for 10 minutes. Season with salt and pepper to taste.

4 Roll the potato dough into a sausage about 1 inch/2.5 cm in diameter. Cut the sausage into 1 inch/2.5 cm lengths. Flour your hands, then press a fork into each piece to create a series of ridges on one side and the indent of your index finger on the other.

5 Bring a large pan of water to the boil and cook the gnocchi, in batches, for 2–3 minutes. They should rise to the surface when cooked. Drain well and keep warm.

6 Stir the basil into the tomato sauce and pour over the gnocchi. Garnish with basil leaves and season with pepper to taste. Sprinkle with Parmesan and serve at once.

VARIATION

The gnocchi can also be served with a Pesto Sauce made from fresh basil leaves, pine nuts, garlic, olive oil, and pecorino or Parmesan cheese.

Fish Dishes

There is no denying that fish and potatoes are a terrific combination. In these recipes potatoes are used in a variety of ways to enhance the fish. They are used to form a crispy coating for cod, and mashed to make the basis of fishcakes and fritters. They are sliced to form part of a

layered pie, and sautéed with shallots to create the perfect accompaniment to a red mullet wrapped in prosciutto. These recipes also include some interesting flavors from France, such as Cotriade, a satisfying stew of fish and vegetables flavored with herbs. For health-conscious cooks, the nutritious value of these delicious dishes is unbeatable.

Fishcakes & Piquant Sauce

The combination of pink- and white-fleshed fish, with a tasty tomato sauce, transforms the humble fish into something special.

NUTRITIONAL INFORMATION

Calories	334	Sugars	.........7g
Protein	........31g	Fat	...........7g
Carbohydrate	...37g	Saturates	......1g

🍧 2 hours   🕐 55 mins

SERVES 4

INGREDIENTS

2 ⅔ cups diced potatoes

8 oz/225 g trout fillet

8 oz/225 g haddock fillet

1 bay leaf

1¾ cups fish bouillon

2 tbsp lowfat unsweetened yogurt

4 tbsp snipped fresh chives

½ cup dry white bread crumbs

1 tbsp sunflower oil

salt and pepper

snipped freshly chives, to garnish

lemon wedges and salad leaves,
    to serve

PIQUANT TOMATO SAUCE

¾ cup strained tomatoes

4 tbsp dry white wine

4 tbsp lowfat unsweetened yogurt

chili powder

1 Place the potatoes in a pan and cover with water. Bring to a boil and cook for about 10 minutes or until the potatoes are tender. Drain thoroughly and then mash well.

2 Meanwhile, place the fish in a pan with the bay leaf and fish bouillon. Bring to a boil and simmer for 7–8 minutes until tender.

3 Remove the fish with a slotted spoon and flake the flesh away from the skin. Gently mix the cooked fish with the potato, unsweetened yogurt, chives, and seasoning. Let cool, then cover and leave to chill for 1 hour.

4 Sprinkle the bread crumbs on to a plate. Divide the fish mixture into 8 and form each portion into a patty, about 3 inches/7.5 cm in diameter. Press each fish cake into the bread crumbs, coating all over.

5 Brush a skillet with oil and cook the fish cakes for 6 minutes. Turn the fish cakes over and cook for another 5–6 minutes until golden. Drain on paper towels and keep warm.

6 To make the sauce, heat the strained tomatoes and wine. Season, remove from the heat and stir in the yogurt. Return briefly to the heat, then transfer to a small serving bowl and sprinkle with chili powder. Garnish the fish cakes with chives and serve with lemon wedges, salad leaves, and the sauce.

Potato-Topped Cod

This simple dish has a spicy bread crumb mixture topping layers of cod and potatoes. It is cooked in the oven until crisp and golden.

NUTRITIONAL INFORMATION

Calories	118	Sugars	.......1.0g
Protein	........9.8g	Fat	..........4.4g
Carbohydrate	..10.5g	Saturates	.....2.6g

5–10 mins

35 mins

SERVES 4

INGREDIENTS

5 tbsp butter

4 waxy potatoes, sliced

1 large onion, finely chopped

1 tsp whole-grain mustard

1 tsp garam masala

pinch of chili powder

1 tbsp chopped fresh dill

1¼ cups fresh bread crumbs

1 lb 9 oz/700 g cod fillets

½ cup grated Swiss cheese

salt and pepper

fresh dill sprigs, to garnish

1 Melt half of the butter in a skillet. Add the potatoes and cook for 5 minutes, turning until they are browned all over. Remove the potatoes from the pan with a perforated spoon.

2 Add the remaining butter to the skillet and stir in the onion, mustard, garam masala, chili powder, chopped dill, and bread crumbs. Cook for 1–2 minutes, stirring and mixing well.

3 Layer half of the potatoes in the base of an ovenproof dish and place the cod fillets on top. Cover the cod fillets with the rest of the potato slices. Season to taste with salt and pepper.

4 Spoon the spicy mixture from the skillet over the potato and sprinkle with the grated cheese.

5 Cook in a preheated oven, 400°F/200°C, for 20–25 minutes or until the topping is golden and crisp and the fish is cooked through. Garnish with fresh dill sprigs and serve at once.

COOK'S TIP

This dish is ideal served with baked vegetables which can be cooked in the oven at the same time.

Layered Fish & Potato Pie

This is a really delicious and filling dish. Layers of potato slices and mixed fish are cooked in a creamy sauce and topped with grated cheese.

NUTRITIONAL INFORMATION

Calories	116	Sugars	.......1.9g
Protein	.......6.2g	Fat	.........6.1g
Carbohydrate	...9.7g	Saturates	.....3.8g

5 mins   55 mins

SERVES 4

I N G R E D I E N T S

2 lb/900 g waxy potatoes, sliced

5 tbsp butter

1 red onion, halved and sliced

⅓ cup all-purpose flour

2 cups milk

⅔ cup heavy cream

8 oz/225 g smoked haddock fillet, cubed

8 oz/225 g cod fillet, cubed

1 red bell pepper, diced

4½ oz/125 g broccoli florets

scant ⅔ cup Parmesan cheese,
    freshly grated

salt and pepper

1 Cook the sliced potatoes in a pan of boiling water for 10 minutes. Drain and set aside.

2 Meanwhile, melt the butter in a pan, then add the onion and cook gently for 3–4 minutes.

3 Add the flour and cook for 1 minute. Blend in the milk and cream and bring to a boil, stirring until the sauce has thickened.

4 Arrange half of the potato slices in the base of a shallow ovenproof dish.

5 Add the fish, diced bell pepper, and broccoli to the sauce and cook over a low heat for 10 minutes. Season with salt and pepper, then spoon the mixture over the potatoes in the dish.

6 Arrange the remaining potato slices in a layer over the fish mixture. Sprinkle the Parmesan cheese over the top.

7 Cook in a preheated oven, 350°F/180°C, for 30 minutes or until the potatoes are cooked and the top is golden.

COOK'S TIP

Choose your favorite combination of fish, adding salmon or various shellfish for special occasions.

Tuna & Cheese Quiche

The base for this quiche is made from mashed potato instead of pastry, giving a softer textured shell for the tasty tuna filling.

NUTRITIONAL INFORMATION

Calories	383	Sugars	.........5g
Protein	........25g	Fat	..........15g
Carbohydrate	...40g	Saturates	......6g

20 mins   1 hour

SERVES 4

I N G R E D I E N T S

SHELL

2 ⅔ cups diced mealy potatoes

2 tbsp butter

6 tbsp all-purpose flour

FILLING

1 tbsp vegetable oil

1 shallot, chopped

1 garlic clove, crushed

1 red bell pepper, diced

6 oz/175g canned tuna in brine, drained

1¾ oz/50 g canned corn, drained

⅔ cup skim milk

3 eggs, beaten

1 tbsp chopped fresh dill

½ cup grated sharp low-fat cheese

salt and pepper

TO GARNISH

fresh dill sprigs

lemon wedges

1 Cook the potatoes in a pan of boiling water for 10 minutes or until tender. Drain and mash the potatoes. Add the butter and flour and mix to form a dough.

2 Knead the potato dough on a floured counter and press the mixture into a 8-in/20-cm flan pan. Prick the base with a fork. Line with baking parchment and baking beans and bake blind in a preheated oven, 400°F/200°C, for 20 minutes.

3 Heat the oil in a skillet, add the shallot, garlic, and bell pepper and cook gently for 5 minutes. Drain well and spoon the mixture into the flan shell. Flake the tuna and arrange it over the top with the corn.

4 In a bowl, mix the milk, eggs, and chopped dill, and season.

5 Pour the egg and dill mixture into the flan shell and sprinkle the grated cheese on top.

6 Bake in the oven for 20 minutes or until the filling has set. Garnish the flan with fresh dill and lemon wedges. Serve with mixed vegetables or salad.

Fish & Potato Pie

This flavorsome and colorful fish pie is perfect for a light supper. The addition of smoked salmon gives it a touch of luxury.

NUTRITIONAL INFORMATION

Calories	523	Sugars	........15g
Protein	........58g	Fat	...........6g
Carbohydrate	...63g	Saturates	......2g

15 mins   1 hr

SERVES 4

INGREDIENTS

2 lb/900 g smoked haddock or cod fillets

scant 2½ cups skim milk

2 bay leaves

4 oz/115 g white mushrooms, quartered

4 oz/115 g frozen peas

4 oz/115 g frozen corn

1½ lb/675 g potatoes, diced

5 tbsp lowfat natural yogurt

4 tbsp chopped fresh parsley

2 oz/55 g smoked salmon, sliced into thin strips

3 tbsp cornstarch

1 oz/25 g smoked cheese, grated

salt and pepper

1 Preheat the oven to 400°F/200°C. Place the fish in a pan and add the milk and bay leaves. Bring to the boil, cover, and then simmer for 5 minutes.

2 Add the mushrooms, peas, and corn, bring back to a simmer, cover, and cook for 5–7 minutes. Let cool.

3 Place the potatoes in a pan, cover with water, bring to a boil, then cook for 8 minutes. Drain well and mash with a fork or a potato masher. Stir in the yogurt, parsley, and seasoning. Set aside.

4 Using a slotted spoon, remove the fish from the pan. Flake the cooked fish away from the skin and place in an ovenproof gratin dish. Reserve the cooking liquid.

5 Drain the vegetables, reserving the cooking liquid, and gently stir into the fish with the salmon strips.

6 Blend a little cooking liquid into the cornstarch to make a paste. Transfer the rest of the liquid to a pan and add the paste. Heat through, stirring, until thickened. Discard the bay leaves and season to taste. Pour the sauce over the fish and vegetables and mix. Cover the fish with the mashed potato, sprinkle with cheese, and bake for 25–30 minutes.

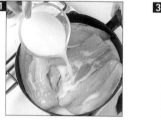

COOK'S TIP

If possible, use smoked haddock or cod that has not been dyed bright yellow or artificially flavored to give the illusion of having been smoked.

Salt Cod Fritters

These tasty little fried fishcakes make an excellent snack or main course. Prepare in advance because the salt cod needs to be soaked overnight.

NUTRITIONAL INFORMATION

Calories	300	Sugars	.........1g
Protein	........16g	Fat	..........22g
Carbohydrate	....11g	Saturates	.......3g

30 mins, plus 48 hrs soaking time

45 mins

SERVES 6

INGREDIENTS

1 lb/450 g salt cod

12 oz/350 g mealy baking potatoes

olive oil, for deep-frying

1 onion, very finely chopped

1 garlic clove, crushed

4 tbsp very finely chopped fresh parsley or cilantro

1 tbsp capers in brine, drained and finely chopped (optional)

1 small egg, lightly beaten

salt and pepper

aïoli, to serve

1 tbsp chopped fresh parsley, to garnish

1 Break the salt cod into pieces and place in a bowl. Add enough water to cover and let stand for 48 hours, changing the water four times.

2 Drain the salt cod, then cook in boiling water for 20-25 minutes until tender. Drain, then remove all the skin and bones. Using a fork, flake the fish into fine pieces that still retain some texture.

3 Meanwhile, boil the potatoes in their skins until tender. Drain, peel, then mash in a large bowl. Set aside.

4 Heat 1 tablespoon of the oil in a skillet. Add the onion and garlic and fry for 5 minutes, stirring, until tender but not brown. Remove with a slotted spoon and drain on kitchen paper.

5 Stir the salt cod, onion, and garlic into the mashed potatoes. Stir in the parsley or cilantro, and the capers if using. Season generously with pepper.

6 Stir in the beaten egg. Cover with plastic wrap and chill for 30 minutes, then adjust the seasoning.

7 Heat 2 inches/5 cm oil in a skillet to 350–375°F/180°–190°C, or until a cube of bread browns in 30 seconds. Drop tablespoonfuls of the salt-cod mixture into the hot oil and cook for about 8 minutes or until golden brown and set. Do not fry more than six at a time because the oil will become too cold and the fritters will become soggy. You will get 18-20 fritters.

8 Drain the fritters on paper towels. Serve at once with aïoli for dipping. Garnish with parsley.

Cotriade

This is a rich French stew flavored with saffron and herbs. Traditionally, the fish and vegetables, and the soup, are served separately.

NUTRITIONAL INFORMATION

Calories . . . . .81 Sugars 0.9g
Protein . . . . .7.4g Fat 3.9g
Carbohydrate . . .3.8g Saturates 1.1g

15 mins   40 mins

SERVES 6

INGREDIENTS

large pinch saffron

2½ cups hot fish bouillon

1 tbsp olive oil

2 tbsp butter

1 onion, sliced

2 garlic cloves, chopped

1 leek, sliced

1 small fennel bulb, finely sliced

1 lb/450 g potatoes, cut into chunks

⅔ cup dry white wine

1 tbsp fresh thyme leaves

2 bay leaves

4 ripe tomatoes, skinned and chopped

2 lb/900 g mixed fish such as haddock, hake, mackerel, or red or gray mullet, roughly chopped

2 tbsp chopped fresh parsley

salt and pepper

crusty bread, to serve

1 Using a mortar and pestle, crush the saffron and add to the fish bouillon. Stir and let infuse for at least 10 minutes.

2 In a large pan, heat the oil and butter together. Add the onion and cook gently for 4–5 minutes until softened. Add the garlic, leek, fennel, and potatoes. Cover and cook for an additional 10–15 minutes until the vegetables are softened.

3 Add the wine and simmer rapidly for 3–4 minutes until reduced by half. Add the thyme, bay leaves, and tomatoes and stir well. Add the saffron-infused fish bouillon. Bring to a boil, then cover and simmer gently for 15 minutes until the vegetables are tender.

4 Add the fish, then return to a boil and simmer for another 3–4 minutes until all the fish is tender. Add the parsley and season to taste. Using a slotted spoon, remove the fish and vegetables to a warmed serving dish. Serve the soup with plenty of crusty bread.

VARIATION

Once the fish and vegetables have been cooked, you could process the soup and pass it through a strainer to give a smooth fish soup.

Broiled Red Mullet

Try to get small red mullet for this dish. If you can only get larger fish, serve one to each person and increase the cooking time accordingly.

NUTRITIONAL INFORMATION

Calories 111   Sugars 0.8g
Protein . . . . . . .10.2g   Fat 5.4g
Carbohydrate . . .5.9g   Saturates 0.7g

🔒 🔒 🔒

🧊 10 mins   ⏱ 20 mins

SERVES 4

I N G R E D I E N T S

1 lemon, thinly sliced

2 garlic cloves, crushed

4 sprigs fresh flatleaf parsley

4 sprigs fresh thyme

8 leaves fresh sage

2 large shallots, sliced

8 small red mullet, cleaned

8 slices prosciutto

salt and pepper

4 tbsp olive oil

generous 5 cups diced potatoes

8 whole garlic cloves, unpeeled

12 small whole shallots

FOR THE DRESSING

4 tbsp olive oil

1 tbsp lemon juice

1 tbsp chopped fresh flatleaf parsley

1 tbsp chopped fresh chives

salt and pepper

1 For the sauté potatoes and shallots, heat the olive oil in a large skillet and add the potatoes, garlic cloves, and shallots. Cook gently, stirring regularly, for about 12–15 minutes until golden, crisp, and tender.

2 Meanwhile, divide the lemon slices, halved if necessary, garlic, parsley, thyme, sage, and shallots between the cavities of the fish. Season well. Wrap a slice of prosciutto around each fish. Secure with a toothpick.

3 Arrange the fish on a broiler pan and cook under a preheated hot broiler for 5–6 minutes on each side until tender.

4 To make the dressing, mix together the oil and lemon juice with the finely chopped parsley and chives. Season to taste with salt and pepper.

5 Divide the potatoes and shallots between 4 serving plates and top each with the fish. Drizzle around the dressing and serve immediately.

Poached Rainbow Trout

This colorful, flavorsome dish is served cold, and therefore makes a lovely summer lunch or supper dish.

NUTRITIONAL INFORMATION

Calories 99   Sugars 1.1g
Protein ....5.7g   Fat 6.3g
Carbohydrate ...3.7g   Saturates 1.0g

🦪 🦪 🦪

🧊 20 mins   🕐 1 hr 15 mins

SERVES 4

I N G R E D I E N T S

3 lb/1.3 kg rainbow trout fillet, cleaned

1 lb 9 oz/700 g new potatoes

3 scallions, finely chopped

1 egg, hard-cooked and chopped

C O U R T - B O U I L L O N

3½ cups cold water

3½ cups dry white wine

3 tbsp white wine vinegar

2 large carrots, roughly chopped

1 onion, roughly chopped

2 celery stalks, roughly chopped

2 leeks, roughly chopped

2 garlic cloves, roughly chopped

2 fresh bay leaves

4 sprigs fresh parsley

4 sprigs fresh thyme

6 black peppercorns

1 tsp salt

W A T E R C R E S S   M A Y O N N A I S E

1 egg yolk

1 tsp Dijon mustard

1 tsp white wine vinegar

1¾ oz/50 g watercress leaves, chopped

1 cup light olive oil

salt and pepper

1 First make the court-bouillon. Place all the ingredients in a large pan and bring slowly to a boil. Cover and simmer gently for about 30 minutes. Strain the liquid through a fine strainer into a clean pan. Bring to a boil again and simmer fast, uncovered, for 15–20 minutes until the court-bouillon is reduced to 2½ cups.

2 Place the trout in a large skillet. Add the court-bouillon and bring slowly to a boil. Remove from the heat and let the fish in the poaching liquid go cold.

3 Meanwhile, make the watercress mayonnaise. Put the egg yolk, mustard, wine vinegar, watercress, and seasoning into a food processor or blender and blend for 30 seconds until foaming. Begin adding the olive oil, drop by drop, until the mixture begins to thicken. Continue adding the oil in a slow steady stream until it is all incorporated. Add a little hot water if the mixture seems too thick. Season to taste and set aside.

4 Cook the potatoes in plenty of boiling salted water for 12–15 minutes until soft and tender. Drain well and refresh them under cold running water. Set the potatoes aside until cold.

5 When the potatoes are cold, cut them in half if they are very large, and toss thoroughly with the watercress mayonnaise, finely chopped scallions, and hard-cooked egg.

6 Carefully lift the fish from the poaching liquid and drain on paper towels. Carefully pull the skin away from each of the trout and serve immediately with the potato salad.

Smoked Fish Pie

This is a classic fish pie with smoked fish, shrimp, and vegetables, in a cheese sauce, with a more unusual grated potato topping.

NUTRITIONAL INFORMATION

Calories 562	Sugars 9g
Protein 42g	Fat 29g
Carbohydrate ...35g	Saturates 16g

🥔 10 mins   🕐 1 hr 30 mins

SERVES 6

I N G R E D I E N T S

2 tbsp olive oil

1 onion, finely chopped

1 leek, thinly sliced

1 carrot, diced

1 celery stalk, diced

½ cup white mushrooms, halved

grated zest 1 lemon

12 oz/350 g skinless, boneless smoked cod or haddock fillet, cubed

12 oz/375 g skinless, boneless white fish such as haddock, hake, or monkfish, cubed

8 oz/225 g cooked, shelled shrimp

2 tbsp chopped fresh parsley

1 tbsp chopped fresh dill

S A U C E

4 tbsp butter

4 tbsp all-purpose flour

1 tsp mustard powder

2½ cups milk

generous ¾ cup Swiss cheese

T O P P I N G

1½ lb/65 g potatoes, unpeeled

4 tbsp butter, melted

¼ cup grated Swiss cheese

salt and pepper

1 For the sauce, heat the butter in a large pan and when melted, add the flour and mustard powder. Stir until smooth and cook over a very low heat for 2 minutes without coloring. Slowly beat in the milk until smooth. Simmer gently for 2 minutes then stir in the cheese until smooth. Remove from the heat and put some plastic wrap over the surface of the sauce to prevent a skin forming. Set aside.

2 Meanwhile, for the topping, boil the whole potatoes in plenty of salted water for 15 minutes. Drain well and let stand until cool enough to handle.

3 Heat the olive oil in a clean pan and add the onion. Cook for 5 minutes until softened. Add the leek, carrot, celery, and mushrooms, and cook for a further 10 minutes until the vegetables have softened. Stir in the lemon zest and cook briefly.

4 Add the softened vegetables with the fish, shrimp, parsley, and dill to the sauce. Season with salt and pepper and transfer to a greased 7½-cup baking dish.

5 Peel the cooled potatoes and grate coarsely. Mix with the melted butter. Cover the filling with the grated potato and sprinkle with the grated Swiss cheese.

6 Cover loosely with aluminum foil and bake in a preheated oven at 400°F/200°C for 30 minutes. Remove the foil and bake another 30 minutes until the topping is tender and golden and the filling is bubbling. Serve immediately with your favorite selection of vegetables.

Herring & Potato Pie

The combination of herrings, apples, and potatoes is popular throughout northern Europe. In salads, beets are often added.

NUTRITIONAL INFORMATION

Calories ....574 Sugars 10g
Protein ....17g Fat 36g
Carbohydrate ...48g Saturates 19g

15–20 mins   1 hr 5 mins

SERVES 4

INGREDIENTS

1 tbsp Dijon mustard

½ cup butter, softened

1 lb/450 g herrings, filleted

1 lb 10 oz/750 g potatoes

2 cooking apples, thinly sliced

1 large onion, sliced

1 tsp chopped fresh sage

2½ cups hot fish bouillon

1 cup crustless ciabatta bread crumbs

salt and pepper

parsley sprigs, to garnish

1 Mix the mustard with a quarter of the butter until smooth. Spread this mixture over the cut sides of the herring fillets. Season and roll up the fillets. Set aside. Generously grease a 8-cup/2-liter pie pan with some of the remaining butter.

2 Thinly slice the potatoes, using a mandoline if possible. Blanch for 3 minutes in plenty of boiling, salted water until just tender. Drain well, then refresh under cold water and pat dry.

3 Heat a third of the remaining butter in a skillet and add the onion. Cook gently for 8–10 minutes until softened but not colored. Remove from the heat and set aside.

4 Put half the potato slices into the bottom of the pie dish with some seasoning, then add half the apple and half the onion. Put the herring fillets on top of the onion and sprinkle with the sage. Repeat the layers in reverse order, ending with potato. Season well and add enough hot bouillon to come halfway up the sides of the dish.

5 Melt the remaining butter and stir in the bread crumbs until well combined. Sprinkle the bread crumbs over the pie. Bake in a preheated oven, at 375°F/190°C for 40–50 minutes until the bread crumbs are golden and the herrings are cooked through. Serve garnished with parsley.

VARIATION

If herrings are unavailable, substitute mackerel or sardines.

Luxury Fish Pie

This is a fish pie for impressing the guests! Try piping the potato topping decoratively over the pie—it looks marvelous when baked.

NUTRITIONAL INFORMATION

Calories 863	Sugars 5g
Protein 66g	Fat 41g
Carbohydrate . . .60g	Saturates 24g

10 mins   1 hr 10 mins

SERVES 4

INGREDIENTS

½ cup butter

3 shallots, finely chopped

4 oz/115 g white mushrooms, halved

2 tbsp dry white wine

2 lb/900 g live mussels, scrubbed and bearded

1 quantity court-bouillon (see Poached Rainbow Trout, page 210)

10½ oz/300 g monkfish fillet, cubed

10½ oz/300 g skinless cod fillet, cubed

10½ oz/300 g skinless lemon sole fillet, cubed

4 oz/115 g jumbo shrimp, peeled

2½ tbsp all-purpose flour

3 tbsp heavy cream

POTATO TOPPING

3 lb 5oz/1.5 kg mealy potatoes, cut into chunks

4 tbsp butter

2 egg yolks

½ cup milk

pinch freshly grated nutmeg

salt and pepper

fresh parsley, to garnish

1 For the filling, melt a third of the butter in a skillet. Add the shallots and cook for 5 minutes until softened. Add the mushrooms and cook over a high heat for 2 minutes. Add the wine and simmer until the liquid has evaporated. Transfer to a 6¼-cup shallow ovenproof dish and then set aside.

2 Put the mussels into a large pan with just the water clinging to their shells and cook, covered, over a high heat for 3–4 minutes, until all the mussels have opened. Discard any that remain closed. Drain, reserving the cooking liquid. When cool enough to handle, remove the mussels from their shells and add to the mushrooms.

3 Bring the court-bouillon to a boil and add the monkfish. Poach gently for 2 minutes before adding the cod, sole, and shrimp. Poach for another 2 minutes. Remove the fish with a slotted spoon and add to the mussels and mushrooms.

4 Melt the remaining butter in a pan and add the flour. Stir until smooth and cook for 2 minutes without coloring.

Gradually, stir in the hot court-bouillon and mussel cooking liquid until smooth and thickened. Add the cream and simmer gently for 15 minutes, stirring. Season to taste and pour over the fish.

5 Meanwhile, make the topping. Boil the potatoes in plenty of salted water for 15–20 minutes until tender. Drain well and mash with the butter, egg yolks, milk, nutmeg, and seasoning. Pipe over the fish, or spread with a palette knife, and roughen the surface of the topping with a fork.

6 Bake the finished fish pie in a preheated oven at 400°F/200°C for 30 minutes until golden and bubbling. Serve straight from the oven, piping hot with a garnish of fresh parsley.

Poultry & Meat

This chapter contains a wide selection of delicious entrées.

The potato is the main ingredient in the majority of these

recipes, but there are also ideas for adding meat, poultry,

fish, and vegetables as the main

ingredients, so that there is sure to be

something for everyone. The recipes

come from all around the world—try

Potato Ravioli or Potato and Lamb Kofta, There are also

hearty dishes including Creamy Chicken and Potato

Casserole, and Lamb Hotpot. Whatever

the occasion, you are sure to find

something here to entice you.

Baked Chicken & Fries

Traditionally, this dish is deep-fried, but the lowfat version is just as mouthwatering. Serve with chunky potato wedge chips.

NUTRITIONAL INFORMATION

Calories	361	Sugars	........2g
Protein	........24g	Fat	..........8g
Carbohydrate	...51g	Saturates	......2g

10 mins   35 mins

SERVES 4

INGREDIENTS

4 small baking potatoes

1 tbsp sunflower oil

2 tsp coarse sea salt

2 tbsp all-purpose flour

pinch of cayenne pepper

½ tsp paprika pepper

½ tsp dried thyme

8 chicken drumsticks, skin removed

1 egg, beaten

2 tbsp cold water

1 cup dry white bread crumbs

salt and pepper

lowfat coleslaw salad and corn relish,
   to serve

1 Preheat the oven to 400°F/200°C. Wash and scrub the potatoes and cut each into 8 equal portions. Place in a clean plastic bag and add the oil. Seal and shake well to coat.

2 Arrange the potato wedges, skin side down, on a non-stick baking sheet. Sprinkle over the sea salt and bake in the oven for 30–35 minutes until they are tender and golden.

3 Meanwhile, mix the flour, spices, thyme, and seasoning together on a plate. Press the chicken drumsticks into the seasoned flour to lightly coat.

4 On one plate mix together the egg and water. On another plate sprinkle the bread crumbs. Dip the chicken drumsticks first in the egg and then in the bread crumbs. Place on a non-stick baking sheet.

5 Bake the chicken drumsticks alongside the potato wedges for 30 minutes, turning after 15 minutes, until both potatoes and chicken are tender and cooked through.

6 Drain the potato wedges thoroughly on paper towels to remove any excess fat. Serve with the chicken, accompanied with lowfat coleslaw and corn relish.

Chicken & Banana Cakes

Potato cakes are usually served plain. Here the potatoes are combined with ground chicken and mashed banana for a fruity main course.

NUTRITIONAL INFORMATION

Calories 439   Sugars 11g
Protein . . . . .22g   Fat 23g
Carbohydrate . . .39g   Saturates 10g

5–10 mins   25–30 mins

SERVES 4

INGREDIENTS

2⅔ cups diced mealy potatoes

8 oz/225 g ground chicken

1 large banana

2 tbsp all-purpose flour

1 tsp lemon juice

1 onion, finely chopped

2 tbsp chopped fresh sage

2 tbsp butter

2 tbsp vegetable oil

⅔ cup light cream

⅔ cup chicken bouillon

salt and pepper

fresh sage leaves, to garnish

1 Cook the diced potatoes in a pan of boiling water for 10 minutes until cooked through. Drain and mash the potatoes until they are smooth. Stir in the chicken.

2 Mash the banana and add it to the potato with the flour, lemon juice, onion, and half of the chopped sage. Season well and stir the mixture together.

3 Divide the mixture into 8 equal portions. With lightly floured hands, shape each portion into a round patty.

4 Heat the butter and oil in a skillet. Add the potato cakes and cook for 12–15 minutes or until cooked through, turning once. Remove from the skillet and keep warm.

5 Stir the cream and bouillon into the skillet with the remaining chopped fresh sage. Cook over a low heat for 2–3 minutes.

6 Arrange the potato cakes on a serving plate. Garnish with fresh sage leaves and serve with the cream and sage sauce.

COOK'S TIP

Do not boil the sauce once the cream has been added because it will curdle. Cook it gently over a very low heat.

Chicken & Potato Casserole

Small new potatoes are ideal for this recipe. If larger potatoes are used, cut them in half before adding them to the casserole.

NUTRITIONAL INFORMATION

Calories	.865	Sugars	.7g
Protein	.35g	Fat	.58g
Carbohydrate	.40g	Saturates	.26g

5 mins   1 hr 30 mins

SERVES 4

I N G R E D I E N T S

2 tbsp vegetable oil

¼ cup butter

4 chicken portions, about 225 g/8 oz each

2 leeks, sliced

1 garlic clove, crushed

4 tbsp all-purpose flour

3¾ cups chicken bouillon

1¼ cups dry white wine

4½ oz/125 g baby carrots, halved lengthwise

4½ oz/125 g baby corn, halved lengthwise

1 lb/450 g small new potatoes

1 bouquet garni

⅔ cup heavy cream

salt and pepper

1 Heat the oil and butter in a large skillet. Cook the chicken for 10 minutes, turning until browned all over. Transfer the chicken to a casserole dish using a perforated spoon.

2 Add the leek and garlic to the skillet and cook for 2–3 minutes, stirring. Stir in the flour and cook for another minute. Remove the skillet from the heat and stir in the chicken bouillon and wine. Season well.

3 Return the pan to the heat and bring the mixture to a boil. Stir in the carrots, corn, potatoes, and bouquet garni.

4 Transfer the mixture to the casserole dish. Cover and cook in a preheated oven, 350°F/180°C, for about 1 hour.

5 Remove the casserole from the oven and stir in the cream. Return the casserole to the oven, uncovered, and cook for a further 15 minutes. Remove the bouquet garni and discard. Taste and adjust the seasoning, if necessary. Serve with plain rice or fresh vegetables.

COOK'S TIP

Use turkey fillets instead of the chicken, if preferred, and vary the vegetables according to those you have to hand.

Potato Crisp Pie

This layered chicken pie with a creamy sauce is topped with a crisp oat layer. Use strips of beef or pork for an equally delicious dish, if preferred.

NUTRITIONAL INFORMATION

Calories 630	Sugars 12g
Protein 25g	Fat 40g
Carbohydrate ...38g	Saturates 24g

10 mins   55 mins

SERVES 4

INGREDIENTS

1 lb 5 oz/600 g waxy potatoes, sliced

5 tbsp butter

1 skinned chicken breast fillet, about
  6 oz/175 g

2 garlic cloves, crushed

4 scallions, sliced

2½ tbsp all-purpose flour

⅔ cup dry white wine

⅔ cup heavy cream

8 oz/225 g broccoli florets

4 large tomatoes, sliced

2¾ oz/75 g Swiss cheese, sliced

1 cup unsweetened yogurt

⅓ cup rolled oats, toasted

1 Cook the potatoes in a pan of boiling water for 10 minutes. Drain and set aside.

2 Meanwhile, melt the butter in a skillet. Cut the chicken into strips and cook for 5 minutes, turning. Add the garlic and scallions and cook for another 2 minutes.

3 Stir in the flour and cook for 1 minute. Gradually add the wine and cream. Bring to a boil, stirring, then reduce the heat until the sauce is simmering and cook for 5 minutes.

4 Meanwhile, blanch the broccoli in boiling water. Drain and refresh in cold water.

5 Place half of the potatoes in the base of a pie dish and top with half of the tomatoes and half of the broccoli.

6 Spoon the chicken sauce on top and repeat the layers in the same order once more.

7 Arrange the Swiss cheese on top and spoon over the yogurt. Sprinkle with the oats and cook in a preheated oven, 400°F/200°C, for 25 minutes until the top is golden brown. Serve the pie immediately.

COOK'S TIP

Add chopped nuts, such as pine nuts, to the topping for extra crunch, if you prefer.

Potato, Leek & Chicken Pie

This pie has an attractive phyllo pastry shell which has a ruffled top made with strips of the phyllo pastry brushed with melted butter.

NUTRITIONAL INFORMATION

Calories ....543 Sugars 7g
Protein ....21g Fat 27g
Carbohydrate ...56g Saturates 16g

🍴 10 mins   🕐 1 hr 15 mins

SERVES 4

INGREDIENTS

225 g/8 oz waxy potatoes, cubed

5 tbsp butter

1 skinned chicken breast fillet, about 6 oz/175 g, cubed

1 leek, sliced

5½ oz/150 g chestnut mushrooms, sliced

2½ tbsp all-purpose flour

1¼ cups milk

1 tbsp Dijon mustard

2 tbsp chopped fresh sage

8 oz/225 g phyllo pastry, thawed if frozen

3 tbsp butter, melted

salt and pepper

1 Cook the potato cubes in a pan of boiling water for 5 minutes. Drain and set aside.

2 Melt the butter in a skillet and cook the chicken cubes for 5 minutes or until browned all over.

3 Add the leek and mushrooms and cook for 3 minutes, stirring. Stir in the flour and cook for 1 minute. Gradually add the milk and bring to a boil. Add the mustard, chopped sage, and potato cubes, then leave the mixture to simmer for 10 minutes.

4 Meanwhile, line a deep pie dish with half of the sheets of phyllo pastry. Spoon the sauce into the dish and cover with one sheet of pastry. Brush the pastry with butter and lay another sheet on top. Brush this sheet with butter.

5 Cut the remaining phyllo pastry into strips and fold them on to the top of the pie to create a ruffled effect. Brush the strips with the melted butter and cook in a preheated oven, 350°F/180°C for 45 minutes, or until golden brown and crisp. Serve hot.

COOK'S TIP

If the top of the pie starts to brown too quickly, cover it with foil halfway through the cooking time to allow the pastry base to cook through without the top burning.

Quick Chicken Bake

This recipe is a type of shepherd's pie and is just as versatile. Add vegetables and herbs of your choice, depending on what you have to hand.

NUTRITIONAL INFORMATION

Calories	496	Sugars	........10g
Protein	........38g	Fat	..........17g
Carbohydrate	...52g	Saturates	......9g

15 mins   45 mins

SERVES 4

I N G R E D I E N T S

1 lb 2 oz/500 g ground chicken

1 large onion, finely chopped

2 carrots, finely chopped

2 tbsp all-purpose flour

1 tbsp tomato paste

1¼ cups chicken bouillon

pinch of fresh thyme

generous 3½ cups mashed potatoes, creamed with butter and milk and highly seasoned

¾ cup grated semihard white cheese

salt and pepper

peas, to serve

1 Brown the ground chicken, onion, and carrots in a non-stick pan for 5 minutes, stirring frequently.

2 Sprinkle the chicken with the flour and simmer for a further 2 minutes.

3 Gradually blend in the tomato paste and bouillon, then simmer for 15 minutes. Season and add the thyme.

4 Transfer the chicken and vegetable mixture to an ovenproof casserole and let cool.

5 Spoon the mashed potato over the chicken mixture and sprinkle with cheese. Bake in a preheated oven at 400°F/200°C for 20 minutes, or until the cheese is bubbling and golden, then serve, straight from the casserole, with the peas.

VARIATION

Instead of plain cheese, you could sprinkle a flavored cheese over the top. There are a variety of cheeses blended with onion and chives, and these are ideal for melting as a topping. Alternatively, you could use a mixture of cheeses, depending on whatever you have to hand.

Country Chicken Hotpot

There are many regional versions of hotpot, all using fresh, local ingredients available all year, perfect for traditional one-pot cooking.

NUTRITIONAL INFORMATION

Calories ....499 Sugars 6g
Protein ....43g Fat 17g
Carbohydrate ...44g Saturates 8g

5 mins

2 hours

SERVES 4

INGREDIENTS

4 chicken quarters

3 lb/1.3 kg potatoes, cut into
¼ inch/5 mm slices

2 sprigs thyme

2 sprigs rosemary

2 bay leaves

1 cup diced smoked bacon

1 large onion, finely chopped

2 carrots, sliced

⅔ cup stout or dark beer

2 tbsp melted butter

salt and pepper

1 Remove the skin from the chicken quarters, if desired.

2 Arrange a layer of potato slices in the base of a wide casserole. Season with salt and pepper, then add the thyme, rosemary, and bay leaves.

3 Top with the chicken quarters, then sprinkle with the diced bacon, and the onion and carrots. Season well and arrange the remaining potato slices on top, overlapping slightly.

4 Pour over the stout or beer. Brush the potatoes with the melted butter and cover with a lid.

5 Bake in a preheated oven, 300°F/150°C, for about 2 hours, uncovering for the last 30 minutes to allow the potatoes to brown. Serve hot.

VARIATION

This dish is also delicious with stewing lamb, cut into chunks. You can add different vegetables depending on what is in season—try leeks and rutabaga for a slightly sweeter flavor.

Gardener's Chicken

Any combination of small, young vegetables can be roasted with this delicious stuffed chicken, such as zucchini, leeks, and onions.

NUTRITIONAL INFORMATION

Calories	674	Sugars	........18g
Protein	........35g	Fat	..........40g
Carbohydrate	...45g	Saturates	......12g

🕙 10 mins   ⏱ 1 hr 40 mins

SERVES 4

INGREDIENTS

4 cups parsnips, peeled and chopped

2 small carrots, peeled and chopped

½ cup fresh bread crumbs

¼ tsp grated nutmeg

1 tbsp chopped fresh parsley

1 chicken, 3 lb/1.5 kg

bunch fresh parsley

½ onion

2 tbsp butter, softened

4 tbsp olive oil

1 lb 2 oz/500 g new potatoes, scrubbed

1 lb 2 oz/500 g baby carrots, washed and trimmed

salt and pepper

1 To make the stuffing, put the parsnips and carrots into a pan. Half cover with water and bring to a boil. Cover the pan and simmer until tender. Drain well, then purée in a blender or food processor. Transfer the purée to a bowl and let to cool.

2 Mix in the bread crumbs, nutmeg, and parsley and season to taste with salt and pepper.

3 Put the stuffing into the neck end of the chicken and push a little of the stuffing under the skin over the breast meat. Secure the flap of skin with a small metal skewer or toothpick.

4 Place the bunch of parsley and onion inside the cavity of the chicken, then place the chicken in a large roasting pan.

5 Spread the butter over the skin and season with salt and pepper. Cover with aluminum foil and place in a preheated oven, 375°F/190°C, for 30 minutes.

6 Meanwhile, heat the oil in a skillet, and lightly brown the potatoes.

7 Transfer the potatoes to the roasting pan and add the baby carrots. Baste the chicken and continue to cook for another hour, basting the chicken and vegetables after 30 minutes. Remove the foil for the last 20 minutes to let the skin crisp. Garnish the vegetables with chopped parsley and serve.

Potato & Turkey Pie

Turkey is especially good with fruit, because it has a fairly strong flavor. The walnuts counteract the sweetness of the fruit.

NUTRITIONAL INFORMATION

Calories	790	Sugars	16g
Protein	28g	Fat	50g
Carbohydrate	60g	Saturates	23g

10 mins   50 mins

SERVES 4

INGREDIENTS

1⅔ cup waxy potatoes, diced

2 tbsp butter

1 tbsp vegetable oil

10½ oz/300 g lean turkey meat, cubed

1 red onion, halved and sliced

2½ all-purpose flour

1¼ cups milk

⅔ cup heavy cream

2 celery stalks, sliced

2¾ oz/75 g dried apricots, chopped

1 oz/25 g walnut pieces

2 tbsp chopped fresh parsley

salt and pepper

8 oz/225 g store-bought pie dough

beaten egg, for brushing

1 Cook the diced potatoes in a pan of boiling water for 10 minutes until tender. Drain and set aside.

2 Meanwhile, heat the butter and oil in a pan. Add the turkey and cook for 5 minutes, turning until browned.

3 Add the sliced onion and cook for 2–3 minutes. Stir in the flour and cook for 1 minute. Gradually stir in the milk and the heavy cream. Bring to a boil, stirring, then reduce the heat until the mixture is simmering.

4 Stir in the celery, apricots, walnut pieces, parsley, and potatoes. Season well with salt and pepper. Spoon the potato and turkey mixture into the base of a 5 cup/1.1 liter pie dish.

5 On a lightly floured counter, roll out the pie dough until it is 1 inch/2.5 cm larger than the dish. Trim a 1 inch/2.5 cm wide strip from the pie dough and place the strip on the dampened rim of the dish. Brush with water and cover with the pie dough lid, pressing to seal the edges.

6 Brush the top of the pie with beaten egg and cook in a preheated oven, 400°F/200°C, for 25–30 minutes or until the pie is cooked and golden brown. Serve at once.

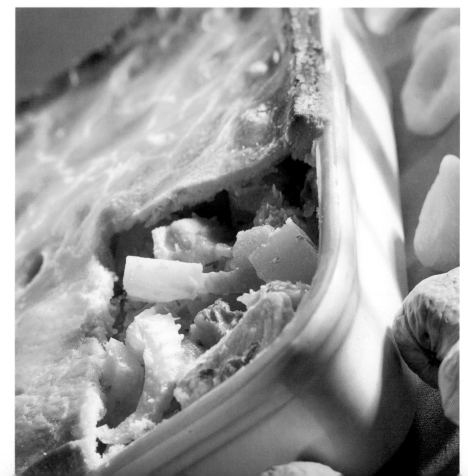

Hotpot Chops

A hotpot is a lamb casserole, made with carrots and onions and with a potato topping. The chops used here are an interesting alternative.

NUTRITIONAL INFORMATION

Calories 250	Sugars 2g
Protein 27g	Fat 12g
Carbohydrate 8g	Saturates 5g

10 mins   30 mins

SERVES 4

INGREDIENTS

4 lean, boneless lamb leg chops, about
   125 g/4½ oz each

1 small onion, thinly sliced

1 carrot, thinly sliced

1 potato, thinly sliced

1 tsp olive oil

1 tsp dried rosemary

salt and pepper

fresh rosemary, to garnish

freshly steamed green vegetables, to serve

1 Preheat the oven to 350°F/180°C. Using a sharp knife, trim any excess fat from the lamb chops.

2 Season both sides of the chops with salt and pepper and arrange them on a baking sheet.

3 Alternate layers of sliced onion, carrot, and potato on top of each lamb chop.

4 Brush the tops of the potato lightly with oil. Season well with salt and pepper to taste and then sprinkle with a little dried rosemary.

5 Bake the hot pot chops in the oven for 25–30 minutes until the lamb is tender and cooked through.

6 Drain the lamb on paper towels and transfer to a warmed serving plate.

7 Garnish with fresh rosemary and serve accompanied with a selection of green vegetables.

VARIATION

This recipe would work equally well with boneless chicken breasts. Pound the chicken slightly with a meat mallet or covered rolling pin so that the pieces are the same thickness throughout.

Beef & Potato Goulash

In this recipe, the potatoes are actually cooked in the goulash. For a change, you may prefer to substitute small, scrubbed new potatoes.

NUTRITIONAL INFORMATION

Calories	477	Sugars	........11g
Protein	........47g	Fat	..........16g
Carbohydrate	...39g	Saturates	......5g

15 mins   2¼ hours

SERVES 4

2 tbsp vegetable oil

1 large onion, sliced

2 garlic cloves, crushed

1 lb 10 oz/750 g lean stewing steak

2 tbsp paprika

14 oz/400 g canned chopped tomatoes

2 tbsp tomato paste

1 large red bell pepper, cored, seeded
   and chopped

6 oz/175 g mushrooms, wiped and sliced

2½ cups beef bouillon

1 lb 2 oz/500 g potatoes, peeled and cut
   into large chunks

1 tbsp cornstarch

salt and pepper

TO GARNISH

4 tbsp lowfat natural yogurt

paprika

chopped fresh parsley

1 Heat the oil in a large pan and cook the onion and garlic for 3–4 minutes until softened.

2 Cut the steak into chunks and cook over a high heat for about 3 minutes until browned all over.

3 Add the paprika and stir well. Add the tomatoes, tomato paste, red bell pepper, and mushrooms. Cook the vegetables for 2 minutes, stirring constantly.

4 Pour in the bouillon. Bring to a boil, then reduce the heat. Cover and simmer for about 1½ hours until the meat is tender.

5 Add the potatoes and cook, covered, for 20–30 minutes until tender.

6 Blend the cornstarch with a little water and add to the pan, stirring until thickened and blended. Cook for 1 minute, then season with salt and pepper. Top with the yogurt, then sprinkle over the paprika. Garnish with chopped fresh parsley and serve.

Potato, Beef & Peanut Pot

The spicy peanut sauce in this recipe will complement almost any meat; this dish is just as delicious made with chicken or pork.

NUTRITIONAL INFORMATION

Calories	559	Sugars	. . . . .5g
Protein	. . . . .35g	Fat	. . . . .37g
Carbohydrate	. . .24g	Saturates	. . . . . .13g

5 mins   1 hour

SERVES 4

INGREDIENTS

1 tbsp vegetable oil

5 tbsp butter

1 lb/450 g lean beef steak, cut into thin strips

1 onion, halved and sliced

2 garlic cloves, crushed

1 lb 5 oz/600 g waxy potatoes, cubed

½ tsp paprika

4 tbsp crunchy peanut butter

2½ cups beef bouillon

1 oz/25 g unsalted peanuts

2 tsp light soy sauce

1¾ oz/50 g sugar snap peas

1 red bell pepper, cut into strips

parsley sprigs, to garnish (optional)

1 Heat the oil and butter in a flameproof casserole dish.

2 Add the beef strips and cook them gently for 3–4 minutes, stirring and turning the meat until it is sealed on all sides.

3 Add the onion and garlic and cook for a further 2 minutes, stirring constantly.

4 Add the potato cubes and cook for 3–4 minutes or until they begin to brown slightly.

5 Stir in the paprika and peanut butter, then gradually blend in the beef bouillon. Bring the mixture to a boil, stirring frequently.

6 Finally, add the peanuts, soy sauce, sugar snap peas, and red bell pepper.

7 Cover and cook over a low heat for 45 minutes or until the beef is cooked right through.

8 Garnish the dish with parsley sprigs, if wished, and serve.

VARIATION

Add a chopped green chili to the sauce for extra spice, if you prefer.

Potato Ravioli

In this recipe the "pasta" dough is made with potatoes instead of the traditional flour. The ravioli are filled with a rich bolognese sauce.

NUTRITIONAL INFORMATION

Calories	559	Sugars	.........4g
Protein	........17g	Fat	..........30g
Carbohydrate	...60g	Saturates	......11g

5–10 mins   1 hr 10 mins

SERVES 4

I N G R E D I E N T S

FILLING

1 tbsp vegetable oil

4½ oz/125 g ground beef

1 shallot, diced

1 garlic clove, crushed

1 tbsp all-purpose flour

1 tbsp tomato paste

⅔ cup beef bouillon

1 celery stalk, chopped

2 tomatoes, peeled and diced

2 tsp chopped fresh basil

salt and pepper

RAVIOLI

2⅔ cups diced mealy potatoes

3 small egg yolks

3 tbsp olive oil

1½ cups all-purpose flour

5 tbsp butter, for frying

shredded basil leaves, to garnish

1 To make the filling, heat the oil in a pan and cook the beef for 3–4 minutes, breaking it up with a spoon. Add the shallot and garlic and cook for 2–3 minutes until the shallot has softened.

2 Stir in the flour and tomato paste and cook for 1 minute. Stir in the beef bouillon, celery, tomatoes, and the chopped fresh basil. Season to taste with salt and pepper.

3 Cook the mixture over a low heat for 20 minutes. Remove from the heat and let cool.

4 To make the ravioli, cook the potatoes in a pan of boiling water for 10 minutes until cooked.

5 Mash the potatoes in a mixing bowl. Add the egg yolks and oil. Season, then stir in the flour and mix to form a dough.

6 On a lightly floured surface, divide the dough into 24 pieces and shape into flat rounds. Spoon the filling on to one half of each round and fold the dough over to encase the filling, pressing down to seal the edges.

7 Melt the butter in a skillet and cook the ravioli for 6–8 minutes, turning once, until golden. Serve hot, garnished with shredded basil leaves.

Veal Italienne

This dish is delicious if made with tender veal. However, if veal is unavailable, use pork or turkey escalopes instead.

NUTRITIONAL INFORMATION

Calories	592	Sugars	........5g
Protein	........44g	Fat	..........23g
Carbohydrate	...48g	Saturates	.......9g

25 mins   1 hr 20 mins

SERVES 4

INGREDIENTS

5 tbsp butter

1 tbsp olive oil

1½ lb/675 g potatoes, cubed

4 veal escalopes, 6 oz/175 g each

1 onion, cut into 8 wedges

2 garlic cloves, crushed

2 tbsp all-purpose flour

2 tbsp tomato paste

⅔ cup red wine

1¼ cups chicken bouillon

8 ripe tomatoes, peeled, seeded, and diced

1 oz/25 g pitted black olives, halved

2 tbsp chopped fresh basil

salt and pepper

fresh basil leaves, to garnish

1 Heat the butter and oil in a large skillet. Add the potato cubes and cook for 5–7 minutes, stirring frequently, until they begin to brown.

2 Remove the potatoes from the skillet with a perforated spoon and set aside.

3 Place the veal in the skillet and cook for 2–3 minutes on each side until sealed. Remove from the pan and then set aside.

4 Stir the onion and garlic into the skillet and cook for 2–3 minutes.

5 Add the flour and tomato paste and cook for 1 minute, stirring. Gradually blend in the red wine and chicken bouillon, stirring to make a smooth sauce.

6 Return the potatoes and veal to the skillet. Stir in the tomatoes, olives, and chopped basil and season with salt and pepper.

7 Transfer to a casserole dish and cook in a preheated oven, 350°F/180°C, for 1 hour or until the potatoes and veal are cooked through. Garnish with fresh basil leaves and serve.

COOK'S TIP

For a quicker cooking time and really tender meat, pound the meat with a meat mallet to flatten it slightly before cooking.

Lamb Hotpot

This classic recipe using lamb cutlets layered between sliced potatoes, kidneys, onions, and herbs makes a perfect meal on a cold winter's day.

NUTRITIONAL INFORMATION

Calories 420   Sugars 2g
Protein . . . . .41g   Fat 15g
Carbohydrate . . .31g   Saturates 8g

15 mins   2 hours

SERVES 4

I N G R E D I E N T S

1½ lb/675 g lean lamb shoulder chops

2 lambs' kidneys

1½ lb/675 g waxy potatoes, scrubbed and thinly sliced

1 large onion, thinly sliced

2 tbsp chopped fresh thyme

⅔ cup lamb bouillon

2 tbsp butter, melted

salt and pepper

fresh thyme sprigs, to garnish

1 Remove any excess fat from the lamb. Skin and core the kidneys and cut them into slices.

2 Arrange a layer of potatoes in the bottom of a 3½ cup/1.7 liter ovenproof dish.

3 Arrange the lamb shoulder chops on top of the potatoes and cover with the sliced kidneys, onion, and thyme.

4 Pour the lamb bouillon over the meat and then season to taste with salt and pepper.

5 Layer the remaining potato slices on top, overlapping to completely cover the meat and sliced onion.

6 Brush the potato slices with the butter. Cover the dish and cook in a preheated oven, 350°F/180°C for 1½ hours.

7 Remove the lid and cook for another 30 minutes until golden brown on top.

8 Garnish with fresh thyme sprigs and serve hot.

VARIATION

Traditionally, oysters are also included in this tasty hotpot. Add them to the layers along with the kidneys, if wished.

Potato & Lamb Kofta

The Greek kofta are traditionally served threaded on to a skewer. Here they are served on a plate with a refreshing tzatziki sauce.

NUTRITIONAL INFORMATION

Calories	490	Sugars	.........5g
Protein	........20g	Fat	..........36g
Carbohydrate	...24g	Saturates	......9g

🐷 🐷 🐷 🐷

🥔 5 mins   🕐 45 mins

SERVES 4

I N G R E D I E N T S

⅔ diced mealy potatoes

2 tbsp butter

8 oz/225 g ground lamb

1 onion, chopped

2 garlic cloves, crushed

½ tsp ground coriander

2 eggs, beaten

vegetable oil, for deep-frying

mint sprigs, to garnish

S A U C E

⅔ cup natural yogurt

2 oz cucumber, finely chopped

1 tbsp chopped mint

1 garlic clove, crushed

1 Cook the diced potatoes in a pan of boiling water for 10 minutes until cooked through. Drain, then mash until smooth and transfer to a mixing bowl.

2 Melt the butter in a skillet. Add the lamb, onion, garlic, and coriander and cook for 15 minutes, stirring.

3 Drain off the liquid from the pan, then stir the meat mixture into the mashed potatoes. Stir in the eggs and season to taste.

4 To make the sauce, combine the yogurt, cucumber, mint, and garlic in a bowl and set aside.

5 Heat the oil in a large pan to 350°F–375°F/ 180°C–190°C, or until a cube of bread browns in 30 seconds. Drop spoonfuls of the potato mixture into the hot oil and cook in batches for 4–5 minutes or until they are golden brown.

6 Remove the kofta with a perforated spoon. Drain thoroughly on paper towels, set aside, and keep warm. Garnish with fresh mint sprigs and serve with the sauce.

COOK'S TIP

These kofta can be made with any sort of ground meat, such as turkey, chicken, or pork, and flavored with appropriate fresh herbs, such as sage or cilantro.

Spanish Potato Bake

A traditional Spanish dish, *huevos* (eggs) are cooked on a spicy sausage, tomato, and potato mixture.

NUTRITIONAL INFORMATION

Calories 443	Sugars 7g	
Protein 21g	Fat 25g	
Carbohydrate ...36g	Saturates 8g	

🥘 5 mins   🕐 35 mins

SERVES 4

INGREDIENTS

4 cups diced waxy potatoes

3 tbsp olive oil

1 onion, halved and sliced

2 garlic cloves, crushed

14 oz/400 g canned plum tomatoes, chopped

2¾ oz/75 g chorizo sausage, sliced

1 green bell pepper, cut into strips

½ tsp paprika

1 oz/25 g pitted black olives, halved

8 eggs

1 tbsp chopped fresh parsley

salt and pepper

1 Cook the diced potatoes in a pan of boiling water for 10 minutes or until softened. Drain and set aside.

2 Heat the olive oil in a large skillet. Add the sliced onion and garlic and cook gently for 2–3 minutes until the onion softens.

3 Add the chopped canned tomatoes and cook over a low heat for about 10 minutes until the mixture has reduced slightly.

4 Stir the potatoes into the pan with the chorizo, green bell pepper, paprika, and olives. Cook for 5 minutes, stirring. Transfer to a shallow ovenproof dish.

5 Make 8 small hollows in the top of the mixture and break an egg into each hollow.

6 Cook in a preheated oven, 425°F/220°C, for 5–6 minutes or until the eggs are just cooked. Sprinkle with parsley and serve with crusty bread.

VARIATION

Add a little spice to the dish by incorporating 1 teaspoon chili powder in step 4, if desired.

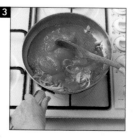

Tomato & Sausage Pan-Fry

This simple dish is delicious as an entrée. Choose good sausages flavored with herbs, or use flavored sausages, such as mustard or leek.

NUTRITIONAL INFORMATION

Calories 458   Sugars 11g
Protein . . . . .21g   Fat 25g
Carbohydrate . . .34g   Saturates 8g

5 mins   30 mins

SERVES 4

I N G R E D I E N T S

1 lb 5 oz/600 g potatoes, sliced

1 tbsp vegetable oil

8 flavored sausages

1 red onion, cut into 8

1 tbsp tomato paste

⅔ cup red wine

⅔ cup strained tomatoes

2 large tomatoes, each cut into 8 pieces

6 oz/175 g broccoli florets, blanched

2 tbsp chopped fresh basil

salt and pepper

shredded fresh basil, to garnish

1 Cook the sliced potatoes in a pan of boiling water for 7 minutes. Drain thoroughly and set aside.

2 Meanwhile, heat the oil in a large skillet. Add the sausages and cook for 5 minutes, turning them frequently to ensure that they are browned on all sides.

3 Add the onion pieces to the pan and continue to cook for another 5 minutes, stirring the mixture frequently.

4 Stir in the tomato paste, red wine, and the strained tomatoes and mix together well. Add the tomato wedges, broccoli florets, and chopped basil to the pan and mix carefully.

5 Add the parboiled potato slices to the pan. Cook the mixture for about 10 minutes or until the sausages are completely cooked through. Season to taste with salt and pepper.

6 Garnish with fresh shredded basil and serve hot.

COOK'S TIP
Omit the strained tomatoes from this recipe and use canned plum tomatoes or chopped tomatoes for convenience.

Potato, Beef & Leek Pasties

Filled with potatoes, cubes of beef, and leeks, these pasties make a substantial meal. They are also perfect snacks for a picnic or barbecue.

NUTRITIONAL INFORMATION

Calories . . . . .419 Sugars 2g
Protein . . . . .18g Fat 23g
Carbohydrate . . .38g Saturates 9g

10–15 mins   50 mins

SERVES 4

INGREDIENTS

8 oz/225 g diced waxy potatoes

1 small carrot, diced

8 oz/225 g beef steak, cubed

1 leek, sliced

8 oz/225 g store-bought pie dough

1 tbsp butter

1 egg, beaten

salt and pepper

1 Lightly grease a baking sheet.

2 Mix the potatoes, carrots, beef, and leek in a large bowl. Season well with salt and pepper.

3 Divide the pie dough into four equal portions. On a lightly floured surface, roll each portion into an 8 inch/20 cm round.

4 Spoon the potato mixture on to one half of each round, to within ½ inch/ 1 cm of the edge. Top the potato mixture with the butter, dividing it equally between the rounds. Brush the pie dough edge with a little of the beaten egg.

5 Fold the pie dough over to encase the filling and crimp the edges together.

6 Transfer the pasties to the prepared baking sheet and brush them with the beaten egg.

7 Cook in a preheated oven, 400°F/200°C, for 20 minutes. Reduce the oven temperature to 325°F/160°C and cook the pasties for another 30 minutes until cooked.

8 Serve the pasties with a crisp salad or onion gravy.

VARIATION

Use other types of meat, such as pork or chicken, in the pasties and add chunks of apple in step 2, if preferred.

Potato & Meat Phyllo Parcels

These parcels will impress your guests. Crisp pastry encases a tasty potato and beef filling which is cooked in red wine for a delicious flavor.

NUTRITIONAL INFORMATION

Calories 388	Sugars 5g	
Protein 15g	Fat 12g	
Carbohydrate ...53g	Saturates 5g	

🥘 10 mins   🕐 35 mins

SERVES 4

INGREDIENTS

1½ cups finely diced waxy potatoes

1 tbsp vegetable oil

4½ oz/125 g ground beef

1 leek, sliced

1 small yellow bell pepper, finely diced

4½ oz/125 g white mushrooms, sliced

1 tbsp all-purpose flour

1 tbsp tomato paste

6 tbsp red wine

6 tbsp beef bouillon

1 tbsp chopped fresh rosemary

225 g/8 oz phyllo pastry, thawed if frozen

2 tbsp butter, melted

salt and pepper

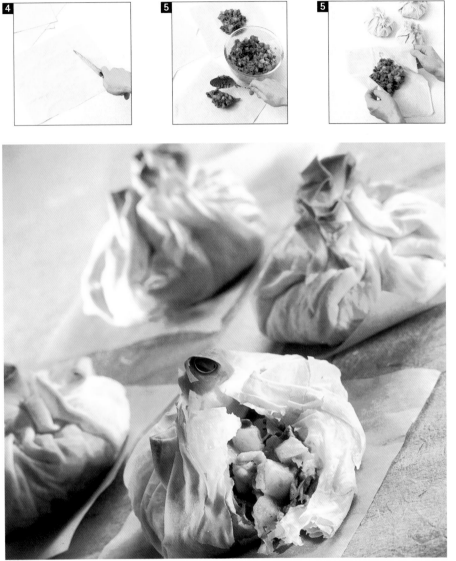

1 Cook the diced potatoes in a pan of boiling water for 5 minutes. Drain and set aside.

2 Meanwhile, heat the oil in a pan and cook the ground beef, leek, yellow bell pepper, and mushrooms over a low heat for 5 minutes.

3 Stir in the flour and tomato paste and cook for 1 minute. Gradually add the red wine and beef bouillon, stirring to thicken. Add the rosemary, season to taste with salt and pepper and let cool.

4 Lay 4 sheets of phyllo pastry on a counter or board. Brush each sheet with butter and lay a second layer of phyllo on top. Trim the sheets to make four 8 inch/20 cm squares.

5 Brush the edges of the pastry with a little butter. Spoon a quarter of the beef mixture into the center of each square. Bring up the corners and the sides of the squares to form a parcel, scrunching the edges together. Make sure that the parcels are well sealed by pressing the pastry together, otherwise the filling will leak.

6 Place the parcels on a baking sheet and brush with butter. Bake in a preheated oven, 350°F/180°C, for 20 minutes. Serve hot.

Carrot-Topped Beef Pie

This is a variation of an old favorite—creamy mashed potato and carrot topping is piled thickly onto a delicious beef pie filling.

NUTRITIONAL INFORMATION

Calories	352	Sugars	........6g
Protein	........28g	Fat	..........11g
Carbohydrate	...38g	Saturates	......6g

10 mins   1¼ hr 15 mins

SERVES 4

INGREDIENTS

1 lb/450 g lean ground beef

1 onion, chopped

1 garlic clove, crushed

1 tbsp all-purpose flour

1¼ cups beef bouillon

2 tbsp tomato paste

1 celery stalk, chopped

3 tbsp chopped fresh parsley

1 tbsp Worcestershire sauce

4 cups mealy diced potatoes

2 large carrots, diced

2 tbsp butter

3 tbsp skim milk

salt and pepper

1 Dry-fry the beef in a large pan set over a high heat for 3–4 minutes, or until sealed. Add the onion and garlic and cook for a further 5 minutes, stirring.

2 Add the flour and cook for 1 minute. Gradually blend in the beef bouillon and tomato paste. Stir in the celery, 1 tablespoon of the parsley, and the Worcestershire sauce. Season to taste.

3 Bring the mixture to a boil, then reduce the heat and simmer for 20–25 minutes. Spoon the beef mixture into a 5 cup/1.1 liter pie dish.

4 Meanwhile, cook the potatoes and carrots in a pan of boiling water for 10 minutes. Drain thoroughly and mash them together.

5 Stir the butter, milk, and the remaining parsley into the potato and carrot mixture, and season with salt and pepper to taste. Spoon the potato on top of the beef mixture to cover it completely; alternatively, pipe the potato on top with a pastry bag.

6 Cook the carrot-topped beef pie in a preheated oven, 375°F/190°C, for 45 minutes or until cooked through. Serve piping hot.

Potato, Beef & Kidney Pie

Steak and kidney has always been a popular pie filling, but this version is particularly good cooked in a beer sauce with added potato.

NUTRITIONAL INFORMATION

Calories 533	Sugars 4g
Protein 36g	Fat 26g
Carbohydrate . . .39g	Saturates 6g

🧈 10 mins   🕐 1 hr 35 mins

SERVES 4

INGREDIENTS

8 oz/225 g waxy potatoes, cubed

2 tbsp butter

1 lb/450 g lean steak, cubed

5½ oz/150 g ox kidney, cored and chopped

12 shallots

2½ tbsp all-purpose flour

⅔ cup beef bouillon

⅔ cup stout

8 oz/225 g store-bought pie dough

1 egg, beaten

salt and pepper

1 Cook the cubed potatoes in a pan of boiling water for 10 minutes. Drain thoroughly.

2 Meanwhile, melt the butter in a pan and add the steak cubes and the kidney. Cook for 5 minutes, stirring until the meat is sealed on all sides.

3 Add the shallots and cook for a further 3–4 minutes. Stir in the flour and cook for 1 minute. Gradually stir in the beef bouillon and stout and bring to a boil, stirring constantly.

4 Stir the potatoes into the meat mixture and season with salt and pepper. Reduce the heat until the mixture is simmering. Cover the pan and cook for 1 hour, stirring occasionally.

5 Spoon the beef mixture into the base of a pie dish. Roll the pie dough on a lightly floured counter until ½ inch /1 cm larger than the top of the dish.

6 Cut a strip of pie dough long enough and wide enough to fit around the edge of the dish. Brush the edge of the dish with beaten egg and press the pie dough strip around the edge. Brush with egg and place the pie dough lid on top. Crimp to seal the edge and brush with beaten egg.

7 Cook in a preheated oven, 450°F/230°C, for 20–25 minutes or until the pastry has risen and is golden. Serve hot, straight from the dish.

Raised Pork & Apple Pie

The pastry in this recipe requires fairly speedy working as it is molded into the pan while it is warm and pliable. It is very easy to make.

🍲 🍲

🍲 2 hrs 20 mins   🕐 2 hrs 35 mins

SERVES 8

I N G R E D I E N T S

FILLING

2 lb/900 g waxy potatoes, sliced

2 tbsp butter

2 tbsp vegetable oil

1 lb/450 g lean pork, cubed

2 onions, sliced

4 garlic cloves, crushed

4 tbsp tomato paste

2½ cups bouillon

2 tbsp chopped fresh sage

2 eating apples, peeled and sliced

salt and pepper

PIE DOUGH

5 cups all-purpose flour

pinch of salt

4 tsp butter

½ cup shortening

1¼ cups water

1 egg, beaten

1 tsp gelatin

1 Cook the potatoes in boiling water for 10 minutes. Drain and set aside. Heat the butter and oil in a flameproof casserole dish and fry the pork until browned, turning. Add the onion and garlic and cook for 5 minutes. Stir in the rest of the filling ingredients, except for the potatoes and the apples. Reduce the heat. Cover and simmer for 1½ hours. Drain the bouillon from the casserole dish and reserve. Let the pork to cool.

2 To make the pie dough, strain the flour into a bowl. Add the salt and make a well in the center. Melt the butter and shortening in a pan with the water; then bring to a boil. Pour into the flour and mix to form a dough. Turn on to a floured counter and knead until smooth. Reserve a quarter of the dough and use the rest to line the base and sides of a large pie pan or deep 8 inch/20 cm loose-bottom cake pan.

3 Layer the pork, potatoes, and apple in the base. Roll out the reserved pie dough to make a lid. Dampen the edges and place the lid on top, sealing well. Brush with egg and make a hole in the top. Cook in a preheated oven, 400°F/200°C, for 30 minutes, then at 325°F/160°C for 45 minutes. Dissolve the gelatin in the reserved bouillon and pour into the hole in the lid as the pie cools. Serve well chilled. Serve with salad.

Potato, Sausage & Onion Pie

This is a delicious supper dish for all of the family. Use good-quality herb sausages for a really tasty pie.

NUTRITIONAL INFORMATION

Calories ....399 Sugars 6g
Protein ....14g Fat 22g
Carbohydrate ...39g Saturates 11g

5–10 mins   40 mins

SERVES 4

INGREDIENTS

1 lb 5 oz/600 g waxy potatoes, unpeeled and sliced

2 tbsp butter

4 thick pork and herb sausages

1 leek, sliced

2 garlic cloves, crushed

⅔ cup vegetable bouillon

⅔ cup hard cider or apple juice

2 tbsp chopped fresh sage

2 tbsp cornstarch

4 tbsp water

¾ cup sharp cheese, grated

salt and pepper

1 Cook the sliced potatoes in a pan of boiling water for 10 minutes. Drain and set aside.

2 Meanwhile, melt the butter in a skillet and cook the sausages for 8–10 minutes, turning them frequently so that they brown on all sides. Remove the sausages from the skillet and cut them into thick slices.

3 Add the leek, garlic, and sausage slices to the skillet and cook for 2–3 minutes.

4 Add the vegetable bouillon, hard cider or apple juice, and chopped sage. Season with salt and pepper. Blend the cornstarch with the water. Stir it into the skillet and bring to a boil, stirring until the sauce is thick and clear. Spoon the mixture into the bottom of a deep pie dish.

5 Layer the potato slices on top of the sausage mixture to cover it completely. Season with salt and pepper and sprinkle the grated cheese over the top.

6 Cook in a preheated oven, 375°F/190°C, for 25–30 minutes or until the potatoes are cooked and the cheese is golden brown. Serve the pie hot.

Potato & Broccoli Pie

This pie's sauce is flavored with dolcelatte cheese and walnuts, which is delicious with broccoli. This recipe makes one large pie or 4 individual pies.

NUTRITIONAL INFORMATION

Calories 616   Sugars 8g
Protein . . . . .22g   Fat 37g
Carbohydrate . . .53g   Saturates 10g

5–10 mins   45 mins

SERVES 4

INGREDIENTS

1 lb/450 g waxy potatoes, cut into chunks

2 tbsp butter

1 tbsp vegetable oil

6 oz/175 g lean pork, cubed

1 red onion, cut into 8 pieces

2½ tbsp all-purpose flour

⅔ cup vegetable bouillon

⅔ cup milk

2¾ oz/75 g dolcelatte, crumbled

6 oz/75 g broccoli florets

1 oz/25 g walnuts

8 oz/225 g store-bought puff pie dough

milk, for glazing

salt and pepper

1 Cook the potato chunks in a pan of boiling water for 5 minutes. Drain and set aside.

2 Meanwhile, heat the butter and oil in a heavy-based pan. Add the pork cubes and cook for 5 minutes, turning until browned.

3 Add the onion and cook for another 2 minutes. Stir in the flour and cook for 1 minute, then gradually stir in the vegetable bouillon and milk. Bring to a boil, stirring constantly.

4 Add the cheese, broccoli, potatoes, and walnuts to the pan and simmer for 5 minutes. Season with salt and pepper to taste, then spoon the mixture into a pie dish.

5 On a floured counter, roll out the pie dough until 1 inch/2.5 cm larger than the dish. Cut a 1 inch/2.5 cm wide strip from the pie dough. Dampen the edge of the dish and place the pie dough strip around it. Brush with milk and put the pie dough lid on top.

6 Seal and crimp the edges and make 2 small slits in the center of the lid. Brush with milk and cook in a preheated oven, 400°F/200°C, for 25 minutes, or until the pastry has risen and is golden.

COOK'S TIP

Use a hard, sharp cheese instead of the dolcelatte, if you prefer.

Potato & Ham Pie

This pie contains chunks of pineapple—a classic accompaniment to ham—with potatoes and onion in a mustard sauce.

NUTRITIONAL INFORMATION

Calories	887	Sugars	........10g
Protein	........31g	Fat	..........57g
Carbohydrate	...68g	Saturates	......34g

10 mins   55 mins

SERVES 12

INGREDIENTS

8 oz/225 g waxy potatoes, cubed

2 tbsp butter

8 shallots, halved

1¼ cups smoked ham, cubed

2½ tbsp all-purpose flour

1¼ cups milk

2 tbsp whole-grain mustard

1¾ oz/50 g pineapple, cubed

PIE DOUGH

2 cups plain all-purpose flour

½ tsp dry mustard

pinch of salt

pinch of cayenne pepper

⅔ cup butter

4½ oz125 g sharp cheese, grated

2 egg yolks, plus extra for brushing

4–6 tsp cold water

1 Cook the potato cubes in a pan of boiling water for 10 minutes. Drain and set aside.

2 Meanwhile, melt the butter in a pan. Add the shallots and cook gently for 3–4 minutes until they begin to color.

3 Add the ham and cook for 2–3 minutes. Stir in the flour and cook for 1 minute. Gradually stir in the milk. Add the mustard and pineapple and bring to a boil, stirring. Season well with salt and pepper and add the potatoes.

4 Sift the flour for the pie dough into a bowl with the mustard, salt, and cayenne. Rub the butter into the mixture until it resembles bread crumbs. Add the cheese and mix to form a dough with the egg yolks and water.

5 On a floured counter, roll out half of the pastry and line a shallow pie dish; trim the edges.

6 Add the filling to the dish. Brush the edges of the pie dough with water.

7 Roll out the remaining dough to make a lid. Press it on top of the pie, sealing the edges. Decorate the top of the pie with the pie dough trimmings. Brush the pie with egg yolk. Cook in a preheated oven, 375°F/190°C, for 40–45 minutes.

Potatoes Cooked with Meat

Khormas almost always contain yogurt and therefore have lovely, smooth sauces. Chapatis or fried rice make a good accompaniment.

NUTRITIONAL INFORMATION

Calories	737	Sugars	.........7g
Protein	........27g	Fat	..........61g
Carbohydrate	...21g	Saturates	......16g

🍲 5 mins   🕐 1 hr 15 mins

SERVES 6

INGREDIENTS

3 onions

3 potatoes

1¼ cups oil

2 lb 4 oz/1 kg leg of lamb, cubed

2 tsp garam masala

1½ tsp fresh ginger root , finely chopped

1½ tsp fresh garlic, crushed

1 tsp chili powder

3 black peppercorns

3 green cardamom pods

1 tsp black cumin seeds

2 cinnamon sticks

1 tsp paprika

1½ tsp salt

⅔ cup unsweetened yogurt

2½ cups water

TO GARNISH

2 green chilies, chopped

fresh cilantro leaves, chopped

1 Peel and slice the onions and set aside. Peel and cut each potato into six pieces.

2 Heat the oil in a pan and cook the sliced onions until golden brown. Remove the onions from the pan and set aside.

3 Add the meat to the pan with 1 teaspoon of the garam masala and cook for 5–7 minutes over a low heat.

4 Add the onions to the pan and remove from the heat.

5 Meanwhile in a small bowl, mix together the ginger, garlic, chili powder, peppercorns, cardamoms, cumin seeds, cinnamon sticks, paprika, and salt. Add the yogurt and mix well.

6 Return the pan to the heat and gradually add the spice and yogurt mixture to the meat and onions and cook for 7–10 minutes. Add the water, then lower the heat and cook, covered, for about 40 minutes, stirring the mixture occasionally.

7 Add the potatoes to the pan and cook, covered, for another 15 minutes, gently stirring the mixture occasionally. Garnish with green chilies and fresh cilantro leaves, and serve at once.

Strained Dhaal with Meatballs

This is a *dhaal* with a difference. After cooking it, add meatballs (*koftas*) and a few fried potato wafers. Serve with fried or plain boiled rice and poppadoms.

NUTRITIONAL INFORMATION

Calories 530   Sugars 1g
Protein . . . . .9g   Fat 44g
Carbohydrate . . .25g   Saturates 5g

5 mins   40 mins

SERVES 6

INGREDIENTS

1½ cups masoor dhaal

1 tsp crushed fresh ginger root

1 tsp fresh garlic, crushed

½ tsp turmeric

1½ tsp chili powder

1½ tsp salt

3 tbsp lemon juice

3½ cups water

1 lb/450 g canned meatballs

TO GARNISH

3 green chilies, finely chopped

fresh cilantro leaves, chopped

BAGHAAR

⅔ cup oil

3 garlic cloves

4 dried red chilies

1 tsp white cumin seeds

POTATO FRIES

pinch of salt

1 lb/450 g potatoes, sliced thinly

1¼ cups vegetable oil

1 Rinse the lentils, and pick over them to remove any stones.

2 Place the lentils in a pan and cover with 2½ cups water. Add the ginger, garlic, turmeric, and chili powder and boil until the lentils are soft and mushy. Add the salt, stirring.

3 Mash the lentils, then push them through a strainer, reserving the liquid. Add the lemon juice to the strained liquid.

4 Stir 1¼ cups of the water into the strained liquid and bring to a boil over a low heat. Drops the meatballs gently into the lentil mixture. Set aside.

5 Prepare the baghaar. Heat the oil in a pan. Add the garlic, dried red chilies, and white cumin seeds and fry for 2 minutes. Pour the baghaar over the lentil mixture, stirring to mix.

6 For the potato fries, rub the salt over the potato slices. Heat the oil in a skillet and fry the potatoes, turning, until crisp. Garnish the meatballs with the fried potatoes, chilies, and cilantro.

Coconut Beef Stir-Fry

This is a truly aromatic dish, blending the heat of red curry paste with the aroma and flavor of the lime leaves and coconut.

NUTRITIONAL INFORMATION

Calories 322	Sugars 9g
Protein 18g	Fat 18g
Carbohydrate ...24g	Saturates 6g

10 mins   25 mins

SERVES 4

INGREDIENTS

2 tbsp vegetable oil

2 cloves garlic

1 onion

12 oz/350 g rump steak

12 oz/350 g sweet potatoes

2 tbsp red curry paste

1¼ cups coconut milk

3 lime leaves

cooked jasmine rice, to serve

1 Heat the vegetable oil in a large preheated wok or large heavy-bottomed skillet.

2 Peel the garlic cloves and crush them in a pestle and mortar. Thinly slice the onions.

3 Using a sharp knife, thinly slice the beef. Add the beef to the wok and cook for about 2 minutes or until sealed on all sides.

4 Add the garlic and the onion to the wok and cook for a further 2 minutes.

5 Using a sharp knife, peel and dice the sweet potato.

6 Add the sweet potato to the wok with the red curry paste, coconut milk, and lime leaves and bring to a rapid boil. Reduce the heat, then cover and let simmer for about 15 minutes or until the potatoes are tender.

7 Remove and discard the lime leaves and transfer the mixture to warm serving bowls. Serve hot with cooked jasmine rice.

VARIATION

If you cannot obtain lime leaves, use grated lime zest instead.

Curried Stir-Fried Lamb

This dish is very filling, and only requires a simple vegetable accompaniment or bread.

NUTRITIONAL INFORMATION

Calories ....375 Sugars 6g
Protein ....26g Fat 19g
Carbohydrate ...27g Saturates 6g

10 mins   1 hour

SERVES 4

INGREDIENTS

2⅔ cups diced potatoes

1 lb/450 g lean lamb, cubed

2 tbsp medium hot curry paste

3 tbsp sunflower oil

1 onion, sliced

1 eggplant, diced

2 cloves garlic, crushed

1 tbsp grated fresh root ginger

⅔ cup lamb or beef bouillon

salt

2 tbsp chopped fresh cilantro, to garnish

1 Bring a large pan of lightly salted water to the boil. Add the potatoes and cook for 10 minutes. Remove the potatoes from the pan with a slotted spoon and drain thoroughly.

2 Meanwhile, place the lamb cubes in a large mixing bowl. Add the curry paste and mix well until the lamb is evenly coated in the paste.

3 Heat the sunflower oil in a large preheated wok.

4 Add the onion, eggplant, garlic, and ginger to the wok and stir-fry for about 5 minutes.

5 Add the lamb to the wok and cook for another 5 minutes.

6 Add the bouillon and cooked potatoes to the wok. Bring to a boil and leave to simmer for 30 minutes, or until the lamb is tender and cooked through.

7 Transfer the mixture to warm serving dishes and scatter with chopped cilantro. Serve immediately.

COOK'S TIP

The wok is an ancient Chinese invention, the name coming from the Cantonese word for a "cooking vessel."

Bread & Desserts

The potato adds an interesting flavor and texture to loaves and cakes. This section includes a range of unusual recipes, and also shows the qualities of the sweet potato in combination with fruit and spices, such  as the Fruity Potato Cake, which is ideal for any special occasion. There is also a tempting braided loaf and some smaller treats, such as Potato Muffins and the delicately spiced Potato and Nutmeg Scones. To finish, the Indian Sweet Potato Dessert, which includes protein-  rich almonds, will provide a satisfying and nutritious end to any meal.

Cheese & Potato Braid

This bread has a delicious cheese and garlic flavor, and is best eaten straight from the oven, as soon as it is the right temperature.

NUTRITIONAL INFORMATION

Calories 387   Sugars 1g
Protein . . . . .13g   Fat 8g
Carbohydrate . . .70g   Saturates 4g

🕐 55 mins

SERVES 8

I N G R E D I E N T S

1 cup diced mealy potatoes

2 x 7 g active dry yeast

5 cups white bread flour

2 cups vegetable bouillon

2 garlic cloves, crushed

2 tbsp chopped rosemary

¼ cup grated Swiss cheese

1 tbsp vegetable oil

1 tbsp salt

1 Lightly grease and flour a baking sheet. Cook the potatoes in a pan of boiling water for 10 minutes, or until soft. Drain and mash.

2 Transfer the mashed potatoes to a large mixing bowl. Stir in the yeast, flour, and bouillon, and mix to form a smooth dough. Add the garlic, rosemary, and ¾ of the cheese and knead the dough for 5 minutes. Make a hollow in the dough, then pour in the oil, add the salt, and knead the dough again.

3 Cover the dough and leave it to rise in a warm place for 1½ hours, or until doubled in size.

4 Knead the dough again and divide it into 3 equal portions. Roll each portion into a sausage shape about 14 inches/35 cm long.

5 Press one end of each of the sausage shapes firmly together, then carefully braid the dough, without breaking it, and fold the remaining ends under, sealing them firmly.

6 Place the braid on the baking sheet, cover and leave to rise for 30 minutes.

7 Sprinkle the remaining cheese over the top of the braid and cook in a preheated oven, 375°F/190°C, for 40 minutes, or until the bottom of the loaf sounds hollow when tapped. Serve warm.

Sweet Potato Bread

This is a great tasting loaf, colored light orange by the sweet potato. Added sweetness from the honey is offset by the tangy orange zest.

NUTRITIONAL INFORMATION

Calories 267   Sugars 7g
Protein ....4g   Fat 9g
Carbohydrate ...45g   Saturates 4g

SERVES 8

INGREDIENTS

1⅓ cups diced sweet potatoes

⅔ cup tepid water

2 tbsp clear honey

2 tbsp vegetable oil

3 tbsp orange juice

generous ⅓ cup semolina

2 cups white bread flour

1 sachet active dry yeast

1 tsp ground cinnamon

grated zest of 1 orange

5 tbsp butter

1 Lightly grease a 1½ lb/675 g loaf pan. Cook the sweet potatoes in a pan of boiling water for about 10 minutes, or until soft. Drain well and then mash until smooth.

2 Meanwhile, mix the water, honey, oil, and orange juice together in a large mixing bowl.

3 Add the mashed sweet potatoes, semolina, three-quarters of the flour, the yeast, ground cinnamon, and grated orange zest and mix thoroughly to form a dough. Let stand for about 10 minutes.

4 Cut the butter into small pieces and knead it into the dough with the remaining flour. Knead for about 5 minutes, until the dough is smooth.

5 Place the dough in the prepared loaf pan. Cover and leave in a warm place to rise for 1 hour, or until the dough has doubled in size.

6 Cook the loaf in a preheated oven, 375°F/190°C, for 45–60 minutes, or until the bottom sounds hollow when tapped. Serve the bread warm, cut into slices.

Potato Muffins

Serve this dish while the cheese is still hot and melted, as cooked cheese turns very rubbery if it is allowed to cool down.

NUTRITIONAL INFORMATION

Calories 100   Sugars 11g
Protein . . . . .3g   Fat 2g
Carbohydrate . . .19g   Saturates 1g

🥔 🥔 🥔

🥔 10 mins   🕐 30 mins

SERVES 12

I N G R E D I E N T S

butter, for greasing

1 cup diced mealy potatoes

3 tbsp self-rising flour, plus extra for dusting

2 tbsp soft light brown sugar

1 tsp baking powder

¾ cup raisins

4 eggs, separated

1 Lightly grease and flour 12 muffin pans and set aside.

2 Cook the diced potatoes in a pan of boiling water for 10 minutes or until cooked. Drain well and mash until smooth.

3 Transfer the potatoes to a mixing bowl and add the flour, sugar, baking powder, raisins, and egg yolks. Mix well.

4 In a clean bowl, whisk the egg whites until standing in peaks. Using a metal spoon, gently fold them into the potato mixture until fully incorporated.

5 Divide the mixture between the prepared pans.

6 Cook in a preheated oven, 400°F/200°C, for 10 minutes. Reduce the oven temperature to 325°F/160°C and cook the muffins for 7–10 minutes or until risen.

7 Remove the muffins from the pans and serve warm.

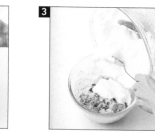

COOK'S TIP

Instead of spreading the muffins with plain butter, serve them with cinnamon butter made by blending 5 tbsp butter with a large pinch of ground cinnamon.

Potato & Nutmeg Scones

These have a slightly different texture from traditional scones, but they are just as delicious served warm and spread with butter.

NUTRITIONAL INFORMATION

Calories ....135 Sugars 6g
Protein ....3g Fat 4g
Carbohydrate ...23g Saturates 2g

5 mins   25 mins

SERVES 8

INGREDIENTS

butter, for greasing

1⅓ cups diced mealy potatoes

⅓ cup all-purpose flour

1½ tsp baking powder

½ tsp grated nutmeg

⅓ cup golden raisins

1 egg, beaten

3 tbsp heavy cream

2 tsp soft light brown sugar

1 Line and grease a baking sheet. Cook the diced potatoes in a pan of boiling water for 10 minutes or until soft. Drain well and mash the potatoes.

2 Transfer the mashed potatoes to a large mixing bowl and stir in the flour, baking powder, and nutmeg.

3 Stir in the golden raisins, egg, and cream, and beat the mixture with a spoon until smooth.

4 Shape the mixture into 8 rounds, ¾ inch/2 cm thick and place on the baking sheet.

5 Cook in a preheated oven, 400°F/200°C, for about 15 minutes or until the scones have risen and are golden. Sprinkle the scones with sugar and serve warm and spread with butter.

COOK'S TIP

For extra convenience, make a batch of scones in advance and open-freeze them. Thaw thoroughly and warm in a moderate oven when ready to serve.

Fruity Potato Cake

Sweet potatoes mix beautifully with fruit and brown sugar in this unusual cake. Add a few drops of rum or brandy to the recipe if you like.

NUTRITIONAL INFORMATION

Calories 275   Sugars 44g
Protein ....6g   Fat 5g
Carbohydrate ...55g   Saturates 2g

15 mins   1 hr 30 mins

SERVES 6

INGREDIENTS

4 cups diced sweet potatoes

1 tbsp butter, melted

4½ oz raw brown sugar

3 eggs

3 tbsp skim milk

1 tbsp lemon juice

grated zest of 1 lemon

1 tsp caraway seeds

4½ oz/125 g dried fruits, such as apple, pear, or mango, chopped

2 tsp baking powder

1 Lightly grease an 7 inch/18 cm square cake pan.

2 Cook the sweet potatoes in boiling water for 10 minutes or until soft. Drain and mash until smooth.

3 Transfer the mashed sweet potatoes to a mixing bowl while still hot and add the butter and sugar, mixing together thoroughly.

4 Beat in the eggs, milk, lemon juice and zest, caraway seeds, and chopped dried fruit. Add the baking powder and mix well.

5 Pour the mixture into the prepared cake pan.

6 Cook in a preheated oven, 325°F/160°C, for 1–1¼ hours or until cooked through.

7 Remove the cake from the pan and transfer to a wire rack to cool. Cut into thick slices to serve.

COOK'S TIP

This cake is ideal as a special occasion dessert. It can be made in advance and frozen until required. Wrap the cake in plastic wrap and freeze. Thaw at room temperature for 24 hours, and warm through in a moderate oven before serving.

Sweet Potato Dessert

This unusual milky dessert is very easy to make and can be eaten either hot or cold.

NUTRITIONAL INFORMATION

Calories	234	Sugars	........23g
Protein	.........5g	Fat	...........3g
Carbohydrate	...51g	Saturates	.......1g

🥔 15 mins 🕐 20 mins

SERVES 10

INGREDIENTS

2 lb 4 oz/1 kg sweet potatoes

3½ cups milk

1¾ cups sugar

a few chopped almonds, to decorate

1 Using a sharp knife, peel the sweet potatoes. Rinse them and then cut them into slices.

2 Place the sweet potato slices in a large pan. Cover with 2½ cups milk and cook over a low heat until the sweet potato is soft enough to be mashed.

3 Remove the sweet potatoes from the heat and mash thoroughly until completely smooth.

4 Add the sugar and the remaining 1¼ cups milk to the mashed sweet potatoes, and carefully stir to blend together completely.

5 Return the pan to the heat and simmer the mixture until it starts to thicken (it should reach the consistency of a creamy soup).

6 Transfer the sweet potato dessert to a serving dish.

7 Decorate with the chopped almonds and serve immediately.

COOK'S TIP

Sweet potatoes are longer than ordinary potatoes and have a pinkish or yellowish skin with yellow or white flesh. As their name suggests, they taste slightly sweet.

Index